P9-CSS-184

JAPAN AND A NEW WORLD ECONOMIC ORDER

JAPAN AND A NEW WORLD ECONOMIC ORDER

KIYOSHI KOJIMA

WESTVIEW PRESS   BOULDER, COLORADO

Published in 1977 in the United States of America by
Westview Press, Inc.
1898 Flatiron Court
Boulder, Colorado 80301
Frederick A. Praeger, Publisher and Editorial Director

First published in Great Britain by
Croom Helm Ltd., London

Library of Congress Cataloging in Publication Data

Kojima, Kiyoshi, 1920-
Japan and a new world economic order.

1. Japan – Economic policy – 1945- 2, Japan – Foreign economic relations. I. Title.
HC462.9.K613 338.954 76-5808
ISBN 0-89158-607-5

Printed in Great Britain
by Redwood Burn Ltd, Trowbridge and Esher

CONTENTS

1 Japan in the World Economy 9

2 Japan and the Multilateral Trade Negotiations 48

3 A Competitive Bipolar Key Currency 64

4 The Role of Foreign Direct Investment 75

5 A Macroeconomic Theory of Foreign Direct Investment 92

6 The Long-Term Path of the Japanese Economy 120

7 The Reorganisation of North-South Trade 148

8 Economic Integration in the Asian-Pacific Region 168

Index 188

PREFACE

Since President Nixon's new economic policy of August 1971, aggrevated by the oil problem since October 1973, the international currency and trade system has been in chaos and uncertainty. There were fears of another 1930s style depression. In addition, world food shortages and strident claims by developing countries for perpetual sovereignty over resources have added to existing difficulties. The search for a new world economic order has become a major pre-occupation throughout the world. This volume represents an attempt from the point of view of the Japanese economy to suggest a new direction for a world and a regional economic order.

Chapter 1 establishes the problems to be explored, by examining the position of the Japanese economy just before the oil crisis in October 1973. In 1968-73, Japan experienced for the first time since the Second World War a large export surplus and in that period undertook almost complete liberalisation of trade and foreign investment. Whether this trend will be entirely changed by the oil crisis is a question of great concern. The answer is given in Chapter 6. The following chapters set out to define the global and regional setting most favourable to furthering Japan's economic and trade development.

In Chapter 2, prospects for the Tokyo Round of trade negotiations and Japan's attitude towards them are briefly put forward. Then a proposal for a GATT 'fair-weather rule of reduction (or elimination) of tariffs and non-tariff barriers' is suggested. That is, a country should reduce tariffs and non-tariff barriers (NTBs) while its balance of payments is favourable, but it should not be allowed to raise them again, even if its balance of payments becomes unfavourable, since at that time some other country would have a favourable balance of payments and would be expected to reduce its own tariffs and NTBs accordingly, allowing tariffs and NTB's in all advanced countries to be eliminated gradually within, say, 10 years. The argument stresses the positive role of tariffs, safeguards, structural adjustment and foreign direct investment in order to facilitate each country's dynamic adjustments toward world trade expansion. Supply access to primary commodities is also examined and international commodity agreements with a buffer stock scheme are recommended.

In Chapter 3, reform of the international monetary system is discussed. Managed floating exchange rates are a necessary evil for the time being. I expect that the European Monetary Union will be completed by, say, 1980. Meanwhile it is desirable that a bipolar key currency system with the Europa and the dollar may emerge. The desirability and operation of the bipolar key currency system is examined, in connection with the position of the yen.

Foreign direct investment and the activities of multinational enterprise are a new dynamic element of world economy. In Chapter 4, an attempt is made to identify the characteristics of two different types of foreign direct investment: trade-oriented (the Japanese model) and anti-trade-oriented (the American model). Foreign direct investment going from a comparatively disadvantageous industry in the investing country (which is a potentially comparatively advantageous industry in the host country) will promote a mutually beneficial upgrading of industrial structure and thus accelerate trade between the two countries. In comparison, American foreign direct investment made from a position of comparative advantage is anti-trade-oriented and results in balance of payments difficulties, the export of jobs, the prevention of structural adjustment and trade protectionism.

This is a unique approach to the foreign direct investment problem. The Japanese approach contributes effectively to the gradual transfer of manufacturing industries to developing countries. This type of direct investment serves a tutoring role and its fade out is unavoidable when it succeeds in the role of tutor.

The different characteristics and functions of the Japanese approach compared with the American approach to foreign direct investments are theoretically examined in Chapter 5, which, though important, some readers may wish to omit.

Chapter 6 analyses the long-term growth path of the Japanese economy in the light of the impact of the oil crisis. Recent discussion between MITI and business circles on the future of the Japanese industrial structure in the context of international division of labour is surveyed. I stress the need for horizontal (intra-industry) specialisation in agriculture, light industry, intermediate goods production and knowledge-intensive industries with Australia and other neighbouring countries in Asia. This leads to the conclusion that it is desirable to promote *functional* integration in the Western Pacific Region.

Thus, ways and means to reorganise 'north-south' relations in the Asian-Pacific region are the subject of Chapter 7.

An urgent need for the economic development of developing countries is to provide ample opportunity for developing countries to export suitable manufactured goods. It is argued that in order to facilitate this, liberalisation of trade in developed countries, structural adjustments, proper use of aid and direct investment, reorganisation of north-south trade and prosperity in the advanced economies are most important.

In the final chapter, I reconsider the proposals for economic integration in the Asian-Pacific region which I have advocated for the last ten years. The original proposal of a Pacific Free Trade Area received a rather cool response but a functional integration in the region has progressed steadily and there are now promising prospects for the further intensification of Pacific economic integration.

Throughout the volume, I have had in mind the need to consider two major issues in international economics. First, traditional international trade theory aims only for *static* maximisation in the use of world human and material resources, but, it seems to me, we have to pay more attention to such dynamic or developmental elements as population growth, immigration, natural resource developments, improvement in and transfer of technology, economies of scale, direct foreign investment and economic integration in order to create development centres or sectors in the world economy, and that we have to systematise the treatment of these subjects.

Secondly, there is the fundamental question of how to combine a global approach (that is worldwide multilateral, non-discriminatory free trade and free investment) and a regional approach to economic integration. Although the latter is not yet well established theoretically, practically those developmental elements just mentioned are taken care of far better in bilateral relations and through regional cooperation than they are through the global free trade approach. Observation leads me to favour dynamic adjustments in trade, aid and investment through closer regional integration within a freer global trade environment.

This volume has been drawn together from an updated collection of essays produced over past three years. I am grateful to the editors of *Hitotsubashi Journal of Economics, Toward A New World Trade Policy – The Maidenhead Papers* and *Prospects for Partnership* who kindly allowed me permission to republish material from their pages.

I am especially grateful for the opportunity to join in the stimulating discussion of the observations put forward in this book at successive Pacific Trade and Development conferences for which I have been privileged to act as general chairman, and conferences on trade policy sponsored by the Trade Policy Research Centre, the World Bank, the

Brooking Institution and the Japan Economic Research Centre. Professors Kaname Akamatsu, H.W. Arndt, Fred Bergsten, Sir John Crawford, Richard Cooper, Hugh Corbet, Edward English, Gottfried Haberler, Sir Roy Harrod, Helen Hughes, Harry Johnson, Hisao Kanamori, Saburo Okita, Hugh Patrick and Robert Triffin all contributed much in this way to the clarification of my ideas.

I am also deeply indebted, in this context, to Dr Peter Drysdale of the Australian National University for devoting his time to going over my English text, and to Dr Makoto Ikema of Hitotsubashi University for improving the theoretical model.

Kiyoshi Kojima

Hitotsubashi University
Tokyo
December 1975

1 JAPAN IN THE WORLD ECONOMY

I INTRODUCTION

Today, the Japanese economy faces an important turning point. First, while the Japanese economy had succeeded in the rapid development of heavy and chemical industries by 1965 and had experienced a phenomenal growth of exports up to 1972 or 1973, the question arises as to what direction the structure of industry and trade should be further upgraded and developed from now on? Heretofore the Japanese economy could simply imitate the development pattern of more advanced American and European economies, but from now on it has to create a new course of its own for further development.

Secondly, the postwar world economy prospered, enjoying a period of rapid growth due to the strong leadership of the USA and the successful liberalisation of trade, exchange and investment of major industrial countries through the General Agreement on Tariffs and Trade (GATT) and the International Monetary Fund (IMF). Japan benefited from this process in the acceleration of her industrial and trade growth and accomplished her own liberalisation by March 1973. However, from the beginning of the 1970s, these favourable international economic surroundings both in the monetary and trading systems turned into uncertainty and disorder and the search for a new world economic order is now a serious preoccupation. As one of the mainstays of the world economy, the Japanese economy should initiate a positive leadership for the benefit of both the Japanese and neighbouring economies.

Thirdly, the oil crisis in October 1973 aggravated the confusion in international monetary and trading systems to the point of creating an atmosphere of crisis. Not only in respect of the petroleum trade but also in respect of other primary commodities, the claims of developing countries have gathered strength and the north-south problem is entering a new phase. Moreover, even advanced countries like the USA, Canada and Australia may, it is feared, control their exports of food and natural resource products. This is a serious problem for the Japanese economy as it depends upon imports of almost every kind of primary commodity. If possible, Japan needs to change the long-term direction of her 'processing trade' economy. But, at the same time, there is an opportunity to solve the primary commodity problem in favour of accelerating the economic development and welfare of developing countries.

At this turning point in the development of the world economy, the Japanese economy must find solutions to three basic problems. First, in what direction will it upgrade and develop its industrial and trade structure compatible with a closer interdependence and mutual prosperity with the world economy, especially with neighbouring Asian-Pacific countries? Secondly, how will it reconcile both a global (i.e. multilateral and non-discriminatory) approach and a regional approach to trade and economic growth? Thirdly, how will it constructively use not only external trade but also overseas direct investment to develop both the Japanese and the world economies? These are the main issues into which this book will enquire.

In this first chapter, the development of the Japanese economy and its interdependent relationship with the world economy up to 1973, just prior to the oil crisis, is briefly reviewed (Section II). The extent of Japan's trade, investment and exchange liberalisation up to that point is clarified (Sections III and IV), and the impact of the oil crisis in October 1973 on the Japanese economy is described. This chapter provides the starting point for our enquiry.

II JAPAN'S POSITION IN WORLD TRADE

The Japanese trade position before the oil crisis appeared to be strong. In 1971 and 1972, Japan experienced an extraordinarily favourable balance of payments with a phenomenal growth of exports and a huge accumulation of foreign reserves. This aroused, first, fierce condemnation from the USA because of her balance of payments difficulties. The USA argued that in 1971 Japan's bilateral trade surplus ($3.2 billion) was much larger than the US world-wide trade deficit ($2.8 billion) although this was the first time in a hundred years that Japan had attained a long desired bilateral trade surplus. Then the fear of a Japanese export explosion moved to Europe (though Japanese exports account for a very small share – less than 2 per cent – of total European imports), due to the increased protectionism in the US, the smaller revaluation of the yen relative to the European currencies than to the dollar, and the shift of Japan's export drive from the American to the European market. Moreover, Japan's foreign exchange reserves increased during 1971 and 1972 by SDR 10.2 billion and SDR 2.7 billion respectively, which surpassed the normal increase of world-wide international liquidity (about SDR 3.0 billion a year). This brought the further complaint that Japan was responsible for international monetary turmoil due to a delayed decision on yen revaluation, in spite of the fact that European countries were forced to receive larger amounts of dollars as a result of America's 'benign neglect' policy.

Japanese exports have increased almost twice as rapidly as world trade. If this trend were to continue, there are fears that the world market might be preempted by Japanese commodities. In addition, Japanese direct investments to developing Asian countries increased in 1970-73, inducing another round of criticism because of the fears of Japanese overpresence and domination.

In reply to these criticisms it should be made clear that Japan's export explosion and huge export surplus in those years will certainly not continue forever but will be a short-lived phenomenon brought about partly by the unhealthy performance of the American economy and partly by the delayed accommodation in Japanese policies.

On the other hand, Japan is said to be the most difficult market for the foreign exporter and investor because of its highly protectionist tariffs, quota restrictions, exchange controls, investment regulations and even administrative guidance. It is true that liberalisation of Japan's trade and investment has been slow, too cautious and delayed and she might deserve criticism on that score. However, as will be shown in Sections III and IV, almost all barriers had been eliminated by 1972.

There still remain a number of suspicions, complaints and fears abroad, not only in advanced but also developing countries, *vis-à-vis* Japan. Money spent in other countries by the Japanese in acquiring race horses, arts and antiques, etc. has been disregarded and an increase in the number of Japanese tourists and investments abroad looked on with ambivalence,[1] although both are an easy fillip to a foreign country's balance of payments.

Why is Japan feared so much? It is to be hoped that such misgivings are subjective – and temporary. An attempt must be made to analyse Japan's foreign economic policy as objectively as possible in order to eradicate any misunderstandings.

Since October 1973, the situation in the Middle East has exploded and an embargo on petroleum exports has followed. The oil crisis – first the shortage of supply and then the large rise in price – has seriously shocked the Japanese economy and forced a re-examination of her foreign economic policy. The balance of payments in 1973 moved into deficit due to rapid progress in import liberalisation and exchange revaluation, and the deficit is expected to increase further in the coming years due to heavily increased payments for oil. Although it is difficult to take into consideration these uncertain factors, their possible effects on the prospects for the Japanese economy and for international monetary and trade order will be touched upon in Section V.

Rapid growth of Japanese trade

The recovery and expansion of the Japanese economy and trade in the post World War II period was remarkably rapid. In the past twenty years, the annual growth rate of the Japanese gross national product, in real terms, was 8 per cent in 1951-55, 9.1 per cent in 1955-60, 9.7 per cent in 1960-65 and 13.1 per cent in 1965-70. Japan's economic growth in the coming decade may decelerate somewhat compared with growth performance in the 1960s, but it will continue at about 6-7 per cent per annum in real terms, as will be explained in detail in Chapter 6.

Owing to a favourable external environment, Japanese exports grew in an almost parallel fashion in dollar terms with domestic economic development. Japan's exports increased from $2 billion in 1955 to $4.1 billion in 1960 and to $19.3 billion in 1970 with the growth rate as rapid as 16.9 per cent in the 1960s, and her imports (in f.o.b. terms) over the same period increased from $2.2 billion to $3.9 billion and then to $15.7 billion with a growth rate of 15 per cent. Since total world trade increased from $128 billion in 1960 to $311 billion in 1970 with a growth rate of 9.3 per cent, Japanese exports grew 1.8 times faster than world trade, Japan's share of world trade thus increasing from 3.2 per cent in 1960 to 6.2 per cent in 1970.

One may question just what it is that is feared or criticised by foreigners. Is it (a) the rapid growth of Japan's exports (i.e. foreign imports of Japanese goods), or (b) the large and ever increasing share of Japan's exports in total world trade, or (c) Japan's unbalanced growth in exports and imports?

The share of Japanese exports in total world trade, i.e. 6.2 per cent in 1970 (the corresponding share for the US and the EEC being 13.7 per cent and 28.4 per cent respectively) may not be too large when it is compared with the share of Japanese GNP in total world GNP which is estimated to be as large as 7.2 per cent. Japan's export/GNP ratio was as low as 9.4 per cent in 1960 and increased slightly to 9.9 per cent in 1970, while her import (c.i.f.)/GNP ratio was as low as 10.4 per cent in 1960 and decreased to 9.5 per cent in 1970 (if imports are valued at f.o.b. terms, the corresponding figures were 8.6 per cent and 7.6 per cent respectively). Despite the fact that Japan needs huge imports of raw materials and food, her dependence on external trade is relatively limited compared with the world average or with other industrialised countries' import/GNP ratios (for example, 18.9 per cent for Canada, 18.5 per cent for the United Kingdom, 15.2 per cent for West Germany and 13.8 per cent for Italy in 1968; the ratio of 4.1 per cent for the United States is an exception).

As long as Japan is exporting good quality products at internationally competitive prices, this should be welcomed by consumers as raising the national welfare of the importing country. As long as the volume of Japanese imports increases as fast as exports in overall economic relations with the rest of the world, Japan contributes to the continued expansion of world trade by providing a profitable export market for foreign goods. Perhaps Japan is criticised for having a rate of export growth which exceeds the capacity of a foreign country to adjust domestic production. But how can we judge whether the rate of growth is 'too fast' or not? This creates problems of 'market disruption', 'voluntary export restraint', 'safeguard', etc. Japan's overall surplus in her trade balance and balance of payments in recent years might only be criticised if it were brought about and prolonged by governmental mismanagement based upon mercantilistic protectionism. This point should be made clear.

Japan suffered for a long time from a trade deficit. Japan's export (f.o.b.)/import (c.i.f.) ratio based upon customs statistics[2] was 81.4 per cent in 1955 and 84.1 per cent in 1964, averaging 82.6 per cent over the ten year period. In 1965, for the first time since World War II, Japan experienced an export surplus, the export/import ratio being 103.5. Since Japan fell back into trade deficit in 1967 and 1968 and then gained a small trade surplus in 1969 and 1970, her trade in the period 1965-70 was actually kept in balance (the export/import ratio being 100.9). The trade balance abruptly changed to a large surplus in 1971 and 1972 amounting to $ 4.3 billion and $ 5.1 billion respectively (the export/import ratio being 121.8 in both years). Then the ratio fell back to 96.4 in 1973 and 89.4 in 1974, reaching a deficit of $ 16.8 billion in overall balance of payments for the two years taken together.

Japan's invisible (or service) trade has yearly suffered from deficit and accounted for 9.4 per cent of merchandise exports in 1970. In order to cover this and to increase aid and net overseas investment it is to be hoped that Japan's trade balance, based upon customs statistics as above, will show a 5-10 per cent surplus. Japan had just reached that position in the period after 1965 but the trade surplus in 1971 and 1972 unexpectedly surpassed that position. In other words, Japan's trade surplus in those two years was partly due to a trend factor, as will be explained presently, but mainly due to an unhealthy economic performance in foreign countries, especially in the United States.

Japan's reserves of gold and foreign exchange which has been just over over $2 billion during most of the 1960s, came to $2.9 billion at the end of 1968 and $4.8 billion two years later. An avalanche of dollars poured into Japan during 1971 and again in 1972. Her official reserves rose from $5.5 billion in March 1970 to $16.7 billion in March 1972, and reached a peak of $18.2 billion in March 1973, falling then to $12.4 billion in March 1974. The net increase in reserves of $12.6 billion in the period from 1971 to March 1973 was too large to be accounted for by the Japanese trade surplus of $9.4 billion in the same period. An abnormal inflow of short-term capital, mainly due to export earnings receipts and delays in meeting import payments, had taken place.

Structural change for industrialisation and trade expansion

Because of a lack of natural resources and the availability of an able and industrious source of manpower, the Japanese economy has developed for the last 100 years basically through 'processing trade' activities, that is, importing raw materials, manufacturing them for domestic use and exporting, except for the exports of staples such as tea and silk in the early days. Concern about balance of payments problems among other things, has produced policies aimed at maximum domestic processing, protection of new industries and restraint in the import of consumer manufactures, although machinery and equipment necessary to import-substituting industrialisation remained an important element in imports.

Successive new industries have been nurtured in the process of Japanese industrialisation over the past 100 years, but there have been two major structural changes.[3] The first was light industrialisation which began around 1900 and accelerated after World War I. The second was heavy and chemical industrialisation which started in the late 1930s and grew rapidly during the years 1953-65. These structural changes, diversification and the upgrading of industrial structure contributed to a decrease in the import (c.i.f.)/GNP ratio from 21 per cent in the 1920s to 9.5 per cent in 1970 due to the lower imported raw materials content of the heavy and chemical industries when compared with the light industries (mainly cotton textiles) and to the substitution of imported machinery and equipment for domestic production. In other words, to save import content and to increase domestic value added have been the major objectives in industrialisation of the processing trade type. Now it is felt that there should be a shift towards knowledge-intensive industrialisation, a third significant structural change.

In Japan's exports, foodstuffs, raw materials and fuels are unimportant. Almost all exports are manufactured goods. The share in total exports of light industrial goods decreased from 53.5 per cent in 1955 to 22.4 per cent in 1970, and is expected to decline further. On the other hand, the importance in total exports of heavy and chemical goods[4] increased rapidly from 38.0 per cent in 1955 to 72.4 per cent in 1970 and will rise further in the coming decade.

How are these changes reflected in the import structure? In 1955, more than half of total imports consisted of raw materials. Besides raw materials, foodstuffs and mineral fuels were essential imports for the development of Japan's processing trade. Only 12 per cent of total imports consisted of manufactures, largely essential machinery and chemicals. Heavy and chemical industrialisation in the 1960s brought about smaller relative dependence on imports of raw materials but this was almost compensated for by the increased dependence on imported mineral fuels. Further savings in these two items is one of the targets of knowledge-intensive industrialisation in the 1970s. On the other hand, the percentage of manufactured goods imported increased from 11.9 per cent in 1955 to 30.3 per cent in 1970, although this increase is still lower than the corresponding ratio for other advanced countries; for example, manufactured goods represent 50.7 per cent of total imports in the UK, 59.2 per cent in West Germany and 66.2 per cent in the United States. If knowledge-intensive industrialisation is successful, it is expected that processed manufactures will amount to about half of total imports, resulting in increased horizontal trade in machinery and chemicals mainly with other advanced countries and also increased trade in other manufactures with developing countries and natural resource processing nations.

Japan has been catching up with American and European economies and reached a similar stage of industrialisation around 1965 through the diversification of manufacturing industries, upgrading them towards more sophisticated and higher quality products and strengthening international competitiveness through large-scale production. Thus, recently (from 1969 through to 1972), Japan's trade balance turned into an export surplus, *vis-à-vis* not only the USA, but also Europe and the rest of the world.

Japan-US trade

Criticism of Japan intensified because of the large overall trade surplus in 1971 and 1972. It coincided with a huge bilateral export surplus first with the United States and then, a year later, with European countries (see Table 1.1).

Though Japan's trade has expanded in all directions, the United States remains by far its most important market and its chief supplier of imports. The structure of trade is very different on the two sides. Ninety-six per cent of Japan's sales to the United States in 1970 was made up of manufactured goods, with electrical machinery and iron and steel products heading the list with annual sales of about $1.3 billion and $0.9 billion respectively. Roughly $2.1 billion a year was accounted for by non-electrical machinery, automobiles and textiles and clothing. In contrast, of Japan's purchases from the United States, manufactured goods came to only 41 per cent of the total although they have been growing in importance, especially in machinery. Japan still depends heavily on the United States for new technology and the best of new machinery that embodies such technology. More than half of American exports consist of food and raw materials such as lumber, coal, coarse grains, oil seeds and scrap metal. Therefore, more than half of the Japan-US trade is a vertical exchange of American primary products with Japanese manufactured goods in which, it is sometimes said, the United States is playing the role of the less developed country.[5] The rest of the trade is made up of a horizontal exchange of various kinds of manufactured goods. This component in bilateral trade is unstable and precarious and depends upon trade policies on both sides.

In 1965, Japan experienced an export surplus in bilateral trade with the United States for the first time, which was one of the major causes of Japan's overall trade surplus. Japan's export/import ratio *vis-à-vis* the United States, calculated in f.o.b. prices on both sides, had for a long time shown an import surplus. This surplus averaged 72 per cent in 1934-6, 44 per cent in 1950, 63 per cent in 1955, 79 per cent in 1960 and 88 per cent in 1964. The ratio rose to 116 in 1965, i.e. Japan had an export surplus in 1965, growing to 179 or $3.2 billion in 1971 and 183 or $4.1 billion in 1972,[6] and declining to 116 of $1.3 billion in 1973 and to 117 or $1.8 billion in 1974. If imports are valued in terms of c.i.f. prices according to Japanese customs statistics, the export surpluses in 1971 and 1972 were much smaller, $2.5 billion and $3.0 billion respectively, and the export/import ratio in 1973 and 1974 was already as low as 102 and 101 respectively – a reasonable level from Japan's point of view.

Table 1.1 Japan's trade by area

(million dollar)

	1970			1972			1973			1974		
	Exports (f.o.b.)	Share in total exports %	Imports (c.i.f.)	Exports (f.o.b.)	Share in total exports %	Imports (c.i.f.)	Exports (f.o.b.)	Share in total exports %	Imports (c.i.f.)	Exports (f.o.b.)	Share in total exports %	Imports (c.i.f.)
USA	5940	30.7	5560	8848	30.9	5852	9449	25.6	9270	12799	23.0	12682
Western Europe	2900	15.0	1934	4279	16.5	2458	6434	17.7	4038	8400	15.1	5208
EEC	1303	6.7	1117	2203	7.7	1359	4400*	11.9*	3177*	5968*	10.7*	3982*
Canada	563	3.0	929	1104	3.9	1149	999	2.7	2015	1587	2.9	2676
Oceania	802	4;2	1812	1030	3.6	2594	1617	3.9	4237	2689	4.8	4888
Middle East	549	2.8	2273	1056	3.7	3430	1774	4.8	4941	3680	6.6	15920
Africa	1423	7.4	1099	2088	7.8	1172	2305	6.2	1067	3539	6.4	1583
Latin America	1187	6.1	1373	1980	6.9	1418	2761	7.5	1955	5065	9.1	2713
Socialist countries	1045	5.4	888	1442	5.0	1226	1954	5.3	2286	3827	7.1	3141
East and Southeast Asia (total)	4902	25.4	3013	6310	22.1	4171	8931	24.2	7953	12695	22.9	12497
East Asia (South Korea, Taiwan, Hong Kong)	2219	11.5	572	2980	10.4	967	4549	12.3	2375	6025	10.8	2796
Southeast Asia (Philippines, Indonesia, Singapore, Malaysia, Thailand, Cambodia, Sputh Vietnam, Burma)	2004	10.4	1888	2720	9.5	2476	3845	10.0	4511	5579	10.0	8024
Other Asia	310	1.6	453	437	1.5	653	537	1.9	1067	1091	2.0	1677
Total	19318	100.0	18881	28591	100.0	23471	36930	100.0	38314	55536	100.0	62110

* Enlarged EEC (9 countries)

Source: *White Paper on International Trade.*

Japanese-European trade

Japan's exports to the six original EEC countries have increased tremendously over the last fourteen years from US $140 million (f.o.b.) in 1957, just before the EEC was established, to $1,635 million in 1971, or more than 11.7 times. At the same time, the EEC's exports to Japan have also increased by as much as 8.6 times from $180 million (f.o.b.) to $1,555 million. The growth of Japanese-European trade has been both rapid and successful. The growth of Japan's exports to the EEC may be compared with (a) Japan's total exports to the world ($2,850 million in 1957 to $24,019 million in 1971, an increase of 8.4 times), (b) Japan's exports to the USA ($597 million to $7,495 million, an increase of 12.6 times), (c) total world exports ($109,740 million to $346,150 million, an increase of 3.15 times), and (d) intra-EEC trade ($7,860 million to $49,220 million, an increase of 6.26 times).

Although Japanese-European trade has been increasing rapidly, Europe and Japan cannot be said to trade as intensively with each other as their mutual trading capacity would suggest was possible. Japan's exports to the six Community countries in 1971 accounted for 6.8 per cent of her total exports and a mere 1.6 per cent of the EEC's total imports. Since the EEC's imports represent a very large market – 27.0 per cent of the world's imports – Japan could direct at least that percentage of her exports to the EEC if its trade were spread more evenly throughout the world. As Japan actually directed only 6.7 per cent of her total exports to Europe, the volume of Japan's export trade with the EEC is as low as 25 per cent of what it could be if her trade were spread, as hypothesised, more evenly around the world. From the EEC's point of view, exports to Japan represent a mere 0.9 per cent of total exports. While Japan's total imports account for 5.8 per cent of world imports. Hence, the EEC's export trade with Japan is only 16 per cent of the total Japanese import market. By contrast, the USA takes 31.2 per cent of Japan's exports, which comprise 15.9 per cent of total American imports, so that the intensity of trade is as high as 258 per cent, since the American share in the world imports is 12.1 per cent. Why the volume of European-Japanese trade is so low and why it remains so low deserves serious study. Existing tariffs and non-tariff barriers are probably one of the causes, and they should be reduced or eliminated so that mutually beneficial trade can be expanded.

In 1971, light manufactures, mainly textiles, tiles, pottery, toys and footwear, accounted for 15.8 per cent of Japan's exports to the EEC; heavy manufactures and chemicals such as steel, general machinery, electronic machinery, automobiles, ships, cameras and other precision instruments accounted for 62.7 per cent; the remainder, 20.5 per cent, was foodstuffs and materials, mainly canned fish. But fourteen years ago, in 1957, the order was quite the reverse: light manufactures accounted for 50.0 per cent, foodstuffs and raw materials for 30.5 per cent and heavy manufactures and chemicals for 19.5 per cent. Such a rapid upgrading of Japan's export pattern towards consumer durable machinery of good quality, with a high income elasticity of demand, has been the major factor in the successful and rapid expansion of her exports to Europe.

In 1971, more than 87 per cent of Japan's imports from the EEC comprised manufactured goods; 44.8 per cent in the form of various kinds of machinery, 22.2 per cent chemicals, and 20.4 per cent light manufactures. This composition of imports has changed little during the last decade. Thus, Japan and Europe have expanded their horizontal trade in manufactured goods with each other. This is a special pattern in Japan's trade which, in other areas, consists mainly of vertical trade. More than 95 per cent of Japanese exports to the world are manufactured goods while 72 per cent of its imports are primary products.

However, Japan's export explosion in Europe in the last few years should be noticed with a warning. Japan's exports to the six EEC countries increased by 41 per cent in 1969 as compared with the previous year, 35 per cent in 1970, 26 per cent in 1971 and 35 per cent in 1972, reaching $2,203 million. Japan's exports to the enlarged EEC continued to increase in 1973 by 33 per cent and in 1974 by 26 per cent, and this left an export surplus as large as $1,230 million.

The main cause of the rapid growth of Japan's exports to Europe, besides the trend factor in Japanese trade, was increased protectionism in American markets, exchange realignment after December 1971 which brought about smaller revaluation of the yen in relation to European currencies than the the dollar, and, as a natural result, Japan's efforts to diversify exports by moving into Europe and any other profitable markets.

Most of the trouble arises, I believe, from the nature of Japanese-European trade. It is said that horizontal trade in manufactured goods has become, and in future will remain, a more prosperous element in world trade than vertical trade (the exchange of manufactures for primary goods) because a larger proportion of income is spent on manufactured goods as incomes rise, product differentiation in manufactures allows different tastes to be met and new products are created progressively for this purpose, economies of scale reduce costs and create mass consumption of manufactures, and so on. On the other hand, horizontal trade in manufactured goods is precarious from the viewpoint of protectionist policy, since cost differences between advanced countries are narrow and new products and production processes are easily transferred from one country to be imitated by another. Thus, horizontal trade has a double edge: it will expand tremendously if free trade is accepted, but it will deteriorate rapidly if protectionism prevails.

It may be safely concluded that tariffs and non-tariff barriers are not the main cause of the present volume of Japanese-European trade – small in comparison to their actual trading *capacity* – although mutual trade liberalisation is both very desirable and feasible. Perhaps the more substantial cause is 'remoteness' between Europe and Japan and sluggish export efforts on the European side. 'Remoteness' implies not only geographical distance but more importantly a gap in cultural background, customs, languages, philosophy of life and so on, adversely affecting opportunities for business communication and advertisement, or personnel and cultural exchange. Europeans have benefited from better, wealthy markets with each other and with nearby North America, and, as a natural result, they have rather neglected their export efforts towards the Japanese market.

Trade with natural resource producers

A huge amount of industrial raw materials and fuel will be required to service Japanese industrial growth; in 1980, Japan will represent 30 per cent of the world market for commodities such as oil, natural gas, coal, uranium, iron ore, copper, bauxite, other non-ferrous metals, timber and pulp (Table 1.2). Securing stable supplies at reasonable prices is now a major task. Increasing imports of cheaper foodstuffs will be another. New sources of supply, both of raw materials and foodstuffs, will have to be developed all round the world, but the Asian-Pacific countries will hold a large share in the growing market.

As a natural consequence, Japan has, and will increase, new trade deficit *vis-à-vis* natural resource suppliers. The United States has long been one of the major suppliers. Australia,[7] Canada and New Zealand have increased their importance as sources of supply for raw materials and foodstuffs, and as export markets, but Japan has a continuing deficit in trade with them (see Table 1.1).

Another area in which Japan has a big bilateral deficit is the Middle East which is the major supplier of petroleum. The natural resource

Table 1.2 Japanese imports in relation to domestic consumption and total OECD imports of selected raw materials, 1971

Product	Imports as a share of Japanese consumption	Japanese imports as a share of total OECD imports	Ranking of Japan in importance as an importer
	(in per cent)		
Crude petroleum	99.7	15.9	1
Coal	58.4	41.0	1
Iron ore	99.3	42.3	1
Manganese ore	91.9	32.3	1
Copper ore	94.2	77.1	1
Zinc ore	78.5	31.2	1
Lead ore	100.0	26.4	1
Bauxite	100.0	12.3	3
Wool	100.0	22.6	1
Cotton	100.0	35.5	1
Rubber	27.4*	15.4	2

* Imports of natural rubber as per cent of consumption of natural plus synthetic rubber.

Sources: Bureau of Statistics, office of the Prime Minister, *Monthly Statistics of Japan*, May 1973 (Number 143); OECD, *Trade by Commodities*, Series C, Vol. I, Jan.-Dec. 1971.

suppliers have recently taken a strong stand, requesting the processing of natural resources and better prices. How to accommodate this is of great concern for Japan.

Japan's trade with Africa, Latin America and socialist countries has been kept relatively stable with a small export surplus in general but Japan envisages a trade deficit with them in the future for they will be important sources of supply for mineral raw materials and Japan has recently increased investment there to develop those materials.

Trade with developing countries with abundant labour

Trade with East and Southeast Asian countries has been as important for Japan as the trade with the United States, each direction accounting for a third of total trade. Japan's trade with Southeast Asia has provided, and will continue to provide her with a large export surplus. In 1970, Japan's exports (f.o.b.) to the area amounted to $4.9 billion and she imported $3.0 billion worth (c.i.f.) of supplies in return, the imbalance in trade ratio being 1.6:1. Filling this gap is another task for

Japan. Moreover, because of the rapid increase in Japan's trade with Southeast Asia, Japanese goods will account for 40 per cent of the area's total imports in the near future. This might well invite renewed Asian antagonism towards Japanese domination.

Looked at more closely by subregion or by country, however, it is found that the situation varies widely. Japan's trade with East Asia, consisting of South Korea, Taiwan and Hong Kong, is large; with Japan's huge export surplus, the export/import ratio was 3.9:1 in 1970. The eight countries in Southeast Asia (the Philippines, Indonesia, Singapore, Malaysia, Thailand, Cambodia, South Vietnam and Burma) kept an almost evenly balanced trade with Japan overall but the Philippines, Indonesia and Malaysia had an export surplus whilst the others had an import surplus. Japan's trade with the rest of Asia, mainly with South Asian countries such as India, Bangladesh and Pakistan, was small, with minor import surpluses. It will be a most important task for Japan, in the coming decade, to open a large market for labour-intensive manufactures from nearby Asian countries so that Japan's trade with them will move to an equilibrium.

Conclusion

The best choice for Japan is, as the government declares, to expand and free mutual trade with every trading region. The present stage of her industrialisation, her dual pattern of trade with developed and developing countries, and her geographical location dictate such a choice. But it is also true that Japan's main interest continues to be directed towards the Asian-Pacific region. It will be Japan's role in the coming decade to promote a harmonious reorganisation of the north-south trade. This will require a large-scale aid, investment-*cum*-preference, structural adjustment scheme.

Japan expects huge import surpluses with those countries endowed with rich and abundant natural resources but she should also import from nearby Asian countries as much as she exports to them. How to expand trade mutually without falling into large imbalance *vis-à-vis* such wealthy countries as the United States and Western Europe should be another important task for Japan's trade policy.

Perhaps the Japanese economy is like a small boy who has suddenly grown up and is thought of as one of the major powers in world trade but who does not know how to behave or how to take the initiative which has become his responsibility. He does not even know how to explain that the export explosion and abrupt export surplus in 1971 and 1972 have been abnormal events. We must enquire into the longer-term trend of Japan's trade and investment and look for appropriate policies for the prosperity of the world economy, a goal requiring cooperation among nations.

III LIBERALISATION OF TRADE

Delayed change in trade policy

Japan's trade entered an important new phase in 1965 when the trade balance (or current account balance) turned into surplus after a long period of deficit. Before 1965, Japanese business expansion was checked on three occasions by the balance of payments ceiling. It was reasonable under those earlier circumstances for Japanese policy makers to endeavour to restrain imports and promote exports vigorously.

Trade policy was justified on grounds of improving the balance of payments position. Not only agriculture but almost all manufacturing industries, old as well as new, were protected from foreign competition through tariffs, quota restrictions and other non-tariff barriers and they were encouraged through lower interest subsidies and tax incentives. Japan's trade liberalisation made its first rapid progress from 1960 to 1963 but another liberalisation phase began only as recently as 1969 to 1972, after the trade balance had turned to surplus.

Since the trade balance position turned to surplus around 1965, trade policy and exchange rate policy should also have changed from the long-enduring protectionist attitude towards a new philosophy. That change, however, took a long time. First, it was thought that the trade surplus was merely a short-term phenomenon and not a long-term trend. Secondly, the economic community was not ready to accept the new philosophy overnight, since it was thought that protectionist policies had been successful in assisting exports to grow almost twice as rapidly as world trade, resulting in a steady export-surplus trend. Although change towards a new philosophy has been taking place gradually since 1965 and occurred dramatically in 1969-72, it was thought to be too slow and too hesitant from the foreigner's point of view.[8]

Progress in tariff reduction

Japan's tariff policy has a long history. In the early Meiji era, import duties were fixed at less than 5 per cent *ad valorem* equivalent rate by the (unequal) Tariff Treaty with foreign powers in 1866. After much effort, Japan was able to revise the treaty and resume tariff autonomy in 1899. Since then, general revisions of the tariff law were successively effected in 1906, 1911, 1926 and 1932 (mostly upwards) and partial revisions were made almost every year.[9] After World War II, the 1961 revision of the tariff law, which shifted the tariff schedule to Brussels Tariff Nomenclature, set up the clearly protectionist principle of tariff policy prevalent up to 1965. The law declared that the tariff rate should be low on primary products, raw materials, intermediate goods and essential consumer goods, whilst it should be high on processed goods, consumer goods and luxury goods. A higher tariff was to be levied on those commodities in which Japanese domestic industry is or will be competitive and which are important from the point of view of employment even if the industry is deteriorating, whereas the tariff would be lower on those commodities in which Japan either has no potential supply or has already grown up to be strongly competitive. Supported by these tariff policies, rapid heavy industrialisation was undertaken successfully.

Japan's agricultural imports have been and still are partially restrained by quota, while manufactured goods are protected mainly by tariffs at present. Recently, Japan reduced tariffs to a fairly low level in accordance with the Kennedy Round reductions. After that reduction was completed, in 1972, tariffs on dutiable manufactured goods averaged only 8.8 per cent in the United States, 8.2 per cent in the EEC, 8.6 per cent in the United Kingdom, and 12.7 per cent in Japan (Table 1.3).

Although the government joined in the Kennedy Round hesitantly, Japanese trade gained considerable benefits from the 'free ride' due to other countries' tariff reductions, and, it is believed that the Kennedy Round worked as one of the causes of the huge favourable balance of trade after 1968. According to my estimates, which were made during the Kennedy Round negotiations on the assumption of a 50 per cent linear cut, the increase in Japan's trade would have amounted to 10.4 per cent for exports and 4.6 per cent for imports.[10]

Although the average level of Japan's tariffs on manufactures did not become excessively high, there was an obvious tariff escalation (shown in Table 1.3), since the big tariff revision of 1961 took escalation of the tariff as its main principle.

In addition, tariffs on finished consumer goods still remain high even after the Kennedy Round reductions, since heavy protection, once imposed on infant industries, has not been reduced sufficiently, while tariffs on traditional products of the labour-intensive type are still relatively high.

Table 1.3 Average tariff rates* of advanced countries after the Kennedy Round tariff reduction

(per cent)

	Raw materials	Semi-manufactured goods	Finished manufactures	Total
Japan	3.4	6.3	12.7	6.3
	(4.2)**	(4.8)	(8.5)	(5.3)
USA	2.5	5.6	8.8	6.8
EEC	0.4	4.8	8.2	4.5
UK	0.2	6.9	8.6	6.2
Canada	0.4	9.8	6.7	6.6
Average of 11 advanced countries	1.6	5.6	8.4	5.9

* An average of tariffs weighted by each country's imports by commodity.

** Figures in brackets are the rate after 20 per cent unilateral reduction in October 1972 was effected. Since tariffs on petroleum were raised meanwhile, the average rate on raw materials rather increased.

Source: GATT, *Basic Documentation for Tariff Study*, Geneva 1971; and the Japanese Ministry of Finance.

Since Japan's trade balance turned apparently from deficit to surplus around 1968, the Tariff Committee of the Finance Ministry began to enquire into the revision of the tariff law in May 1972 and finalised a recommendation in December 1972. Meanwhile, in October 1972, the government reduced tariffs unilaterally by 20 per cent on almost all imports except primary agricultural products (1,865 items). The average tariff rate on finished manufactures is now as low as 8.5 per cent which is equivalent to the tariff rates of other advanced countries (see Table 1.3). The Tariff Committee strongly recommended the revision of tariff escalation, further reduction of tariffs on manufactured goods in general and agricultural products in particular, the abolition of the concept of luxury tariff and the encouragement of those imports which contribute to curbing domestic inflation and pollution. It also recommended the extension of general preferences to developing countries and the increase of value added tariff items. Some of these recommendations were given effect by the 1973 annual tariff revision.

Actually the benefits of Japan's general preferences have so far been rather limited and the quota ceiling is so small that it was mostly filled within one or two months.[11] The system improved somewhat in 1973 as the preference margin became more generous.

The general preferences to developing country products are not sufficient for opening wider markets in advanced countries, although the longer-term effects might be more significant. Thus, it should be stressed that the extension of trade preferences is unlikely to be practicable or effective unless complementary adjustment policies are implemented in both advanced and less developed countries alike. It can also be said that the elimination of tariffs, even though it would phase out preferential trade arrangements, is preferable as a means of promoting trade for both advanced and developing countries.

Progress in the liberalisation of NTBs

In the forthcoming international negotiations in GATT, non-tariff barriers (NTBs) to trade are expected to be a matter of top priority but there are even more cumbersome trade deterrent factors to be dealt with than the remaining tariff barriers. The elimination of NTBs would be a major breakthrough in expanding not only trade among advanced countries but also their imports from the less developed nations.

Non-tariff barriers have major implications, particularly for Japan. Misunderstandings of and attacks on Japan's import restrictions and export incentives as manifested, for instance, in the Japan-United States textile negotiations, the dumping problem, the strong request for liberalisation of agricultural product imports, pervade the economic world. Japan's non-tariff barriers are not well enough understood and are rather overestimated by foreign countries. A thorough examination will show that, taken as a whole, Japan's non-tariff barriers are surprisingly few in number, though there are some which are highly conspicuous, for example, the residual import restrictions.

Japan's trade liberalisation made its first rapid progress from 1960 to 1963. This might be regarded as the spurt which allowed movement into GATT Article XI and IMF VIII status country. Liberalisation was forced along again from 1969 to 1972,[12] prompted by a desire to bring the liberalisation of trade and capital to completion first before revaluing the yen, since large surpluses of international payments had been accumulated. However, from 1964 to 1969, the pace of liberalisation was extremely slow. During this period residual import restrictions were maintained with few positive initiatives, placing some industries in a state of over-protection. It must be admitted that Japan's trade liberalisation has been too slow, although the above-mentioned intermediate period coincided with the time of Kennedy Round tariff negotiations and the Japanese government may have been too busily occupied in those negotiations to give attention to its own trade liberalisation.

Remaining import quota restrictions

Until a few years ago, Japanese imports were under watertight control through import quota (IQ), automatic import quota (AIQ) and automatic import approval (AA) systems, on the one hand, and exchange control of standard and non-standard methods of settlement on the other.[13] However, by the end of 1972, the AIQ system was abolished and the AA system was changed to a mere import declaration system.

Although there are several kinds of non-tariff barriers, the most important in Japan are the import quota restrictions. The number of items under the residual import restriction was 120 in April 1969 and was rapidly reduced to 33 (24 agricultural, 1 mineral (coal) and 8 manufactured items, in terms of the BTN 4-digit classification) by April 1972. Further liberalisation was undertaken in April 1973 and in October 1973. Therefore only 29 items in total (22 agricultural, 1 mineral (coal) and 6 manufactured items) are still under quota restriction at the present time.[14]

The problem of residual import restrictions on manufactured goods might be said to have nearly come to an end with only six items remaining unliberalised.[15] Of these, four items are raw hide and leather (bovine cattle leather, equine leather, sheep, and lamb skin leather, and goat and kid skin leather) and one is leather footwear. The liberalisation of these items is said to be difficult because of the protection that will have to be accorded to subsistence producers in the so-called 'dowa' districts where a minority group depends on this work. The one other item consists of parts of, and terminal machines for, digital-type electronic computers and integrated circuits. Protection for this item has been justified on the grounds that it is a new industry in need of such protection. The government decided – and businessmen agreed – in March 1973, that those items are to be liberalised gradually within three years.

In the agricultural field, in addition to the twenty-two items, several other items are controlled under state trading which is undertaken by quantitative restrictions. The items set aside for state trading are rice and wheat, barley and rye, major dairy products excluding natural cheese, butter, tobacco, salt, alcohol, poppy, cannabis and raw opium. They differ from other ordinary import quota items in that their transactions are monopolised by particular government agencies (such as the Food Agency of the Public Monopoly Corporation).

The liberalisation of agricultural imports presents a difficult problem for Japan. Agricultural products under the residual import restrictions are of a wide range and variety. The most important items of interest are meat, meat products and fruit. Overall consideration will have to be given to the problem, taking into account the state traded goods such as rice, wheat and barley and milk products, though the number of items is limited. There is a strong view that it is not justifiable that Japan alone should be blamed for protecting agriculture and imposing trade barriers on agricultural imports for that purpose when all other advanced countries do the same. It is also argued that while the United States was granted a waiver by GATT to restrict agricultural imports, and the EEC and the United Kingdom obstruct imports by other, less conspicuous, means such as variable surcharges, Japan depends solely on residual import restrictions and state trading, which attract attention. It is thus considered that the United States, the EEC and the United Kingdom apply restrictive measures which have actually a larger trade deterrent effect than the Japanese measures.

However, with the exception of rice, which is a state traded item for the present, there is little justification for positively maintaining the quantitative import restrictions on other items. It is suggested that imports of ham, bacon, canned beef and pork should be liberalised from direct control. Even if total abolition is difficult, an effort should be made to remove import quota systems on agricultural products other than rice gradually and to shift towards more objective measures such as tariffs, tariff quota systems or fixed surcharges.

Inconveniences in trade

There are cases where regulations which have been introduced with other major policy objectives have trade-inhibiting effects, even though they are not directly designed to have such effects. They are called 'induced non-tariff barriers'. Since they do not make trade regulation their prime objective, institutionally they are not non-tariff barriers. However, if their real trade deterrent effect is considerable, we have to identify them as non-tariff barriers. In such cases we call them *indirect* non-tariff barriers. When no real trade deterrent effect is obvious they are classified as *illusory* non-tariff barriers. They are all minor cases and mostly mere conveniences which might be better identified as illusory non-tariff barriers.

One type of induced NTB for which Japan has been criticised is the high internal excise tax on automobiles and whisky. These taxes, however, were really progressive taxes on luxury goods rather than discriminatory measures against imported products in favour of domestic goods. They were necessary in the past when the income level was low. It has become less necessary, however, to regard large cars or high-quality whisky as luxury goods. In fact excise taxes on luxury cars and whisky were lowered in 1972.

Another similar NTB is government procurement. In Japan, since the law does not discriminate against public purchases from abroad there is no problem legislatively. In practice, however, government contracts are hardly ever given on a competitive basis and governments invite only certain contractors to submit their bids, or give contracts to suppliers on a non-competitive basis. This practice might result in the exclusion of foreign suppliers. However, in so far as public contracts do not involve procurement of goods of great value, these restrictions are not of great importance.

A second type of induced NTB covers such technicalities as customs valuation, industrial standards and safety regulations, domestic animal infectious disease control and plant sanitation acts, the food sanitation act, the measuring system and anti-dumping restrictions and countervailing duties. All such troubles belong to the category of inconveniences which will mostly disappear if an international code or uniform criteria on these technicalities is established. Japan has tried hard recently to get rid of these inconveniences.

A third type of NTB, more apparent than real, is based on the suspicion that exports to Japan are hindered because there is strong administrative guidance (or pressure) which culminates in 'Japan Inc'.[16] In fact there are fewer actual cases of this sort of 'administrative guidance' than foreigners suspect. An administrative guidance was once given, regarding the instalment of larger thermo-electric generators, advising that the first generator be imported but the second be manufactured domestically. The government has also been suggesting that domestic oil refiners should purchase from the Arabian Oil Company (100 per cent Japanese-owned) a certain percentage of their crude oil imports. Criticism has been raised against both cases. However, it is doubtful whether protectionism of this sort should be judged as a non-tariff barrier, since the businesses involved would have acted in this way had they not been given such guidance.[17] If this measure is to be condemned as a non-tariff barrier, the regulations stipulating the domestic content ratios in import-substitution industries, which many countries apply at present, should be taken up as a problem of more importance.

We cannot deny that complaints might be raised that Japanese customs, such as right hand drive in automobiles, are different, and thus constitute trade barriers. In the extreme case the Japanese language itself is the most important barrier of this kind. It can be said that these are mere inconveniences and not non-tariff barriers. It has to be understood that the expenses incurred in overcoming these inconveniences are part of marketing costs which exporters to Japan naturally have to pay.

To sum up, there are no major non-tariff barriers against imports to Japan, especially from the viewpoint of American and European interests. What Japan might be blamed for is not the present level of restrictions, but the fact that her trade liberalisation has been too cautious, too slow and undramatic. Because of this, Japan could not eradicate her bad image in foreign countries, as a most restrictive country. Perhaps Americans and Europeans still complain about the difficulty of increasing exports to Japan more from vague reasons like remoteness, the differences in customs, and even the Japanese language. However, there are equivalent difficulties which Japanese businesses encounter in American and European markets. They should not be called non-tariff barriers but mere inconveniences which can be overcome by keen export efforts.

Measures promoting exports

Another characteristic of Japanese trade policy was the asymmetric governmental intervention in exports on the one hand and imports on the other. There was a sharp contrast between the measures favouring, encouraging and promoting exports and those restricting imports. A number of incentive measures were applied to exports, such as tax and credit incentives which were designed to make export business more profitable. However, almost all the export incentives have already been abolished recently.

In Japan, general trading firms played an important role. After World War II, the Japanese government established JETRO (Japan External Trade Organisation) for trade promotion and information services. The government also provided effective incentives for export promotion through tax reductions for export earnings (first 'export income exemption' and later a 'reserve fund for development of overseas markets' and an 'export depreciation allowance') and subsidised interest rates for export financing, long-term export credit on a deferred payment basis, and subsidies for export and export-oriented production which were designed to encourage exports by influencing the profitability of enterprises engaged in export activity. Even reparations payments and the provision of tied aid worked to give export activity extra profit.

Export interest subsidisation, particularly, worked very effectively in Japan. Incentive interest rates were accorded to foreign exchange bills which conformed to the rule of standard settlement. Such trade bills became eligible to be discounted by, or qualified as collateral acceptable to, the Bank of Japan, and enjoyed the benefit of discount or borrowing at interest rates lower than those prevalent in the country. Early availability of export earnings discounted at lower interest rates benefited business when compared with longer deferred payments in domestic marketing, for their own capital was very limited and availability of money from outside the firm was critical for business expansion.[18] Thus, with other export incentives, it was profitable for businesses to export goods at prices, say, 10 to 15 per cent lower than domestic prices. This incurred not only a waste of resources but also the condemnation of dumping from abroad and provoked discrimination against Japanese goods abroad. Such practices were abolished in August 1971.

Even without such export subsidisation, *de facto* dumping is easily fostered in new industries which depend heavily on economies of scale. In a 'catching-up' country like Japan, the product cycle starts from the importation of a new product of superior quality. A learning process follows and is assisted by the importation of technological knowhow and/or foreign direct investment. The expansion of production then leads to the exploitation of economies of scale, increases in productivity, improvements in quality and reductions in costs. This involves an import-substitution process. But as domestic costs reach the international competitive cost threshold, foreign markets are developed, the scale of production is extended further and costs are reduced again through greater economies of scale. Thus, the expansion of exports, originally made possible by the growth of domestic demand, in its turn provides a stimulus to industrial development. It is even quite profitable to export at a lower price than in the domestic market so as to cover only marginal cost since exporting makes further exploitation of economies of scale possible.

Discrimination against Japanese exports

Needless to say, the non-tariff barriers imposed by foreign countries, which have an import inhibiting effect, work against Japanese exports.

Of particular interest to us are the discriminatory restrictions which foreign countries impose on exports from Japan alone. The more important of these discriminatory restrictions against Japan are: (a) the invocation of Article XXXV of the GATT, and (b) the discriminatory import restrictions against Japanese exports applied by some Western European countries.

When Japan was granted admission to GATT in 1955, fourteen countries, including the United Kingdom, France and Austria, invoked Article XXXV, withholding their application of the Agreement, based on most favoured nation treatment, to Japan. In addition, in the early 1960s, when the British and French colonies gained independence and were admitted to GATT, they followed the United Kingdom and France and withheld their application of the Agreement to Japan, bringing the number of coutries which invoked Article XXXV to nearly thirty. However, major Western and British Commonwealth countries withdrew their invocation later. As of January 1975, eight countries (most of them less developed countries) still deviate from GATT rules in their trade with Japan.

Those still invoking Article XXXV have no real trade-deterrent effect. There will be no significant consequence whether or not they withdraw their invocation of Article XXXV, but apparently they either do not dare to proceed with withdrawal, or they may be reserving their right as a possible bargaining item, to be exchanged for some reciprocal concession by Japan. For Japan this is a matter of international prestige rather than of economic interest. Therefore, it is more than ever desired that they should withdraw the invocation voluntarily, although it might be far better if GATT eliminates Article XXXV which already has become unnecessary.

The problem is important, however, in the sense that the invocation played a role in inviting discriminatory treatment by Western countries against Japan. Although the leading Western European countries have withdrawn their invocation of Article XXXV, they have retained discriminatory treatment against Japan in the form of quantitative restrictions or licensing. In addition such countries as Germany, Italy and Sweden, which had not invoked Article XXXV in their trade with Japan, came to adopt various forms of discriminatory treatment against Japan.

Apart from the invocation of Article XXXV of GATT, which both Austria and Ireland practise, Japanese officials condemn such European non-tariff barriers as discriminatory import restrictions against Japanese exports through quantitative restrictions in some countries and licensing and price surveillance systems. It is rather difficult to give an exact number of items affected. But according to the 4-digit classification of the Brussels Tariff Nomenclature, West Germany applies discriminatory quantitative restrictions against Japan, aside from global quota restrictions, on 21 items; Italy restricts 46, Benelux 27, Denmark 3, Ireland 47, Austria 57, Norway 23 and France 38. Licensing systems discriminate generally against Japanese goods in Sweden, Spain and Portugal, and an import price surveillance scheme against Japan operates in Switzerland. Border tax and variable import levies are another worry for Japan.

Although Japanese officials also mention many other barriers and inconveniences, businessmen do not complain about European practices, saying that there are no problems and that such practices are merely inconveniences, easily overcome with export effort. Actually, those NTBs are mostly retained on our exports of traditional light manufactures in which Japan has been losing interest. Japan is not interested in flooding the European market with these goods. It is, therefore, time for Europeans to eliminate discriminatory restrictions on those goods in so far as the reason for them was, indeed, to prevent 'market disruption'. If Europeans retain those restrictions because they have the impression that access to Japanese markets is barred by residual import restrictions on a wide range of commodities, then it is an appropriate time to bargain for the further liberalisation of import restrictions on both sides.

Another problem for Japanese exports is the system of so-called 'voluntary export restraints'. There is a large variety of voluntary export restraints, and it is not easy to identify the countries concerned or ascertain the number of commodities affected with any precision. It is said that the number of items which are under voluntary export control imposed at the request of importing countries and reported to GATT by the Japanese government as non-tariff barriers reaches 264 according to the BTN 4-digit classification, of which 51 are at the request of the United States, and including double counting of items requested by other countries. One criterion for identifying non-tariff barriers is governmental intervention in export trade via the Export-Import Transaction Act or the Export Trade Control Ordinance. There are also cases of voluntary restraints of steel exports to the United States which involve no governmental intervention.[19]

The responsibility for imposing trade restrictive measures of such an intermediate character as voluntary export restraints, where it is not clear whether they are imposed by the importing countries or by Japan, lies with both parties. First, when a country's imports from Japan increase or threaten to increase sharply, Japan is accused of causing market disruption, and the importing country sometimes threatens to raise tariffs or impose import quotas, although its real intention is to furnish protection to competing domestic industries (in most cases declining industries) within that country. Secondly, Japan for her part accepts the request to impose voluntary export controls on the grounds that voluntary export restraints are less damaging and more palatable than import restrictions by the importing country. The reason why Japan judges voluntary control 'more palatable' is that voluntary actions leave Japan with wider room for discretion. For instance, as has been seen in the course of the Japan-United States textile negotiations, if the United States were to put a product-by-product quantitative import restriction into its trade legislation, Japan could do nothing but obey it, leaving the quantitative ceilings to be decided by the United States, even though Japan could invoke GATT on the grounds that the practice undeniably constituted a non-tariff barrier. On the other hand, voluntary restraints allow Japan to use her discretion. For instance, even though the rate of total export growth may be restricted to a certain percentage, the export of items to a rapidly growing market could be increased and the growth of items not in such demand could be held down or reduced. If subjected to product-by-product regulations, it is often true that in the aggregate even the permitted growth rates cannot be attained.

However, there is one more specifically Japanese problem. It is a fact that there have been cases of excessive competition, where Japanese exporters engaged in cut-throat selling competition with each other, thus inviting a fall in prices. Voluntary export restraints are sometimes applied in order to avoid such excessive competition and to guarantee orderly marketing. Furthermore, there are many cases where voluntary export controls have been introduced on the pretext of avoiding excessive competition even if there is no threat of import restrictions being imposed by the importing countries. This is an abuse of export restraints.

In any event, there are too many items under voluntary export control and a reduction in the number of such items should be considered. Since the greater part of them have been introduced to avoid excessive competition, voluntary export controls on these items should be removed and some other measures to avoid excessive competition should be devised.

All of these discriminatory measures come from the foreigner's fear of sharp increases in Japan's (and other developing countries') exports to particular markets of particular commodities[20] which do not give importing countries sufficient time to reduce or convert their non-competing industries. Thus they think some safeguard is indispensable, as will be discussed in the following chapter.

IV LIBERALISATION OF INVESTMENT

Liberalisation of capital inflow

'Japan can be described as, at best, a reluctant host to foreign direct investment. This follows directly from the long tradition of Japan's suspicion of foreigners and wish to be independent of foreign control.'[21] This is a cynical but substantially correct observation. As with Japan's liberalisation of trade, in the liberalisation of capital inflow, Japan is not criticised for the present degree of liberalisation, which by now allows almost free entry of capital, but for the cautious and slow progress towards that liberalisation.

In the early postwar period, there was intense concern over the weakness in the balance of payments. This led to the enactment in 1949 of the Foreign Exchange Control Law and its extension in 1950 with the Law Concerning Foreign Investment. Under this law a licensing procedure was established whereby the Foreign Investment Council could validate foreign investment in Japan. Investment was permitted only when it contributed to the attainment of Japanese self-sufficiency and to the improvement of the balance of payments, and then only up to 49 per cent ownership of the enterprise. The so-called 'administrative guidance' was used more often, and more effectively, in capital inflow control rather than in import restriction.

The liberalisation scheme began in 1963 when Japan accepted Article VIII status on the IMF and began participation in the Organisation for Economic Cooperation and Development. Since then, four rounds of a 'capital-decontrol' programme have been undertaken in July 1967, March 1969, September 1970 and August 1971. The government virtually assisted on a '50-50 principle' which automatically allows up to a 50 per cent participation for foreign capital in new ventures.[22] These were category I industries. In the four rounds of decontrol, the number of category I industries was gradually increased to more than 700. Some were shifted to category II industries (228) in which 100 per cent foreign ownership is allowed, and the number of excepted (non-liberalised) industries, i.e. category III, was decreased to only 7. Takeovers of existing companies were restricted more rigorously than in the case of new ventures.

A big change in capital inflow policy occurred in May 1973 with the fifth round of the decontrol scheme. Foreign companies undertaking both new ventures and takeovers of existing companies are allowed 100 per cent ownership if they wish, in all kinds of industries, with five exceptions: agriculture, mining, oil refining, leather manufacturing and retailing. In addition, liberalisation was postponed in the integrated circuits industry until December 1974 and in sixteen other industries until May 1975.[23]

Therefore, it can be said that restrictions on capital inflow have been almost completely liberalised. But one should ask why Japan has so severely controlled capital inflow and delayed its control for so long. The main reason was a nationalistic protectionism towards domestic enterprises based on an 'infant industry' type of argument. The bigness and monopolistic behaviour of American multinational corporations were frightening to Japanese business. It was feared that the multinationals would challenge small-sized Japanese enterprises, seriously disturb Japanese technology and oppress the growth of such promising industries as automobiles and computers. These Japanese industries have been overprotected until very recently. Now they have become competitive and capital inflow has been liberalised. What incentives, then, are left for foreign investors to come into Japan? This might be a genuine cause for complaint against Japan.

Instead of foreign direct investment, Japan was successful in stimulating the massive inflow of foreign technology[24] which in the eighteen years between 1950 and 1968 represented about 10,000 contracts and payments in excess of $1.4 billion. Technology inflow permitted the modernisation of old and the creation of new industries under extremely favourable conditions.[25]

Exchange rate realignment

The revaluation of December 1971 was the logical outcome of what had clearly become an untenable position in the balance of payments. The yen, following nearly four months of floating after the announcement by the United States of the August measures, was officially revalued by 7.65 per cent against gold (and by 16.88 per cent against the US dollar) on 21 December 1971. As the year went by and economic recovery gathered speed in the United States, there was little visible progress towards a sustainable equilibrium indicating that the initial exchange rate adjustment had been perhaps insufficient to produce the desired swing in time, thereby fuelling market expectations for a further exchange rate change. Already in October and November signs of speculative transactions became more apparent, increasing in importance in the following two months until the February 1973 devaluation of the US dollar and the subsequent decision to float the yen. Following small fluctuations after the reopening of the exchange markets, the nominal margin of appreciation for the yen in April through October averaged about 16 per cent or 265 yen per dollar (on the basis of the central rate, 308 yen per dollar, established in December 1971). Thus in little over eighteen months the Japanese currency recorded a nominal cumulative appreciation with respect to the dollar of almost 36 per cent. But, since the trend towards balance of payments deficit became obvious in 1973, the value of the yen in the floating exchange market fell from 265 yen per dollar to 275 yen on 2 November 1973 and to 300 yen on 7 January 1974, keeping this level with minor fluctuations throughout 1974 up to November 1975.

Should the Japanese accommodation in exchange rate policy be criticised as being too slow and uncooperative in the move towards international monetary realignment? It is true that the Japanese government and monetary authority tried hard to prevent the revaluation by promoting first trade liberalisation and tariff reduction. These were quite reasonable policies. But the development of monetary turmoil was too great and too abrupt. Japan had had no experience of exchange rate adjustment since the war and it was quite natural that the monetary authority hesitated to revalue the yen since the huge capital loss for the Bank of Japan and the big companies which accumulated overseas credits was so tangible.

By now, Japan has learnt a lot about international monetary turmoil and exchange rate adjustment policy and we may be able to take a more positive attitude towards the reform of the international monetary system. This is touched upon in Chapter 3. Also we are now confident that exchange rate adjustment, though cumbersome, is quite effective as a remedy for Japan's balance of trade and investment.

Conclusion

In the period from 1968 to 1972, the Japanese balance of payments has undergone a fundamental change, from a condition of worrisome periodic deficit to one of abrupt surplus. This change has freed Japan from an external constraint and changed her policy of export-encouraging and import-discouraging to a policy aiming in the reverse direction, shifting the emphasis away from a rapid growth of production and export to the development of a welfare state. The government twice declared dramatic promotion of trade liberalisation in an 'Eight Point Programme' in June 1971 and then a 'Seven Point Programme' in October 1972, in the hope that those policies might make unnecessary, or at least reduce, the revaluation of the yen. Thus, during 1969-73, import quota restrictions were reduced drastically, tariffs were halved through the Kennedy Round and the 20 per cent unilateral reductions, and capital inflow and outflow were also rapidly liberalised. The remaining restrictions are small in number and minor but they are a hard core to be eliminated. The present level of Japan's restrictions by tariffs and non-tariff barriers is very low and roughly equivalent to that of other advanced countries. Therefore, perhaps Japan might not be blamed for the remaining restrictions but rather for her delayed, slow and rather undramatic liberalisation process.

Because of those rapid liberalisation measures, coupled with a large revaluation of the yen, Japan's imports have been increasing overwhelmingly since the second half of 1972, especially in whisky, fashion clothes, furnitures and other consumer goods which were once thought to be luxuries, consumer durable machinery, new machines, equipment and knowhow for the preparation of a third structural change and various kinds of food. In 1973, imports (c.i.f.) increased by 63.2 per cent as compared with the previous year while exports (f.o.b.) were up by only 29.2 per cent, resulting in an import surplus of $1,384 million. In 1974, imports again increased by 62.1 per cent while exports increased by 50.4 per cent, resulting in a heavy import surplus of $6,574 million.

Therefore, Japan will not in future be as comfortable as she was with an abnormal surplus trade in 1971 and 1972, although the heavy additional burden on her balance of payments brought in by the oil crisis may be overcome within a few years.

V THE IMPACT OF THE OIL CRISIS

Since Nixon's new economic policy of August 1971 the international currency and trade system has been plunged into confusion and it is proving a struggle to build a new economic order. The announcement in September 1973 of the Tokyo Declaration for the start of a new round of GATT multilateral trade negotiations, followed by the general meeting of IMF in Nairobi, brought hopes of progress towards the formation of a new world economic order. But with the oil export cutbacks by OPEC countries in October of that year and a four-fold rise in price, the world economy was gripped by the oil crisis. The reconstruction of an international system of currencies and trade seemed to become a forlorn hope. Meanwhile with a world food shortage and strident claims by the developing countries for perpetual sovereignty over resources and concerning the law of the sea, the world economy fell into complete confusion and there were fears of another 1930s depression.

The Japanese economy, dependent on imports from overseas for the bulk of its raw materials and energy and much of its food, felt its existence and development threatened and was shocked into overreaction. A crisis mentality developed. There was a wave of withholding and hoarding not only of oil and related products but even of toilet paper. When on top of all this the 1974 Spring Offensive brought a 35 per cent wage increase, prices rose markedly. By the end of 1974, however, drastic restriction of total demand brought hope that a new price structure adjusted to the rise in oil prices would emerge and would stabilise at that level. The sudden expansion of oil payments in 1974 was met through an enormous Eurodollar loan (some $8 billion) and by direct borrowing from the Arab countries. Such short-term borrowings, however, provided no basic solution and did no more than postpone repayment. The fact that we were able to get by with the aid of borrowings in Year 1, however, does not mean that same process can be repeated in Year 2 and Year 3. There are already signs that eventually we shall need to generate a favourable balance of trade with America and Western Europe and use that to pay for imports of Arab oil and Australian raw materials. So long, however, as the oil importers as a whole are unable to overcome their deficit, such action by Japan would merely serve to increase the burden on other oil importing countries and disrupt their balance of payments and might well invite new charges of Japanese aggression and trade warfare. That prospect is causing concern. Another solution would be to attract long-term Arab investment for productive purposes, but this inflow is unlikely to exceed or even match Japan's obligations for direct foreign investment. Thus there is no easy alternative for Japan other than to balance her global international payments by means of an export surplus to Europe and America.

For the moment, everything depends on solving the oil problem.[26] The basic objective must be to reverse the present balance of bargaining power between the oil producers and the oil importers and change the situation from a sellers' market to a buyers' market. Unless the price of oil can be reduced in this way and the surplus of oil money brought down to a manageable level there can be no solution to the problem. We must do our best to bring the oil price down to, say, seven to eight dollars and achieve within the next one or two years a situation in which the oil producers' import expenditure is, say, $15 billion and the excess oil money some $20 billion.

In the longer term it is essential to develop alternative sources of energy such as gasification of coal, extraction from oilsands and shale, atomic power generation, use of solar energy and so on. Over the short and medium (7-10 years) term, however, until these alternatives come into large-scale commercial production, we should concentrate our energies on the following measures: (a) economise in oil consumption and the building up of buffer stocks; (b) increasing production from existing oil fields and developing new fields (Alaska, North Sea, the continental shelf, etc.); (c) changing over to an oil- and resource-saving industrial structure.

The oil producers have adopted the cartel tactics of jacking up prices by cutting back production and exports. This has strengthened the view that it will not be easy to reduce oil prices. Nevertheless, while tactics vary from one oil producing country to another, overall it seems likely that increased production will be stimulated. More and more developing countries are likely to succeed in developing new oil fields. Some of the current oil producers that have large populations will be anxious to sell oil for industrialisation, while some of those with small populations and smaller requirements for development capital may be anxious for long-term stable sales of oil at moderate prices. There is some hope of an internal split among the oil producers. At the margin the world oil supply situation will be influenced largely by the attitude taken by Saudi Arabia which holds the largest reserves in the world.

Thus, if the short- and medium-term policies of the consumers are successful and there is some breakdown on the side of the producers, it might well be that the interaction of the two might be so phased as to produce a cyclical up-and-down movement of world oil supplies and prices. It may in fact be that the good days experienced by oil producers from the oil shock of October 1973 until today will not continue forever but that oil prices will turn down with a subsequent period of hard times. We recall that the skyrocketing of primary products during the Korean War period lasted less than two years. Past experience indicates that primary product prices go through a succession of such short-term but wide-amplitude cycles. Is there any reason why oil should be an exception?

We must assume that oil is like any other primary product and that its price will be subject to continued wide cyclical fluctuation according to variations in supply and demand at the margin. In the current situation, however, the majority do not seem prepared to concede this. We should stop and think about the over-pessimistic view of oil availability and the consequent rush to obtain it. Oil reserves are still sufficient to support consumption for a long time yet and there is no question of their being unavailable. The important thing is to have confidence in that. Oil will continue to be an 'economic good' for a long time to come and will undergo cyclical variations in price so long as the policies of consumers and producers are out of step, producing swings in the world supply and demand situation. If consumers are patient for a little longer and encourage consumption cuts, oil prices are bound to fall some day. I should also like to make the following point: it is precisely because people do expect cyclical movements that they stress the importance of stockpiling on the principle that if we can survive for one, two or at the most three months, the oil market will ease and prices turn down.

If my assessment that oil is subject to cyclical price variation like any other primary product is correct, then the best solution would be to apply a multilateral international commodity agreement approach to oil. This should be combined with the pooling of individual countries' buffer stocks to form an international buffer stock with perhaps the addition of separate buffer stocks held by international organisations. The idea would be that ceiling and floor prices for oil would be fixed by international agreement and that when the market price fell below the floor price the international organisation would buy and increase its stocks while when the market price went above the ceiling, the international organisation would release stocks onto the market. Stabilising the oil price within a fixed band in this way would be attractive not only to consumers but also to producers. If a substantial fall in oil prices is coming, as there are signs that it is, then the oil producers should be happy to join an international oil agreement of this kind.

We are left with the problem of recycling oil money. Short-term borrowing of oil dollars through the Eurocurrency market or the New York market may be unavoidable in the first year, but it cannot continue through the second and third years. Establishment of the oil facility in the IMF and of the Kissinger Fund (Financial Cooperation Fund) in OECD are no more than emergency finance to cover deficits in the international balance of payments (the role that the IMF was designed to play) and cannot provide a basic answer to oil deficits. Leaving aside the possibility of long-term investment which I shall discuss below, sooner or later each oil importing country must pay for its oil and bring its current balance of payments into balance. In this connection, the argument that oil deficits should be treated specially contains a fallacy and contributes nothing to the fundamental solution of the problem. That argument runs that the oil importing countries as a whole cannot avoid a deficit of $50-60 billion a year. If each country adopts adjustment policies designed to balance its own individual current account, we will have competitive devaluation, export promotion, import restrictions and so on, producing chaos in international currency and trade. Beggar-thy-neighbour policies by which each country tries to shift the burden of the oil problem onto the others, could not cover the deficits to the oil producers. For this reason, the argument runs, it is better to borrow the amount of the oil deficit from abroad.

The advanced countries of OECD should do their utmost to bring their current accounts into balance. This will still leave (if we include the non-oil-producing developing countries) a huge deficit *vis-à-vis* the oil producers. It would be quite an achievement to get it down to, say, $20 billion a year with some fall in oil prices. This excess oil money should be employed in productive long-term investment to promote the economic development of the developing countries, including the Arab region, and the most desirable solution would be to devise a system of long-term recycling of oil money for that purpose.

From the oil producers' point of view, the safest long-term investments would probably be in American treasury bills, British gilt edged or in Japanese or West German government bonds. Japan could float national loans in the Euromarket or the Arab region, or could borrow through flotations by government institutions like the Export-Import Bank, the Overseas Economic Cooperation Fund or the Development Bank. We might well consider, moreover, making these more attractive to the Arabs by guaranteeing a return linked to the rate of inflation by a sliding scale.

Since the whole point is to divert excess oil money into productive long-term investment in the developing countries, we should actively promote a long-term recycling plan by which oil money would be absorbed (by facilitating loan flotations and long-term investment) through a World Bank group consisting of the World Bank, the Second World Bank, or International Development Corporation, and regional development banks like the Asian Development Bank which would then channel these funds into long-term investment in the developing countries. This plan for long-term recycling of oil money through the World Bank group is the main point, although it seems to have been overshadowed to some extent by the growing interest in the IMF's oil facility idea. There are some problems in long-term investment in developing countries through the World Bank group. Firstly, while the oil producers are anxious for high returns, the developing countries who are borrowing are unable to bear a high interest burden and some means will have to be devised to bridge this interest gap – for example by provision of aid funds from the advanced countries. Secondly, however efficiently the World Bank group may operate, the economic development of the developing countries, including the Arab region, will take time and will not require such enormous amounts immediately – perhaps no more than $10 billion a year. In other words, capacity to absorb such funds is limited. Even aggregate overseas direct investment by the United States over the past few decades is said to be only $100 billion. That may well indicate the sort of tempo at which highly profitable and safe investment could be expanded. Nevertheless, we should certainly promote the plan for long-term recycling of oil money through the World Bank group including means of raising the developing countries' capacity for absorbing long-term investment.

Measures through the World Bank group will not, by themselves, be sufficient to absorb the whole of the enormous amount of excess oil money. We must therefore ask whether there are not ways of long-term recycling that will mobilise imaginative direct investment by private enterprise. One can think of a number of varieties.

Firstly, there is the formation in the developing countries, including the Arab region, of joint ventures combining the funds of the oil producers with the technology and managerial capacity of firms in the advanced countries to promote agricultural development and industrialisation. Where joint ventures are formed in the oil producing countries themselves this may not be so important, but where they are formed in other countries it may be necessary to make their establishment more profitable by providing low-interest finance for exports of plant on credit through the Export-Import Bank or the Overseas Economic Cooperation Fund. This is one form of interest subsidisation for developing countries.

Secondly, there is the long-term recycling of oil money via a triangular route. First, firms in the advanced countries borrow oil money long term at the market rate of interest to expand their own activities. These funds will, of course, be applied to productive activities which yield a rate of profit higher than the interest paid. At the same time, the advanced countries transfer an equivalent amount of funds in the form of aid or low-interest investment to the developing countries for productive activities there. Use of this triangular route will not only achieve long-term recycling of oil money to the developing countries but at the same time will provide for subsidisation of the interest gap by the advanced countries. I would suggest that this plan is worthy of full consideration and early implementation. My point is that although the major impact of the oil crisis has been on the long-term future of the economies of Japan and the other advanced countries, it cannot be solved within the advanced countries alone. The way to a solution lies in conscientiously tackling the promotion of economic development in the developing countries including the Arab region and reorganisation of north-south trade; spare oil money should be employed as an appropriate source of funds for that purpose. We should keep this firmly in mind in rethinking the long-term future of the Japanese economy.

NOTES

1. 'To hear some anguished Europeans tell it, the Japanese are not just bartering, but begging, borrowing and stealing European's markets, Europe's profits, even Europe's art – in addition to its fashions, its wines, its thoroughbreds, indeed its very cultural heritage.' 'The Japanese in Europe', *Time* European Edition, 6 August 1973, p. 6. Also see, *The Japanese Challenge in Europe*, prepared and published by Business International S.A. Geneva (reprinted from *Business Europe*), 1973.

   As an example of Asian developing countries' criticisms against Japan, it is reported that: 'Today Japan does more business, gives more aid, sends more tourists and even plays more golf in the region than any other country. Her steel builds virtually all the buildings, her cars and motor-cycles dominate the roads, her ships fill the ports, her radios bring the news, and her advertising keeps both the region's press afloat and its cities lit up at night . . . The Japanese tend to move in bunches, frequenting Japanese bars, restaurants, night clubs, and hotels. Because of this, Japanese restaurants find it profitable to fly in raw fish from Tokyo once a week via – naturally – Japan Air Lines.' James P. Sterba, 'Japan Tightens Her Economic Grip on Nations of East and South Asia', *New York Times*, 28 August 1972.
2. This is not, however, an appropriate index for the denominator since it involves a value approximately 10 per cent higher than the f.o.b. term.
3. Kiyoshi Kojima, *Japan and a Pacific Free Trade Area*, Macmillan, London, 1971, pp. 9-12.
4. The main export items of chemical goods are: synthetic plastics, organic chemicals, chemical fertilisers, inorganic chemicals, dyeing and colouring materials, and medical and pharmaceutical products. They are sensitive to the shortage of petroleum.
5. Warren S. Hunsberger, 'Japan-United States Trade – Patterns, Relationships, Problems', Jerome B. Cohen, ed., *Pacific Partnership: United States-Japan Trade*, Japan Society Inc., 1972, p. 128.

6. *Ibid.*, p. 120.
7. Cf. Kiyoshi Kojima, ed., *Economic Cooperation in the Western Pacific*, Japanese-Australian Project, Report No. 1, Japan Economic Research Centre, Tokyo, June 1973.
8. It has been observed that the policy making and decision making processes in Japan are at first slow to move but, having begun, move in a highly concerted fashion. Government bureaucrats are an elite, efficient and dedicated to their assigned task. In order to set up an important policy, long discussions and meetings are needed in order to coordinate and adjust the diverse views and interests of the various ministries, especially between the ministers of finance, foreign affairs, international trade and industry, agriculture, and the economic planning agency. It is a democratic process and good as a system of mutual checking, but compromise is often delayed, as a result of cautiousness, until pressure from foreign powers becomes strong and irrefutable. When the situation becomes serious the decided policy is enforced quickly and in a highly concerted manner. However, it often overshoots the target or, on other occasions, works in the wrong direction since the policy is already out of touch with the current situation. Cf. Richard Halloran, 'The 24 Unseen Bureaucrats who Decide Japan's Course', *International Herald Tribune*, Paris, 2 January 1974.
9. See Ippei Yamazawa, 'Industrial Growth and Tariff Protection in Prewar Japan', *Keizai Kenkyu* (Hitotsubashi University), January 1973.
10. Kiyoshi Kojima, *Japan and a Pacific Free Trade Area*, Macmillan, London, 1971, pp. 35-7.
11. On the EEC preferences, see Richard N. Cooper, 'The EEC Preferences: A Critical Evaluation', *Inter Economics*, April 1972, pp. 122-4. Japan's preferences are basically similar to the EEC's and could be subjected to the same critical evaluation.
12. There is a rough indicator of the progress of trade liberalisation, the so-called 'liberalisation ratio', which is the ratio of the value (in 1959) of imports on which quantitative restrictions are removed to the total imports. The liberalisation ratio jumped from 44 per cent in 1960 to 92 per cent in 1963 and stayed at the same level until 1969. It rose again after 1970 and reached 97 per cent in 1972.
13. More detailed explanations are given in Kiyoshi Kojima, *Nontariff Barriers to Japan's Trade*, Japan Economic Research Centre, December 1971, pp. 25-30.
14. This may be compared with other countries' quota restrictions as of November 1972: West Germany 39, France 74, Italy 20, United Kingdom 25, Benelux 8, and United States 7 plus 16 waived items.
15. 'With respect to both tariffs and quotas, therefore, Japan's protectionist barriers in 1971 had been brought more or less into line with those of major Western industrial countries.' Patricia H. Kuwayama, 'Japan's Balance of Payments and Its Changing Role in the World Economy', Jerome B. Cohen, ed., *Pacific Partnership: United States-Japan Trade*, Japan Society Inc., 1972, p. 60. See also Ryutaro Komiya, 'Japan's Non-Tariff Barriers in Manufactured Products', H. E. English and Keith Hay, eds., *Obstacles to Trade in the Pacific Area*, Carleton University, Ottawa, 1972, pp. 225-6.
16. See, *Japan, The Government-Business Relationship*, Department of Commerce, Washington, D.C., USA, April 1972. See also William Diebold, Jr., *The United States and the Industrial World*, The Council on Foreign Relations, New York, 1972, Chap. 3.

    It seems to me that there is a broad misunderstanding in foreign countries of Japan's business-government relations and administrative guidance. Bureaucrats, businessmen and academics naturally work together in the Council of Economic Planning Agency, MITI, etc., for the better planning of economic growth and welfare. The Chairman of this Agency is often a businessman or an academic leader. The business circle exercises a big influence and brings pressure to bear upon the government, not the reverse. Business abuses and ignores the 'administrative guidances', which do not actually exist or cannot be enforced, in its negotiations with foreigners and competitors.

17. Dr Kuwayama expresses it in this way: 'The view is often expressed that Japanese imports have failed to respond to liberalisation of formal barriers like quotas and tariffs because of remaining informal policies, perhaps the most frequently mentioned being "administrative guidance" of purchases by major Japanese corporations. How widespread and important such informal barriers are is an empirical question which is difficult to answer.' Patricia H. Kuwayama, 'Japan's Balance of Payments and Its Changing Role in the World Trade', Jerome B. Cohen, ed., *Pacific Partnership: United States-Japan Trade*, Japan Society Inc., 1972, p. 71.

18. The interest subsidisation to the shipbuilding industry which is criticised by foreign sources as a non-tariff barrier is of quite a different nature. Under this policy the government subsidises part of the interest which shipowners have to pay on loans to finance the domestic building of ships. This system is a scheme which is deemed necessary to offset the long-term, low-interest, deferred-payment loans granted on ship exports. In other words if no such scheme operated, all ocean going vessels would be built for export alone and none built for domestic use, because of profit disadvantages. In this sense, the interest subsidisation of shipbuilding can be said to be a non-tariff barrier which is a necessary evil to assure equal treatment with exports.

19. Since 1 October 1971, exports of wool and synthetic textiles are subject to governmental agreement between Japan and the USA (also Canada), i.e. product-by-product regulations.

20. It is difficult to explain why Japanese exporters turn up in the same markets at the same time and engage in excessive competition. Certainly it is easier for a firm to follow a pioneer firm who successfully enters a new market and it is even profitable as long as there is a large market to be exploited. However, it cannot be denied that there is a characteristic element in Japanese enterprises that is apt to give rise to excessive competition. For instance, there are too many small enterprises. With a low ratio of owned to total capital, they rely on borrowings from outside sources and consequently have no financial cushion in case of a downturn in sales. Small margins and large turnover is their motto. They lack initiative and blindly follow other enterprises who have succeeded. They are only keen on forestalling their competitors with no consideration of results upon mutual situation. Trading firms, which are unique to Japan, are not exceptions. Changes are needed in the philosophy of business behaviour.

21. Lawrence B. Krause, 'Evolution of Foreign Direct Investment: The United States and Japan', in Jerome B. Cohen, ed., *Pacific Partnership: United States-Japan Trade*, Japan Society Inc., 1972, p. 162.

22. More detailed explanation is given by Ryutaro Komiya, 'Direct Foreign Investment in Postwar Japan', Peter Drysdale, ed., *Direct Foreign Investment in Asia and the Pacific*, Australian National University Press, Canberra, 1972.

23. Meat products, processed tomato products, feeds, precooked foods for

distribution to restaurants and other eating houses, manufacturing and wholesales of clothing, pharmaceutical and agricultural chemicals, ferro-alloys, hydraulic equipment, packaging and wrapping machines, electronic precision instruments, records, real estate, manufacturing, sales and lease of electronic computers, data processing, fruit juices and fruit beverages, and photographic film.

24. Cf. Terutomo Ozawa, 'Imitation, Innovation, and Japanese Exports', Peter B. Kenen and Roger Lawrence, eds., *The Open Economy*, Columbia University Press, New York, 1968, pp. 190-212.
25. The outflow of Japanese capital will be analysed in Chapter 7.
26. Cf. K. Farmanfarmain, A. Gutowski, S. Okita, R. V. Roosa and C. L. Wilson, 'How Can the World Afford OPEC Oil?', *Foreign Affairs*, January 1975.

2 JAPAN AND THE MULTILATERAL TRADE NEGOTIATIONS

I PROSPECTS FOR THE TOKYO ROUND NEGOTIATIONS

A new round of multilateral trade negotiations in GATT was initiated with the declaration of ministers approved in Tokyo on 14 September 1973, and after a lengthy wait for authorisation of the US Trade Act of 1974, actual negotiations resumed in early February 1975.

The new Tokyo round will be effective in preventing a further increase in protectionist pressures – at least during the negotiation period. It will be a difficult and lengthy negotiation.

This round of trade negotiations has reopened under the worst possible circumstances: a world whose monetary system has been shot to pieces by the oil producers, most of whose trading nations are deep in deficit, and whose largest single economy is in recession, with all the protectionist pressure that implies. Add to this the American presidential election in late 1976.

There is a view that no negotiation is worth undertaking and that little serious progress in trade liberalisation is expected under such uncertainty in world monetary, trade and investment regimes as at present. Rather than further trade liberalisation, reform of the international monetary system is more urgently demanded in order to calm the turmoil since August 1971, to remove the fear of a crisis like the 1930s, and in order to cope with the aggravated difficulty created by the oil crisis and world-wide inflation since October 1973.

It is true that a sound international monetary system is a prerequisite to further trade liberalisation. But it may also be true that now is a good time to establish a clear division of functions and co-operation between the monetary and trade systems, or between the IMF and GATT, so that further trade liberalisation will facilitate the orderly function of a durable and equitable monetary system.

The success of the Tokyo round negotiations depends in large part on the attitude of the three trading giants: the USA, the European Economic Community and Japan.

The American intentions are clearly shown in the Trade Act of 1974 which gives the American administration a reasonably free hand on tariffs. It can dispense with tariffs of up to 5 per cent, which cover about half of the United States' manufactured imports, and it can cut higher tariffs by up to 60 per cent of the rate. But on non-tariff barriers to trade, the American negotiators' hands will be tied. They can negotiate what they like, but they will need the subsequent approval of Congress to put their promises into effect.

The EEC, as shown in 'Conception d'ensemble', will insist again on harmonisation, instead of the linear-cut, in the tariff structure, and will not eliminate common tariffs and common agricultural protection policies.

What then are the interests and attitudes of Japan? Unfortunately, multilateral trade negotiations are a highly confidential matter for the Japanese administration and an economist like myself is not privy to such information. But I would guess that Japan's attitude is positive in promoting further trade liberalisation[1] for she is one of the initiators of the new round and was the host country for the Tokyo ministerial meeting in September 1973. And perhaps Japan expects a favourable result from tariff reductions, as far as they are undertaken on an equitable, reciprocal basis, which would increase her exports more than her imports, as was the case in the Kennedy Round tariff cut.[2] Japan may be keenly interested in setting up a rule for export control or supply access of primary commodities.

We envisage in the coming negotiations that tariffs on manufactured goods will be reduced to a certain extent as the second phase of the Kennedy Round, though this will necessarily result in decreasing returns. On non-tariff barriers, discussion in the GATT committee has been undertaken to develop codes of conduct in such areas as industrial standards, customs valuations and import licensing; the codes will be extended to other areas, such as those concerning subsidies and countervailing duties, quantitative import restrictions and voluntary export restraints, government procurements, packaging and labelling and import documentation. A real difficulty will be the reduction of those non-tariff barriers, especially QRs, which are immune from quantifying, through multilateral negotiations on a reciprocal basis. Negotiations on reducing barriers to agricultural trade will be toughest. There needs to be much debate on export controls (supply access), safeguard mechanisms, and favourable trade opportunities for less developed countries (LDCs).

Since I am not able to handle the complexity of multilateral trade negotiations as a close observer, I would like instead to present a view of a new world trade order which, it is hoped, is more impartial and internationalistic than negotiators have in mind now.

II A 90 PER CENT FREE TRADE OF MANUFACTURED COMMODITIES

The steady liberalisation of world trade since 1945, which owes much to the contributions of GATT, has played an integral role in the unparalleled growth in world production, employment and prosperity which virtually all developed nations have enjoyed since that time.

The starting point of my observation is to ask whether the remaining tariffs and non-tariff barriers are really large and still a deterrent to trade expansion. Legally, the answer is yes. Practically, it can be said that trade liberalisation has been almost finalised. Even in the 1860s free trade was never complete. The present tariffs and NTBs appear to be large because comparative cost differences in manufactured trade have become much narrower than those of nineteenth-century vertical trade, but, in fact, they are not large barriers and can be easily overcome by export efforts. Thus, world trade must now make a bold attempt to find fresh directions for GATT.

In the present situation, in which only a hard core of trade barriers is retained by each country, it should be asked whether it is right to push hard for further trade liberalisation in the coming GATT negotiations or whether we should rather stop the 'liberalisation war' and wait for the effect of monetary realignments to become more obvious. To attack partner countries' hard core barriers in the present situation may be merely to invite antagonism and resentment. Usually, in order to eliminate hard core barriers, GATT negotiation is useless and domestic structural adjustment in each country and harmonisation of domestic policies between them are indispensable. A complete reorganisation of GATT into a new organisation *à la* the larger European Community might be required – this is unquestionably difficult.

Therefore an attempt to reduce by half the present low levels of tariffs (less than 10 per cent on average)[3] in advanced countries does not present an attractive target when the time and labour required are compared with the expected result, which, as a runner-up to the Kennedy Round, will necessarily result in decreasing returns. Rather, a complete and stage-by-stage elimination within say, ten years, of tariffs on manufactured goods should be aimed at. If this were attained, many non-tariff barrier problems, such as customs valuation and procedures, tariff preferences of customs unions and preferences toward developing countries, etc., would automatically disappear.

However, complete tariff-free trade is too idealistic and neither practicable nor reasonable if the positive role of tariffs in dynamic structural adjustment of international trade, as explained in the next section, is taken into consideration.[4] Therefore I would like to propose 'a 90 per cent free trade of manufactured commodities'. In other words, each trading nation must eliminate tariffs and quantitative restrictions on at least 90 per cent of manufactured imports.

The proposal presupposes that tariffs and other trade policy measures should not be used for balance of payments difficulties, the adjustment of which can be left entirely with overall adjustment measures, such as prompt and effective adjustment of exchange rates. A clear division of labour between trade policies and overall adjustments should be established.

Although the Japanese government and business circles stressed the difficulty of reducing tariffs during the Kennedy Round negotiations, it could, in fact, be done without any difficulty or harm to our national economy (this remark is applicable not only to tariff reduction, but also to the gradual elimination of quota restrictions and to the revaluation of the yen). On the contrary, Japan benefited considerably from the Kennedy Round tariff reduction. In October 1972, the Japanese government unilaterally reduced tariffs by 20 per cent on almost all manufactured imports. If we could do this then, why could we not implement gradually a 100 per cent tariff cut? The reduction of the escalation of the tariff system will also be completed very soon. In the EEC and EFTA, they were able to eliminate intra-area tariffs. There is, perhaps, no reason why they could not abolish external tariffs as well.

In order to bring about a substantial abolition of non-tariff barriers and a furtherance of tariff reductions, it is necessary to change the mistaken concept of 'national interest' in which exports are gains and imports losses. The true concept of the gains from trade is that the real gain is to import cheaply and in great quantity, while exports, which are not a gain *per se*, should reach the level where they can finance imports efficiently. Japan will have to shift its objectives toward the realisation of this true gain from trade. Needless to say, such a change of philosophy is required not only of Japan, but of all other countries, too. Dismantling of non-tariff barriers and tariff reduction will not be realised unless all countries act voluntarily on the basis of the true concept of gains from trade, irrespective of what their partners do.

It is not only in regard to trade that the change of philosophy is necessary. Too many resources have been poured into export activities in Japan. Furthermore, import restrictions have acted to protect less efficient industries within the country. In this way, the Japanese economy attained and maintained full employment and has continued to grow at a rapid pace. When compared with the possible state of a nation in which the optimal allocation of resources had been attained, industrial efficiency and the welfare of the people have been distorted. Abandoning the pursuit of mere high growth of aggregate national product irrespective of its quality and content, Japan ought to change its philosophy toward the attainment of economic growth by utilising its resources more efficiently.

It is time to expect a unilateral reduction[5] and elimination of trade barriers from each country in its own interest, i.e. in order to achieve better reallocation of resources, to curb inflationary pressures, and so forth. All nations should get rid of mercantilistic attitudes. This is especially needed in the case of non-tariff barriers. Non-tariff barriers can hardly become a subject of bargaining in accordance with the principle of reciprocity, since they are not measurable in their effect, not comparable with each other and differ from country to country in their motivation and intent. However, such a rule as 'overtime reciprocity' might be established in order to facilitate unilateral, stage-by-stage trade liberalisation.

In order to realise 90 per cent free trade, I would like to propose to GATT 'a fair-weather rule of reduction (or elimination) of tariffs and non-tariff barriers'. That is, a country should reduce tariffs and NTBs while its balance of payments is favourable, but it should not be allowed to raise them again, even if its balance of payments becomes unfavourable, since at that time some other country will have a favourable balance of payments and will be expected to reduce its own tariffs and NTBs. Thus, tariffs and NTBs in all advanced countries will be eliminated gradually within, say, ten years.[6] The fair-weather reduction rule may be implemented in a more detailed fashion as a counterpart to the exchange rate adjustment rule which is now under discussion in the arena of international monetary reform.

All countries should abolish non-tariff barriers, which are direct and selective restrictions on trade, as soon as possible and shift to the tariff system. If it is possible to measure the tariff equivalent effect of non-tariff barriers, then there is no reason why a shift to tariff systems is impossible. If it is not possible to measure such an effect, then it might be well to permit countries to levy or raise tariffs to the extent that they can feel safe or secure by doing so. This might be unavoidable even if it temporarily raises tariff barriers to some extent. However, it will eventually be recognised that high tariffs are unnecessary. Then it might be appropriate to set about a 'Kennedy Round' of tariff cutting negotiations. This method, as suggested by some experts,[7] is worth thorough consideration.

III DYNAMIC ADJUSTMENTS TOWARDS WORLD TRADE EXPANSION

The primary aim so far of GATT has been to achieve a global free trade – multilateral, non-discriminatory free trade – by reducing tariffs and non-tariff barriers as far as possible, and this aim has almost been realised. Although global free trade realises the most efficient allocation and utilisation of world resources and the maximum welfare in a static sense under given conditions, it may not assure steady growth of world production and trade without such dynamic forces as growth of the work force, technological progress, capital accumulation, natural resources development, etc., and with steady and harmonious structural adjustments of industries in each national economy and of the international division of labour. To facilitate those structural adjustments, the contribution of foreign direct investments is evaluated.

We must pay attention to how the structural adjustments can be promoted by tariffs and other trade policies. This must be the proper and positive role of trade policies in the dynamic expansion of world trade. Sheer global free trade is not a sufficient and sole aim of GATT. The positive contribution of trade policies, which have been regarded only as negative trade deterrent factors, must be built into the GATT system. How properly to make those two aims consistent in the world trade order should be investigated.

Even the present GATT rule could not avoid such exceptions to the global free trade principle as customs unions and free trade areas (Article XXIV), import restriction of those items under state trading and other specific reasons (Articles XVII, XX, XXI), safeguard (Article XIX), special treatment for less developed countries (Articles XXXVI-XXXVIII), and so forth. To re-examine these exceptions is one thing: to sanction positively some tariffs as far as they are properly necessary for dynamic trade expansion is quite another. Then, multilateral trade negotiations may be undertaken to achieve equitable reciprocity on exceptional items, leaving the further liberalisation of trade with the '90 per cent free trade' principle. Certainly, the admission of tariffs and other trade policies in exceptional cases may be dangerous if they are increased only for protectionist purposes. Therefore, strict criteria are required to identify what kind, when and how long such trade policies would properly foster structural adjustments contributing to dynamic world trade expansion. Under strict criteria, exceptional items should be reduced to as few as possible.

Compared with such overall adjustments as changes in the exchange rate, wage rate, general price level, etc. – the most effective ways to adjust balance of payments – a trade policy of tariffs, quota restrictions and subsidies is selective and discriminatory in the industries to be protected. Such trade policy is discriminatory, not only against foreign commodities imported, but also among domestic industries. This is the merit as well as the demerit of such a trade policy. Because trade policy is discriminatory against foreign commodities, it should be abolished in order to achieve the optimum allocation of world resources under static conditions. But because it is industry-specific, it is useful to foster structural adjustments of industries in order to achieve dynamic world trade expansion.

Even in international economic theory, which is usually critical of almost all protectionist theories, arguments for 'infant' industries are supported with strict qualifications. Practically, in order to develop proper new manufacturing industries in developing countries, protection is inevitable, and industrialisation in latent comparative advantage lines is the most promising way for the LDCs economic development and for dynamic world trade growth.

Moreover, even if developing countries have succeeded in developing manufacturing production, there are huge barriers to entry into advanced countries' markets by LDCs. Assistance to 'infant trade', in addition to infant industry, may be justified.

Barriers to new entry in advanced economies, besides tariffs and other ordinary barriers, include: (1) economies of scale enjoyed by advanced countries' companies, but not yet realised by developing countries' enterprises; (2) advanced technology which is monopolised by industries in the advanced countries and which the developing countries can only use through royalties or foreign direct investment; (3) product differentiation in brand or design which makes adaption by developing countries difficult; and (4) other barriers, such as marketing and information networks, vertical and horizontal integration in production and sales with which only the big multinational corporations are equipped. Because of these barriers to entry for developing countries, they may better utilise the advantages and excellent facilities of multinational enterprises through direct investment both in production and marketing until they can succeed in developing new manufacturing production and in finding new openings in advanced markets. And advanced countries might have to provide special treatment favourable to the entry of developing countries' exports.[8]

The above argument for 'economies of scale' is also applicable to the latecomer industrialised country. A new, high technology manufactured product is preempted by the most advanced country, who is the innovator. But a latecomer may, due to more suitable factor endowments and demands, be able to produce that product at comparatively cheaper cost if it achieves production with optimum economies of scale through learning or foreign direct investments. Protection of such an industry until it achieves the appropriate economies of scale may be justified.

There is another practical, not theoretically justified, need for protection of senescent industries. Retirement of the industry or transfer to another more promising sector should be undertaken according to changes in the comparative advantage pattern, but it must be done in a gradual and harmonious way for reasons of employment and social justice. The need for protection is aggravated when a large increase occurs suddenly in specific manufactures which are usually the product of senescent industries which have already lost a comparative advantage. These justify a safeguard mechanism.

Although free trade is beneficial for the whole national economy, individuals within each country can be hurt as a result of changes in trade patterns. Complementary policies are needed to give those individuals who are displaced time to adjust to the new conditions and to help them do so. These policies should be of two types: (1) temporary limitations (safeguards) on the rate of imports to protect against a rise too rapid to be readily absorbed; (2) government assistance to help affected individuals adjust comfortably to the new circumstances. However, there is great concern that the safeguards might easily be abused for protectionist purposes. It is in Japan's interest that, as an amendment to Article XIX, the safeguard clause should include an obligation that 'application of the safeguard measures should be accompanied by action to bring about domestic adjustment so that the use of the safeguard mechanism will in fact be temporary'.[9]

The Maidenhead Communiqué defines this more precisely:

> Temporary limits on the growth of imports should be available in cases where examination of all relevant facts shows clearly that injury to firms and workers, beyond their capacity to adjust with reasonable assistance, has been caused by imports. Such restrictions should be strictly limited in duration and degressive over time. In addition, an adjustment program which will enable the injured either to continue their present occupations or shift into new

> endeavours should accompany any such import limitations, to permit those limitations to expire on schedule. All these features of a new safeguard system should be subject to international surveillance. The new system should cover all policy instruments used to restrain trade, including the so-called 'voluntary' export restraints, most of which have heretofore operated outside any international framework.[10,11]

Perhaps sharp increases in Japan's (and some developing countries') exports of particular goods to particular markets are the object of the new safeguards. Japan must reconsider this since this reaction is the result of the Japanese style of export competition. Once export of a particular commodity to a particular market is alleged to be promising, firms follow each other blindly, flooding the market and waging a cut-throat price war. To cope with such practices, control through use of minimum export prices might be most useful. Another cause of excessive competition in export markets has been export credit incentives. On domestic sales, it takes considerable time to collect bills. In the case of exports, exporters were able to receive payment immediately after shipment of goods by discounting bills at subsidised interest rates. Therefore, the abolition of export interest subsidisation which was carried out in August 1971 will help to prevent excessive export competition.

Japan needs (and will agree to) new safeguards for she has already faced and will continue to face a sharp increase in imports from developing countries in the not too distant future. But she strongly insists, as shown in the last Tokyo meeting, that safeguards should be multilateral and non-discriminatory. In other words, Japan cannot accept safeguards under bilateral treaties which exist between Japan and some European countries, the United Kingdom, France and Benelux, and such safeguards as perhaps the EEC has in mind which discriminate against a specific country (perhaps Japan).

To sum up, both protection of a new industry which facilitates the development of a comparative advantage line, and safeguards against sudden increases in specific imports which assure gradual retirement of a comparative disadvantage industry, may be justified in order to promote structural adjustment in each trading economy which results in a new growth of world trade.

Structural adjustment policy usually focuses its attention on contracting old, comparatively disadvantageous sectors of the economy, but a way of promising the growth of new, comparative advantage sectors is an equally important task for structural adjustment policy. Overall unemployment is another problem which relates directly to the degree of flexibility and cost of adjustment programmes. This may be the most serious problem for such mature economies as those of the United States and the United Kingdom, but not for Japan's which is still young and suffers from a labour shortage. Structural adjustment in declining, inefficient sectors is undertaken successfully only in a dynamic economy in which the growth sectors develop so rapidly as to absorb resources from contracting sectors. This is the general position of the Japanese economy today in respect of the rising ability of developing countries to export manufactured goods. A third structural change, knowledge-intensive industrialisation,[12] which the Japanese economy intends to attain is just what is required to allow adjustment with developing countries.

However, exceptional protection measures for these structural adjustments should be limited to, for example, less than 10 per cent of manufactured trade. Multilateral negotiations may be done so as to achieve reciprocity of minimum exceptions under tariff protection, including safeguard and state trading items. Exceptions are sanctioned through examination with strict criteria which are appropriate only for structural adjustment purposes.

Although it is theoretically right that subsidies are a more effective measure than tariffs in developing new industries, practically speaking, tariffs may be preferable because subsidies are not allowed in the GATT system (Article XVI) and are hidden from foreigners' eyes. Also tariffs are preferable to quotas as a safeguard measure because tariffs may be as high as is sufficient, induce structural adjustment according to the price mechanism, and tariff revenue may be used for adjustment assistance (although quotas seem effective in improving a trade imbalance, this should be left to exchange rate adjustment). The ideal is that trade barriers should be confined to tariffs and that the adjustment of international balance of payments be left with overall adjustment measures.[13]

Since the forces behind both protection for new industry and safeguards for emergency are dynamic in their character, tariffs for those purposes should be temporary and should be gradually eliminated within a given period, although this does not exclude the possibility of new tariffs for different imports if it becomes necessary to make another structural adjustment. These exceptional tariffs should also be subject to the process of review, periodic report and other multilateral surveillance.

One of the implications of the above arguments is that measures designed to protect industrialisation in less developed countries are to be permitted, although improvements to present inefficient protective systems should be recommended. Developed countries do not expect reciprocity for commitments made by them in negotiations to reduce or remove tariffs and other barriers to trade with developing countries. The generalised system of preferences must be improved and adopted by many developed countries in addition to the EEC and Japan. However, to provide preferences for developing countries, because non-tariff free trade and the elimination of an escalated tariff structure are more effective than restrictive preferences in opening market access for the manufactured products of LDCs. The real difficulty in almost all developing countries, except some industrially developed ones such as Hong Kong, Singapore, Korea, Taiwan, etc., is the lack of capacity for producing appropriate, good quality manufactured exportables and the lack of trading channels to developed markets.

At this point, direct foreign investments play an important role, if they are undertaken in the proper way. Direct foreign investment, that is, the transmission to the host country of a package of capital, managerial skill and technical knowledge, is a potent agent of economic transformation and development. I differentiate 'trade-oriented' (or Japanese) and anti-trade-oriented (or American) foreign direct investments.[14] Japanese foreign investment has to date been 'trade-oriented'. It was aimed at complementing Japan's position of comparative advantage.

The point is that it is better for Japan, as she has done, to transfer, one by one, out of those industries in which she is losing her comparative advantage, and to invest in developing countries. In other words, foreign direct investment to developing countries should be, as Japan's was, 'trade-oriented', that is, aimed at complementing and strengthening comparative advantage in investing and receiving countries respectively.

In contrast to Japan, it seems to me that the United States has transferred abroad those industries which ranked at the top of her comparative advantage and has thus brought about balance of payments difficulties, unemployment and the need for protection of her remaining industries.

'Anti-trade-oriented' direct investment in manufacturing industries, particularly by US multinational corporations, has increased rapidly since the war. It has mainly been motivated by a desire to overcome the existence of tariffs and other trade barriers and to maximise monopolistic profits. This raises a serious question for the world economy. Should free trade policy be a basic rule and the role of foreign direct investment subordinate to it, or should it be the reverse? This may be the most important question to be decided in considering the relationship between trade and foreign direct investment policy. It seems to me that the former should be taken as the basic policy attitude. Unfortunately, however, recent developments seem to have been in quite the reverse direction.

From the point of view of the relation between trade policy and investment policy, it is essential to liberalise all the tariff and non-tariff barriers to trade in order to realise potential comparative costs. Because of the existence of trade barriers, much foreign direct investment has the object of getting around trade barriers and obtaining extra profits from protection. To put it more generally, because of market imperfections accelerated by trade barriers, there is a stimulus to anti-trade-oriented direct investment and the desire of multinationals dominates and twists trade policy. Furthermore, because of the trade barriers in advanced countries against exports from developing countries, true comparative costs are hidden, lowering profits from, and thus hindering, much needed 'trade-oriented' direct investment, as well as blocking the reorganisation of international trade.

The monopolistic or oligopolistic nature of multinationals, internal as well as global, should be rectified, for it results in a waste of world resources. Therefore, to promote the genuine role of foreign direct investment and to reduce and/or eliminate the monopolistic element should be a major objective of investment policy and this conforms to free trade policy. A new role for, and form of, foreign direct investment should be encouraged in order to maximise the benefits from it.

For example, multinational corporations are particularly useful and efficient for promoting horizontal trade in parts and components, each of which is produced in a different country with economies of scale greater than the minimum optimum. The trouble with horizontal trade is the difficulty of reaching agreement on specialisation between countries. This difficulty is easily overcome in the multinational corporation, since specialisation is decided upon by the central decision-making body of the firm. However, a rational specialisation programme is made possible in a free trade area only where there are no trade barriers and where no fear exists of increased barriers. Certainly, monopolistic behaviour should be strictly controlled and this may be feasible if the integrated market is so wide that many enterprises in each industry have to compete with each other.

Policies toward direct foreign investment and the role of multinational corporations are an essential part of trade reorganisation and should be integrated with trade policies in the GATT regime.

To recapitulate, the establishment of rules of free trade which will merely assure a static optimal resource allocation is not enough. Comparative costs of various countries change as time goes on. Measures have to be provided which would promote dynamic, long-term optimal resource allocation. The protection of new industries is justified from such a dynamic viewpoint. If this is recognised then policies aimed at structural adjustment and assistance in shifting resources from mature and declining industries to those which are gaining comparative advantage should be internationally approved and instituted.

Instead of harshly attacking other country's trade barriers, we should look for a dynamic outlet for increasing world trade and appropriate measures for this purpose should be built into the GATT rules. Possible policies which come to mind are the creation of new products and a new growth centre in world trade, structural adjustment to changing comparative advantages, agreed specialisation in those products in which economies of scale dominate costs of production, and better utilisation of foreign direct investment.

IV SUPPLY ACCESS TO PRIMARY COMMODITIES

The oil supply cutback by the Organisation of Arab Petroleum Exporting Countries since October 1973 has had a profound effect on the Japanese economy, as noted in Chapter 1. It over-reacted too seriously at first, since it depends almost entirely (up to 99.7 per cent) upon imported oil of which 81 per cent comes from the Middle East (and 40 per cent from the OAPEC countries). Japan's successful economic growth, especially rapid heavy and chemical industrialisation since the war, has been sustained by access to a stable and cheap source of petroleum. Petroleum has been so much more economical and efficient than coal both as an energy source and a raw material that Japan has reduced production of coal fuel to a negligible amount.

By March 1974, the panic reaction had calmed down. It has become obvious that the physical shortage of petroleum is only a short-term phenomenon and that, in the long term, the price problem (with the posted price of crude rising four times since 1972, to $11.651 per barrel and the producers' price rising to $7) will be more difficult to solve. The abrupt rise of the crude oil price brought about a general inflation, first in oil-related products and electricity, then in other manufactured goods. This was compounded by a rise in wages. The

Japanese economy experienced a chaotic price rise for several months from November 1973. By the end of 1974, however, various prices were shifted to a higher level and an equilibrium price system is more or less established and stabilising at that level.

But even oil is probably no exception to other primary products which experience cyclical fluctuations in the margin of demand and supply and in prices. This may be true as long as oil is kept as an economic good and not turned into a political weapon. Therefore, I propose an international commodity agreement on petroleum as the most desirable solution. The plan must be integrated with the stockpiling policy of each consuming country, and be international in scope.

As a long-run policy, Japan should transform her economic structure into a more 'oil-saving' one than at present by moving ahead in knowledge-intensive industrialisation. This target had already been set in 1971 by the MITI council but the restructuring should be intensified and speeded up to deal with the problem of petroleum.[15] It is envisaged that the elasticity of oil consumption to GNP, which has been falling from 2.5 since 1955-60, will decline to about unity. If this is realised, coupled with increased alternative energy sources, a 5-6 per cent annual increase of imported oil, no larger than in other developed countries, would make a 6-8 per cent growth of GNP possible.

It should be remembered that the non-oil producing developing countries have been severely hit by the quadrupling of oil prices. The extra oil payments for 1974 amount to more than $10 billion which surpasses the official development aid that they receive. The shortage of oil and the rising price of chemical fertilisers, plastics and other intermediate goods hinders industrialisation and food production in developing countries. Furthermore, aid might be reduced as a result of the balance of payments difficulties of donor countries and markets for their exports might narrow because of reduced economic activity in developed countries.

Thus, it becomes an urgent and fundamental task for Japan and other developed countries in the 1970s to promote the steady economic development of developing countries, including the Arab oil producers, and to reorganise north-south trade on an harmonious and prosperous basis. A grand integrated policy of aid, investment-*cum*-preferences, structural adjustment should be developed.[16]

The success of OPEC provoked other natural resource countries to claim a strong position in selling copper, tin, iron ore, bauxite and even sea bed resources. Prior to the oil crisis, the United States had sharply limited agricultural exports in 1973, especially its sale of soybeans in order to avoid 'unacceptable' domestic price rises. In addition to this, because of the world-wide shortage of grains for the last two years, supply access to foods has become a serious problem for Japan. It naturally stimulates agricultural protectionist pressures to increase domestic production of grains and meats even though it is inefficient. The situation may be similar for the EEC, which may solidly maintain its Common Agricultural Policy. Therefore, trade negotiations in agricultural products could be toughest and little progress is expected.

Export embargoes on petroleum, grains and other primary products are of great concern to the Japanese economy which depends heavily upon imports from abroad of essential raw materials and food. At present, we do not know how to deal with such a situation. Retaliation may not only be ineffective, but also result in the multiplication of trade barriers.

Some rule of export controls may be established in the Tokyo round. Perhaps, as in the case for petroleum, an international commodity agreement incorporating a buffer stock plan may be a desirable solution for sugar, wheat, soybean, timber, etc., although the stockpiling of these is more difficult than is the case of minerals. Also long-term purchasing contracts on a bilateral basis (for example, iron ore and sugar between Japan and Australia) may be promoted. However, as a multilateral trade negotiator, Japan should not be too harsh, since the need for export controls would easily turn to a reverse situation as far as primary products are concerned. It is most important to avoid politicising the problem of primary products.

NOTES

1. The basic policy aims of multilateral trade negotiations which the Japanese government decided on 31 August 1973 are:

   1. The negotiations should be conducted in accordance with the objectives and principles of GATT and with a view to securing overall reciprocity.

   2. Substantial reductions (including elimination) of tariffs will be sought for.

   3. The elimination or reduction of non-tariff measures, or the trade-restricting or trade-impeding effects of these measures will be sought for.

   4. With a view to seeking a further promotion of trade liberalisation and preserving such results, multilateral safeguards having in mind the principle of non-discrimination, will be examined.

5. In respect to trade in agricultural products, in line with the general objectives of the negotiations, considering the special nature of the agricultural sector and based upon mutual benefits through cooperation of exporting and importing countries, a steady expansion under stable market conditions will be sought for.

6. Taking into account the development needs of the developing countries, due attention will be paid to securing additional benefits for the international trade of these countries.

At the same time, reciprocity will not in principle be expected of the developing countries.

7. If it proves necessary during the course of the negotiations that the GATT provisions should be reviewed, it will be dealt with in line with the objectives and principles of the trade negotiations.

2. See Chapter 1, Section III.
3. See Table 1.3, Chapter 1.
4. Even the common tariffs which the EEC insists on retaining as the symbol of integration may be admitted if they come to be a uniform rate as low as, say, 5 per cent, for they then have no trade deterrent effects and can be easily overcome by a few per cent change in the exchange rate.
6. The Japanese government supports the gradual elimination of tariffs, but insists that negotiations be conducted in accordance with the provisions of GATT including those on 'most favoured nation treatment', and on the basis of the principles of mutual benefit and overall reciprocity. It is a question as to whether my 'overtime reciprocity' is taken as a concept of 'overall reciprocity'.
7. See Gerard and Victoria Curzon, *Hidden Barriers to International Trade*, Trade Policy Research Centre, London, 1970, p. 63; Harold B. Malmgren. *Trade Wars or Trade Negotiation?*, the Atlantic Council of the United States, Washington, D.C., 1970, pp. 66 and 70; Hans H. Glismann and Axel Neu, 'Towards New Agreements on International Trade Liberalisation – Methods and Examples of Measuring Nontariff Trade Barriers', *Weltwirtschaftliches Archiv*., Band 107, 1971, Heft 2.
8. These points are further developed in Chapter 7.
9. OECD, *Policy Perspective for International Trade and Economic Relations*, Paris, 1972, p. 84.
10. Fred Bergsten, ed., *Toward a New World Trade Policy: The Maidenhead Papers*, Lexington Books, D. C. Heath and Co., 1975, p. 375.
11. See also, *World Trade and Domestic Adjustment*, A tripartite report by fourteen economists from Japan, the European Community and North America, The Brookings Institution, 1973, pp. 17-18.
12. See Chapter 6.
13. See Chapter 3.
14. See Chapter 4.
15. See Chapter 6.
16. See Chapter 7.

3 A COMPETITIVE BIPOLAR KEY CURRENCY SYSTEM

I A NEW INTERNATIONAL MONETARY SYSTEM

The ideal would be that trade barriers should be confined to tariffs and that the adjustment of international balance of payments be left with overall adjustment measures. However, the reality is that overall adjustment measures *per se* do not work promptly and effectively with the result that some countries have an unfavourable trade balance while others have a favourable balance for prolonged periods. Hence the difficulties in removing non-tariff barriers and the fears that they might, instead, be increased. Thus, more than anything else, the streamlining of the international monetary system and foreign exchange rates so that overall adjustment measures can function promptly and effectively is necessary. Though it is not clear what sort of cooperative relation exists between GATT and the IMF, it is difficult to see how trade liberalisation can be negotiated with GATT as its focus and how it can be prompted by means of tariff cuts or the reduction and removal of non-tariff barriers without regard to the international monetary situation. If the latter is in a state of confusion, liberalisation of trade can only regress.

The Tokyo GATT ministerial meeting declared, after a long discussion between the USA and France, that:

> The policy of liberalising world trade cannot be carried out successfully in the absence of parallel efforts to set up a monetary system which shields the world economy from the shocks and imbalances which have previously occurred. The ministers will not lose sight of the fact that the efforts which are to be made in the trade field imply continuing efforts to maintain orderly conditions and to establish a durable and equitable monetary system. The ministers recognise equally that the new phase in the liberalisation of trade which it is their intention to undertake should facilitate the orderly function of the monetary system.[1]

In the near future, it is almost certain that effective new rules and procedures to assure sufficiently prompt adjustment of payments imbalances by both surplus and deficit countries will be set up in the IMF. The new rules would be exchange parities subject to frequent and relatively small adjustment according to some objective indicators, with provision for wider margins and options for temporary floats under appropriate circumstances.

More fundamental reform in the international monetary system may not be easy and will take a longer time, for the United States supports the present floating exchange rate system as a means of continuing her 'benign neglect' policy.

My view is that a bipolar key currency system should be set up between the dollar and the 'Europa' which will be established before long under the European currency integration scheme. A central cross rate would be set between the two currencies and they could be used as reserve assets, intervention currencies and vehicle currencies. The central exchange rate between the two key currencies would be adjustable according to new rules for exchange adjustment.

If the country in surplus wants to avoid revaluation or make a smaller revaluation, it would be required to lend to the IMF. International liquidity should not be increased either through the balance of payments deficit of a key currency country, as it was under the dollar standard, nor through arbitrary control without any backing as it has been in the present SDRs. Rather international liquidity should be increased through investments by surplus countries.

If the country in deficit wants to avoid devaluation or make a smaller devaluation, it would be required to borrow the counterpart key currency through the IMF and to submit to international surveillance by the IMF.

Because of competition between the two key currencies, the result of which would be revealed in the cross rate between them, the two sides would be forced to pursue monetary and balance of payments disciplines. In addition, other countries would have freedom as to which key currency they chose as a peg, in what proportion they held the two key currencies and even the freedom to switch the key currency to which they peg. Thus, the behaviour of other countries helps to enforce further discipline upon the two key currency countries.

This is a brief outline of my proposal of a competitive bipolar key currency system as a new international monetary system. In what follows I first examine the reasons for putting forward this proposal for reform of the international monetary system (Section II); secondly, the working of the proposed system is analysed in more detail (Section III); finally, the feasibility of the bipolar key currency system between the US dollar and the European common currency is briefly assessed (Section IV).

II DILEMMA OF A SINGLE KEY CURRENCY SYSTEM

It is obvious that the present 'floating' exchange rates of almost all major currencies throughout the world is not a sound and durable solution but a necessary evil resulting from the turmoil in the international monetary system. The IMF will set up new rules for exchange rate adjustment within wider bands so that exchange rates are adjusted both in deficit and surplus countries equitably, more often, and promptly, according to movements on objective indicators such as the foreign reserve position.[2] Then, there will be little difference between the present managed floating rate and the IMF's adjustable peg except for revised rules for exchange rate adjustment. The floating rate effectively equilibrates the balance of payments and prevents speculative movements of short-term capital. But the floating rate neglects the other important role of the exchange rate, namely, to facilitate steady growth of trade and foreign investment and to maintain a desirable composition in the balance of payments (i.e. without maintaining balance through large short-term borrowing). Therefore, the adjustable peg, though it should be more flexible than heretofore, may be reinstituted as soon as possible when the present confusion due to the oil crisis calms down.

Consideration of more basic reforms of the international monetary system requires examination of the characteristics of an international key currency. The proper functioning of a genuinely international reserve currency requires the development of a currency that is both privately useful and used, and one that can serve as an 'intervention asset' in exchange markets. As a corollary, securities denominated in that currency must be available for private transactions of a higher yielding form of wealth convertible on predictable terms into other currencies.[3] Only a national currency like the US dollar meets these conditions. That country is the largest and most economically diversified trading and financial centre in the world, and its national currency is widely used and accepted as vehicle and intervention currency throughout the world. Every other nation has confidence in the value of the key currency which is backed by huge productivity, assets and resources of the key currency country. In other words, the backing of key currency, which should be a *national* currency, is not gold or other international money like the SDR but huge national economic power. Besides these, the centre country has to have a stable price level, keeping stability in purchasing power over goods and services.[4]

There is the view, however, that 'the use of *national* currencies as *international* reserves constitutes indeed a built-in destabiliser in the world monetary system',[5] and, therefore, that the internationalisation of the foreign exchange component of monetary reserves is necessary. Triffin's World Central Bank, Bernstein's composite reserve unit and other plans were proposed in order to create an 'international money', besides gold, under an internationally managed currency system along these lines. The Special Drawing Right (SDR) of the IMF is one form of international money, which created about $9.3 billion international liquidity in 1970-2.

The SDR is useful as a numeraire along with gold and may increase international liquidity somewhat in so far as it is acceptable among monetary authorities. But the SDR does not work as a key currency for it cannot be used as a vehicle and intervention currency. Moreover, the value of the SDR may be doubted and confidence in it lost if the volume of SDRs is increased cumulatively, for it lacks any solid backing[6] except the IMF's prestige or the name 'international monetary cooperation'.

Thus, a reformed international monetary system drawn up on the IMF-SDR lines may not be a preferable solution. Instead of that, I prefer the reconstruction of the exchange standard with two key competitive currencies. The gold exchange standard in the IMF was not itself unsound, but it became unhealthy and precarious because it relied on a single key currency, the dollar, and worked as a *de facto* dollar standard, although before World War II the pound sterling was used together with the dollar.

The soundness of a competitive key currency system compared with a single key currency system may be analysed from the viewpoint of the dilemma between liquidity, confidence and adjustment, the three main issues in the international monetary system. The single key currency system fails in all three respects while the competitive key currency system works independently of them.

First, there is the dilemma between increases in international liquidity and loss of confidence in the key currency. Sufficient growth in international liquidity is required to sustain an optimum growth of world trade and investment. It is obvious that supply of new gold which increases at 1-1.5 per cent annually (in addition, demand for non-monetary use has been increasing rapidly) is far from sufficient. The monetary system has in a long history improved in the direction of 'gold saving' and evolved into the gold exchange standard. The IMF has contributed to some extent to increased international liquidity through increased total fund quotas, relaxed conditions for general drawings, etc., but the contribution has been limited for the IMF has been based upon a fund principle which does not allow any creation of international money – the SDR representing a significant deviation from this principle. Therefore, a national currency, the dollar, filled the gap in fulfilling a rapidly increasing need for international liquidity and a *de facto* dollar standard prevailed during the post World War II era up to August 1971.

But as the dollar was spread too much throughout the world and the dollar holdings in foreign countries exceeded American gold reserves, confidence in the dollar was to weaken. International liquidity, the dollar, was supplied only through continued deficits in the American balance of payments, a further source of loss of confidence in it. While the USA keeps her balance of payments in balance or surplus, international liquidity will not increase at all or rather decrease, although confidence in the dollar strengthens. This is the so-called 'liquidity dilemma', which appeared in the late 1950s and became gradually more serious, resulting in uncertainty in the international monetary system.

From 1968, the USA followed inflationary policies to mitigate the unemployment problem at home and a policy of benign neglect abroad, spreading the dollar glut throughout the world. This was possible for the dollar was a sole key currency which enjoyed the privilege of 'seigniorage'. In the end, the redemption of dollars in gold was stopped *de facto* in 1968 and *de jure* in 1971. No international measures were able to restrain American inflation and balance of payments deterioration. The USA forced surplus countries to revalue exchange rates instead of devaluing the dollar. A compromise was engineered through the Smithsonian negotiations in December 1971, the agreements from which did not last long. The result was the general float in exchange rates after February-March 1972.

Now, imagine that there is a system of competitive two key currencies, and that the dollar and the Europa (a common currency in the European Community) are used in the framework of the IMF system. The dollar is not able to avoid taking action on the balance of payments problem, for, if it were to do so, the hegemony in the international monetary system would be taken over by the Europa through competitive market mechanisms (which will be explained in the following section). The two key currencies restrain each other so as to maintain a stable international monetary system.

How to increase international liquidity in the new system remains a problem. A spillover from the fact that the national economic activities (domestic production and foreign trade and investment) in the two key currency countries grow steadily, will be the increased use between the two centres and among other countries of the two key currencies as international liquidity.[7] The IMF must enhance its genuine function of balance of payments financing through increased fund quotas and further softening conditions of drawing. The country in balance of payments surplus, either a Europa surplus or a dollar surplus, may invest or lend its surplus to the IMF which, in turn, finances the deficit of other countries under its surveillance. This is similar in concept to the oil facility which the IMF inaugurated in 1974.

Secondly, there is the dilemma between increased liquidity and delayed balance of payments adjustment. It is desirable to maintain stable exchange rates as long as possible and to limit adjustment only to the case of fundamental disequilibrium in a country's balance of payments. This is the case of the adjustable peg system in the IMF. To maintain stable exchange rates in non-fundamental disequilibrium, each country needs international reserves and facilities to borrow which the IMF was intended to supplement. But as the international liquidity which each country holds increases sufficiently, the necessary adjustment in exchange rates and/or demand controls even in the case of fundamental disequilibrium are delayed or postponed, resulting in a large and disruptive attack of speculative capital movements. The USA, the reserve centre, overcame its fundamental disequilibrium by a policy of benign neglect up to December 1971 (and even afterwards), spreading inflation throughout the world. Generally, floating rates were the only measure able to cope with speculative capital movements but this system damaged other important functions of stable exchange rates and did not reduce the necessary volume of international liquidity.

Under a system of two key currencies, neither of the two reserve centres would be able to continue a balance of payments maladjustment and pursue a 'benign neglect' policy for the cross exchange rate between the two key currencies would be continuously adjusted in the exchange market. If the surplus centre allowed its exchange rates to revalue at less than market forces demanded, it would have to invest the surplus with the IMF, whereas if the deficit centre were to devalue its exchange rate at less than the appropriate level, it would have to borrow the other key currency through the IMF. Such investment and borrowing should be within the range which would not jeopardise confidence in the two key currencies. International liquidity would be increased adequately through such a new facility in the IMF.

Thirdly, there is the dilemma between adjustment and confidence. The USA insisted for a long time that devaluation of the dollar was neither possible (for other countries might follow suit to the devaluation of the gold par value of the dollar), nor desirable, for the devaluation of the dollar – the sole international key currency working as reserve asset and intervention as well as vehicle currency – would seriously impair confidence in the international monetary system. Therefore, the USA sought revaluation of other strong currencies like the German mark and the Japanese yen.

The dollar standard is a system of *n* national currencies with one (the dollar) serving as the numeraire. The position of the numeraire currency is necessarily asymmetrical with those of the other currencies, because to fix the price of other currencies in terms of the numeraire requires using the numeraire currency as an intervention currency, and also promotes its use as a medium of international exchange and a store of international value.[8] It is impossible to keep for a long period the value of a key currency intact in terms of gold or an artificial international money like the SDR. Moreover, it is not necessary to do this but it is important to maintain the purchasing power over goods and services of the key currency as stable as possible.

In the two key currency system the devaluation of the dollar is the revaluation of the Europa and *vice versa*, and the value of the two key currencies taken together may be kept stable if the competition between them acts as a restraint and discipline. This is somewhat similar to the value of the present SDR which is the weighted sum of a standard package of major currencies. But in the new system neither gold nor artificial international money like the SDR is needed as a numeraire. Since there is only one cross rate between the two currencies, one key currency is used as a numeraire for the other key currency. Other countries use either the dollar or the Eurodollar as numeraire. Gold is not a numeraire but may be used for settlement of payment between the two reserve centres at market price as a highly liquid asset.

III WORKING MECHANISM OF A BIPOLAR KEY CURRENCY SYSTEM

The working of the proposed two key currency systems may be explained more systematically as follows:

(1) A cross rate is established between the two key currencies, say the dollar and the Europa. The cross rate is preferably fixed (i.e. a central cross rate) within wider bands but adjustable in the case of fundamental disequilibrium as the IMF envisages in its new rules for

adjusting exchange rates. But the cross rate may, if necessary, be a managed floating rate as at present.

(2) Devaluation of one key currency in the central cross rate is synonymous with revaluation of the other one. Thus, the value as a numeraire of the two key currencies taken together is maintained unchanged. It is of no significance which side, either the deficit or surplus centre, takes the initiative in changing the central cross rate.

(3) In order to stabilise the cross rate within the wider band, the reserve centres may intervene in the exchange market by using the counterpart key currency and may, if necessary, pay and receive gold which is not numeraire but a highly liquid asset at market prices.

(4) If the side in surplus wants to avoid revaluation of the central cross rate or make revaluation smaller, it has to invest through a special facility (similar to the oil facility) in the IMF. International liquidity would be increased through such investments by the surplus country, instead of through the balance of payments deficits of a key currency country, as it was under the dollar standard, or through the increased issue of the SDRs which lack any real backing.

(5) If the side in deficit wants to avoid devaluation of the central cross rate or make devaluation smaller, it has to borrow the counterpart key currency through the IMF special facility and to submit to international surveillance by the IMF.

(6) Because of the competition between the two key currencies, the result of which is revealed in the cross rate, the two sides are forced to follow monetary and balance of payments disciplines. If one of the key currencies failed to measure up over a sufficiently long period, it would lose its hegemony in the international monetary system and be taken over by a third currency which might eventually emerge as an alternative key currency.

(7) In so far as the key currency economy grows steadily and the value of the key currency is not subject to speculation, the rest of the world, including the counterpart key currency country, will want to accumulate the key currency as foreign exchange reserves in the range that each country considers safe and optimal. Within that range, the key currency country is able to maintain a balance of payments deficit which is actually its short-term foreign investment, bringing about an increase in international liquidity.

(8) Other countries have freedom as to which key currency they choose as a peg, in what proportion they hold the two key currencies and even when to switch the key currency to which they peg. Since they take these choices according to the cross rate between the two key currencies, the behaviour of these other countries further enforces the discipline of the key currency countries.

(9) Other countries may choose one key currency as a peg originally because of trade and investment interdependence with that key currency country and neighbouring other countries. Other countries have to adjust exchange rates according to the new IMF rules when they fall into payments disequilibrium in relation to the pegged currency. They can obtain financing from the IMF through its general drawing right as well as the special facility proposed. However, if other countries switch their pegged currency frequently and exercise other freedoms excessively, this may disturb the smooth working of the two key currency system. This danger may be prevented if two optimum currency areas are established: one, the European currency area as already presumed in our argument and the other the dollar (or Pacific) currency area.[9] Then, other countries in a currency area may be able to overcome their balance of payments difficulties more easily by the support of the key currency. Moreover, because each optimum currency area covers a wide and diversified market area, fluctuations in area balance of payments *vis-à-vis* the counterpart currency area will be smaller and the cross rate more stable. This may be properly called a bipolar key currency system.

IV PROSPECTS FOR THE BIPOLAR KEY CURRENCY SYSTEM

The bipolar key currency system proposed in this chapter is not only soundly based theoretically but it is also a feasible prospect.

First, its feasibility depends upon the progress in European Monetary Union. Already the European Monetary Cooperation Fund and a common currency unit called Eurco have been established. The common float of European Community countries in March 1973 was seen as an important step towards the bipolar key currency system. While France's withdrawal from the EEC common float in January 1974 cast some doubt on the solidarity of European currency integration, she returned to it in July 1975, showing her enthusiasm for the completion of integration by 1980. In the light of past experience in the EEC, the realisation could be earlier than that.

Secondly, the argument for setting up two optimum currency areas using flexible exchange rates between them has a long history[10] and advocates urge that the time has now come to put the idea into practice.

Thirdly, it has been recently suggested that a new world economic order should involve tripolar coordination, between North America, Western Europe and Japan, the three major powers in the western capitalist world.[11] The international monetary system could be stabilised and a standard package of SDRs arranged through closer cooperation in exchange rate management between the dollar, the mark and the yen.[12] My proposal is on the same lines in principle but I prefer the two key currency system for in the case of more than two currencies, an international money like SDR is necessarily required as a numeraire. Some advocate that Japan should establish a yen currency area.[13] I think this is premature, for the Tokyo exchange and financial market is not only too narrow but also still subject to stringent exchange control with which the government is unwilling to dispense. Japan might do far better to remain under the umbrella of the dollar.

Fourthly, the reform of the international monetary system depends upon the attitude of the United States. She prefers the continuation of the *de facto* dollar standard using the dollar as intervention and vehicle currency and reserve assets. But the European Community might inaugurate the gold exchange standard with its common currency, the Europa, redeemable in gold. Then, the USA would have to resume the gold exchange standard competitively for otherwise the Europa could be considered the superior key currency and the hegemony of the USA in the international monetary system might be taken over. This could happen fairly soon, as one variant of the bipolar key currency system, and might be far better than the present uncertain international monetary situation although our proposal is preferable. In that case trouble in setting the appropriate price of gold could become one source of world-wide inflation.

NOTES

1. Declaration of Ministries, approved at Tokyo on 14 September 1973, Ministerial Meeting, GATT.
2. See, for example, Robert Triffin's 'fork plan' in his 'International Monetary Collapse and Reconstruction in April 1972', *Journal of International Economics*, September 1972.
3. Harry G. Johnson, 'Issues in International Monetary Reform', *Portfolio*

International Economic Perspectives, Vol. 2, No. 3, pp. 6-7.

4. Cf. Harry G. Johnson, 'Political Economy Aspects of International Monetary System', *Journal of International Economics*, September 1972, p. 419.
5. Robert Triffin, *Gold and the Dollar Crisis*, Yale University Press, 1960, p. 87.
6. The issue of a national currency is a creation of credit backed by national products, while that of an international money in addition to national currencies results in double creation of credit without any backing.
7. The total exports of the USA and the enlarged EEC in 1973 amounted to $240 billion which accounted for 53 per cent of the world trade. Suppose a third of that amount or $80 billion is used as international liquidity. This may be sufficient for international liquidity but not too large a portion in total national money circulation of the two centres. As trade increases steadily in the two centres, international liquidity increases too.
8. See Harry G. Johnson, p. 417.
9. See Kiyoshi Kojima, 'A Pacific Currency Area: A New Approach to International Monetary Reform', in his *Japan and a Pacific Free Trade Area*, Macmillan, London, 1971.
10. More important are: *The United States Balance of Payments in 1968*, the Brookings Institution, 1963, p. 259; R. I. McKinnon, 'Optimum World Monetary Arrangements and the Dual Currency System', *Banca Nazional del Lavoro Quarterly Review*, Vol. 16, 1963, pp. 379-85; Robert A. Mundell, *The International Monetary System: Conflict and Reform*, The Private Planning Association of Canada, July 1965, pp. 47-8; Richard N. Cooper, *Sterling, European Monetary Unification, and the International Monetary System*, British-North American Committee, 1972; Richard I. McKinnon, 'The Dual Currency System Revisited', H. G. Johnson and A. K. Swoboda, eds., *The Economics of Common Currencies*, George Allen and Unwin, London, 1973; Robert A. Mundell, 'A Plan for a European Currency', *The Economics of Common Currencies*; Harry G. Johnson, 'SDRs: The Link that Chains', *Foreign Policy*, No. 8, Fall 1972.
11. Cf. Ernest H. Preeg, *Economic Blocs and US Foreign Policy*, National Planning Association, Washington, D.C., 1974.
12. See, Ronald I. McKinnon, 'A New Tripartite Monetary Agreement or a Limping Dollar Standard', Princeton University, *Essays in International Finance*, No. 100, October 1974.
13. See, for example, Nihon Keizai Chosa Kyōgikai, *A New International Monetary System and the Yen* (in Japanese), Tokyo, July 1973. Hiroshi Shibata, 'Japan and Yen Currency Area', unpublished paper read at the thirtieth general meeting of the Japanese Society of International Economics held at Nagasaki, 3 November 1971. Sachio Kohjima, 'Moves Towards Internationalisation of the Japanese Yen and Japan-Australia Currency Relations', Kiyoshi Kojima, ed., *Harmonisation of Japanese and Australian Economic Policies*, Japan Economic Research Centre, June 1975.

4 THE ROLE OF FOREIGN DIRECT INVESTMENT

I INTRODUCTION

One of the most serious omissions in the study of foreign direct investment or the operation of multinational corporations to date is in the area of macroeconomic theory. For an individual firm the objective of maximising its profits and/or enlarging its market share through widening territorial horizons towards global logistics is well justified from a microeconomic point of view. However, foreign direct investment has produced a conflict of interests with national objectives in both investing and host countries alike, since national (macro) economic objectives remain paramount under circumstances where national populations (labourers, by and large) cannot practically and institutionally, move internationally with ease. Resolution of this conflict so that foreign direct investment may contribute harmoniously both to investing and recipient country development, requires a new macroeconomic approach to the problem.[1]

In this chapter, a survey of the motivation and role of foreign direct investment is presented (Section II); then an attempt is made to identify the characteristics of two different types of foreign direct investment – trade-oriented (the Japanese model) and anti-trade-oriented (the American model) foreign investment (Sections III and IV).

It will be shown that comparative profitabilities in trade-oriented foreign direct investment conform to the direction of potential comparative costs and, therefore, complement each other. In other words, foreign direct investment going from a comparatively disadvantageous industry in the investing country (which is potentially a comparatively advantageous industry in the host country) will promote an upgrading of industrial structure on both sides and thus accelerate trade between the two countries.

In comparison, the American model of foreign direct investment does not conform to this comparative profitabilities formula, mainly due to the dualistic structure of the American economy – the dichotomy between the new, oligopolistic industries and the traditional, price competitive industries. This type of foreign direct investment is anti-trade-oriented and results in balance of payments difficulties, the export of jobs, the prevention of structural adjustment and trade protectionism. Further theoretical elaboration of the two types of foreign direct investment will be undertaken in the next chapter.

Thus, in Section V, a new approach to foreign direct investment policy is formulated and its relationship to trade policy made clear, and in Section VI a new form of foreign direct investment is recommended.

II THE MOTIVATION FOR FOREIGN DIRECT INVESTMENT

It is usual to classify the motives for foreign direct investment into resource-oriented, labour-oriented and market-oriented investment. *Natural resource-oriented* investment is obviously trade-oriented or trade-generating for it results from the investing country's desire to increase imports of its comparatively disadvantageously produced or domestically unavailable commodities, and causes growth in vertical specialisation between producers of manufactures and primary products. However, there is the problem that integrated production and marketing are monopolised or oligopolised by big multinationals in oil, copper and other resource goods, leaving smaller benefits to those countries endowed with natural resources.

Labour-oriented investment is also trade-oriented or trade-reorganising. As wages in the advanced investing country become higher year by year relative to capital and as new products – usually more capital – and knowledge-intensive than traditional goods – are created one after another, it becomes profitable and rational for the advanced country to contract its own traditional, labour-intensive industries and transfer the location of production to low wage countries where cheaper labour costs prevail. Thus, corresponding to a dynamic change in comparative advantage, such foreign investment assists the reorganisation of the international division of labour and promotes the harmonious growth of trade between labour scarce and labour abundant countries. It should be noted, however, that such foreign direct investment may transfer either traditional labour-intensive industries which are well standardised, or new goods which utilise cheap labour intensively from the advanced to the low wage country. It should also be noted that the labour-oriented investment aims at establishing an export base, rather than import-substitution, and the development of exports to the investing country as well as other markets.

Market-oriented investment can be subdivided into two categories. Foreign direct investment induced by trade barriers in the host country is mostly trade-oriented but in a different way from the trade-oriented investment mentioned above. In this case, heavier tariffs on final products, for example, lead to the substitution of exports of final products for the export of parts and components, intermediate materials, machinery, equipment and technology necessary to the production of final goods from the investing country. This type of foreign direct investment meets the recipient country's interest in promoting import-substituting activity, not necessarily intended to be competitive in the international market, and therefore results in some waste of resources because of the degree of protection provided to the final goods production. But, if the import-substitution industry grows successfully towards export-orientation, then foreign direct investment of this type turns out to be labour-oriented investment. Therefore, there is no essential difference between labour-oriented and *trade-barrier induced* investment except in so far as one aims at world-wide markets and the other is confined to protected domestic markets.

There is another type of market-oriented investment which may be called *oligopolistic* foreign direct investment. This is typically found in American investment in new manufacturing product industries in recent decades, as will be seen presently, and is anti-trade-oriented.

Finally, it is probably wise to add a fifth type of foreign direct investment: that is the *internationalisation of production and marketing* through vertical and horizontal integration of big multinational enterprises. Whether this is anti-trade-oriented or not depends upon whether the main activity comprises oligopolistic investment.

III THE JAPANESE DIRECT INVESTMENT MODEL

Direct foreign investment, that is, the transmission to the host country of a package of capital, managerial skill and technical knowledge, is a potent agent of economic transformation and development. A large increase in Japanese direct investment in developing countries, in so far as it is welcomed by them, will contribute significantly to the development of their natural resources, their agricultural production and their processing industries, on the one hand, and, on the other, to transferring from Japan to developing countries those manufacturing industries suitable to each developing country.

Japan has endeavoured to invest in developing countries with the object of securing increased imports of primary products which are vitally important for her economy. This is called 'development assistance for import'. It was first directed (and is still being directed in increasing amounts) towards natural resource development projects such as oil, natural gas, iron ore, coal, copper, bauxite and other metals.

Wood and timber also have high priority. The benefits of such development assistance are limited, however, to those countries where abundant natural resources are available, and the employment and training effects are small in so far as the goods are exported in the form of raw materials. If we can extend our development investment for import to agricultural products, benefits will be spread more widely in developing areas. Thailand's successful development of exports to Japan of maize is a good example. Since February 1970, the Asian Trade Development Corporation has been providing subsidies to development assistance for import, with regard to various agricultural products produced in the wider Asian area. The government is also considering whether to provide low interest rate foreign exchange loans to those enterprises which venture to develop new natural resource deposits.

Japan's direct investment for creating manufacturing capacity in developing countries is important and is of mutual benefit, always provided that the appropriate manufacturing industries are selected. The industries to be chosen should be those in which Japan is losing comparative advantage while developing countries are gaining it (or are expected to gain it). Such industries should preferably be export-oriented, not merely serving the benefit of the economically privileged classes in recipient countries.

Thus, Japan's foreign investment has to date been 'trade-oriented'. It was aimed at complementing Japan's comparative advantage position. The major part of investment was directed towards natural resource development in which the Japanese economy is comparatively disadvantaged.[2] Even investment in manufacturing has been confined either to such traditional industries as textiles, clothing and processing of steel in which Japan has been losing its comparative advantage, or the assembly of motor vehicles, production of parts and components of radios and other electronic machines in which cheaper labour costs in Southeast Asian countries are achieved and the Japanese firms can increase exports,[3] substituting for exports of final products, exports of machinery and equipment for the factory and technological knowhow.[4] In this sense, Japanese foreign direct investment is complementary to changes in its comparative advantage position.

A substantial proportion of Japanese direct foreign investment in manufacturing is undertaken by small- and medium-sized firms and on a smaller scale than by American firms[5] which transferred technology suitable to local factor proportions with larger employment and training effects than those characteristic of 'enclave' investments.

Joint ventures have been preferred to wholly-owned subsidiaries.

Suppose that a textile industry which is losing comparative advantage in Japan moves away from Japan through increased direct investment in developing countries. This will promote structural adjustment in Japan and open wider markets for the developing countries' products. If other advanced countries do the same, markets for developing countries' products will become very large. The Japanese textile industry has a long experience of excellent management and technology which is more suitable to developing countries than that of America or Europe. When abundant relatively cheap labour is combined with this expertise in developing countries, the joint venture products will certainly succeed in international competition.

The point is that it is better for Japan, as she has done, to transfer out of those industries in which she is losing her comparative advantage, and to invest in developing countries which are gaining a comparative advantage in the same industries. In other words, foreign direct investment to developing countries should be, as Japan's has been, 'trade-oriented', that is, aimed at complementing and strengthening comparative advantage in investing and receiving countries alike.

In Asia, the success of free trade and investment zones in Kaoshiung, in Taiwan, and the development of a similar area at the Jurong Industrial Estate, Singapore, as well as the successful industrialisation in Korea and Hong Kong is impressive. These demonstrate the need for step-by-step transfer of manufacturing industries from advanced to developing countries.

Foreign direct investment, in harmony with changes in comparative advantage, will accelerate structural adjustment in Japan, and lead to a contraction of traditional industries of the labour-intensive type. It is in the parent company's interests to make investment activity prosperous by opening markets both in Japan and other advanced countries even through taking advantage of general preferences provided only for the developing country's products. The parent company's marketing facilities are indispensable for the new entry of the developing country's products to advanced country markets. Foreign direct investment for Japanese small- and medium-scale firms, which played a major part in manufacturing investments in the past, are a promising outlet for their survival and accelerate internal structural adjustment.

IV THE AMERICAN DIRECT INVESTMENT MODEL

In contrast to Japan, it seems to me that the United States has transferred abroad those industries which ranked at the top of her comparative advantage and has thus brought about balance of payments difficulties, unemployment and the need for protection of her remaining industries.

The typical American foreign direct investment is well characterised by Raymond Vernon and Stephen Hymer. The concern of Vernon and others[6] was to explain how a new product is invented and manufactured on a large scale in leading industrial countries. Exports of this product grow in so far as a 'technological gap' exists between the product-developing country and foreign countries. Foreign producers imitate the new technology and follow suit. Then exports slow down and through direct investment an attempt is made to secure foreign markets. When the technology is standardised and widely disseminated and the limit of scale economies is reached, trade based on wage costs, or factor proportions, starts and the country turns to import this product from abroad.

According to Vernon, 'the US trade position in manufactured goods is based heavily on a comparative advantage in the generation of innovations, rather than on the more conventional notion of relatively cheap capital' and 'the big post-war increase in US overseas investment in manufacturing subsidiaries has come about mainly in the kind of industry that would be expected to have participated in such a process: industries associated with innovation and with oligopoly. It explains why so much of the investment is found in the chemical industries, the machinery industries, the transportation industries, and the scientific instrument industries'.[7] They are 'highly innovative and strongly oligopolistic', and 'multinational enterprises are found principally in industries that devote a relatively high proportion of their resources to research and advertising and that tend to be dominated by very large firms'.[8]

It should be noted that the product cycle or industrial organisation approach to foreign direct investment is essentially microeconomic and deals with one commodity, partial equilibrium analysis. The approach suggests that, once low labour cost becomes beneficial to the firm, the whole industry does better to invest in a low-wage labour country. According to the comparative advantage theory of Heckscher-Ohlin, only less capital- and knowledge-intensive industry profitably invests abroad. There must be some special reason why new industries of the more capital- and knowledge-intensive type move abroad through foreign direct investment from America.

A similar view is seen in Stephen Hymer. After noting the association of multinational corporations with a few large firms, in oligopolistic industries – industries with special characteristics (heavy industry rather than light, i.e. in industries characterised by large firms, high capital intensity, advanced technology, differentiated products, etc.) – Hymer points out three factors which determine whether an industry invests abroad or not:

> firstly, there must be some kind of barrier to entry in the industry (technological, economies of scale, differentiated products) so that local firms cannot compete with profits below a level which compensates the multinational corporation for the extra costs of operating in a foreign country and integrating geographically dispersed operations; secondly, it must be advantageous to produce locally rather than export from a single production centre (this depends upon tariffs, the size of the market, and the threat of local competition); and, thirdly, the firm must find it more profitable to exploit the foreign advantage through direct investment rather than licensing. Hence a technological lead is not a sufficient explanation of foreign investment. One must also explain why the technology is not sold like other commodities. The answer lies usually in the marketing characteristics of the advantage, that is, the difficulty of extracting full quasi-rent where markets are imperfect.[9]

Hymer comes to the striking conclusion that 'on the assumption that the internationalised sector grows at 8 per cent and the non-internationalised sector at 4 per cent, international production will account for 50 per cent of the total world production by the year 2005 and 80 per cent by the year 2040'.[10]

Thus the American economy is split into a dualistic structure: (a) innovative and oligopolistic industries, or, in brief, new industries; and (b) traditional industries (textiles, steel, agriculture, and so on) which are price competitive and stagnant. The genuine product cycles and direct foreign investment take place successively only within the innovative and oligopolistic industry group. Foreign direct investments from these new industries which ranked at the top of American comparative advantage are 'anti-trade-oriented' or involve foreign direct investments which work against the structure of comparative advantage. Those new industries would strengthen exports of their final products if they were conscious of national economic interests, but actually they set up foreign subsidiaries, cutting off their own comparative advantage and inducing increased imports of those products from abroad where they invest. Both the loss of foreign markets and reverse imports later on result in balance of payments difficulties and the 'export of job opportunities'.

It may be true, as many researchers[11] claim, that the new industry sector contributes on balance to foreign exchange earnings, due to increased exports of intermediate goods and equipment, the return flow of earnings from past investment, and the like. It should be stressed, however, that if they had been conscious of national economic interests, by refraining from foreign investment and strengthening export promotion those new industries would have earned greater export surpluses and covered import surpluses in other sectors.

If American foreign manufacturing investment was 'trade-oriented', rather than new industries-oriented, it would be welcomed by developing countries and accelerate the reorganisation of north-south trade, as in the case of Japan's investment.[12]

Moreover, since innovation and foreign direct investment cycles are confined to the new oligopolistic industry sector, the inflow of resources from the traditional sector is restricted and structural adjustment hindered. An increased labour force was available for employment in traditional industries but traditional industries have been losing their comparative advantage. In consequence, there has been a rise in protectionist attitudes. Thus the American economy has fallen into a vicious circle due to foreign direct investment of the anti-trade-oriented kind.

V TRADE POLICY VERSUS DIRECT INVESTMENT POLICY

Should free trade policy be a basic rule to follow and the role of foreign direct investment be subordinate to it *or* should it be the reverse? This may be the most important question to be decided in considering the relationship between trade and foreign direct investment policy. It seems to me that the former should be taken as a basic policy attitude.

The decisions and performance of US-based multinationals may be rational and, perhaps wise, in terms of the firm for its profit maximisation. But investment of an anti-trade-oriented type is in conflict with the national economic development as explained above. Labour is still internationally immobile and, therefore, economic development and welfare should be considered in terms of national economy.

Foreign direct investment should be trade-oriented and since this is of greater mutual benefit to the countries involved, this type of investment should be encouraged so as to accelerate the reorganisation of north-south trade.

International trade theory aims at clarifying a rational national economic development and the mutual prosperity of trading nations when international factor movements are absent. The Heckscher-Ohlin-Samuelson theorem proves the possibility of international factor price equalisation, although under strict assumptions, without international factor movements. The international movement of capital, technological and managerial knowledge which some country is lacking or lagging, is desirable to complement and facilitate the process of international factor price equalisation and thus national economic development. It should be subordinate to, but not master of, international trade and trade policy.

Unfortunately, however, recent developments seem to have been in the reverse direction.

Stephen Hymer warns:

> Multinational corporations, because of their favourable position (large size, wide horizons and proximity to new technology) and the favourable environment (the initial large gold reserves of the United States, the formation of the Common Market, the small size of foreign investment), were in the vanguard of the revolution in world economic structure. The next round is likely to be characterised by increased emphasis on politics rather than economics and a much less free hand for business. The conflict is not so much between nationalism and internationalism, as the supporters of the multinational corporations like to put it; or between corporations and nation states, as others prefer; but between groups of people within corporations and nation states struggling over who decides what and who gets what – that is, between large corporations over their share of the world market, between big business which is internationally mobile and small business and labour which are not, between the middle classes of different countries over managerial positions, between high-wage labour in one country and low-wage labour in another, and between excluded groups in each country and their elites in that country.[13]

> During the next ten years, the challenge of European and Japanese firms to American corporations will increase the manoeuverability of the third world. But increasingly as firms interpenetrate each others' markets and develop global outlooks, competition will turn to collusion as dominant firms of the center present a united front.[14]

This means the spread of the dualistic structure of the American economy between the traditional, price competitive sector and the new, oligopolistic sector into the entire world economy. International prices are eroded and twisted by the cost reducing advantages of economies of scale, marginal costing, product differentiation, intra-corporation pricing, tax havens, oligopolistic competition, etc., all of which are characteristic of big multinationals. There is, therefore, considerable disillusionment with the relevance of the free trade theory and policy, requiring 'the political economy of the second best'.[15]

From the point of view of international trade policy in relation to investment policy, it is essential to liberalise all the tariff and non-tariff barriers to trade, realising potential comparative costs. First, because of the existence of trade barriers, much foreign direct investment has as its motive the object of getting behind trade barriers and obtaining extra profits from protection. To put it more generally, market imperfections accelerated by trade barriers stimulate anti-trade-oriented direct investment and the desire of multinationals dominates and twists trade policy. Because of the trade barriers in advanced countries against exports from developing countries, true comparative costs are hidden, lowering profits from and thus hindering much needed trade-oriented direct investment, as well as blocking the reorganisation of north-south trade.

This leads to a comment on present American foreign economic policy. Many economists recognise that American comparative advantage lies only in agriculture and some of the new products which, however, rapidly lose their comparative advantage due to hasty foreign direct investment. America has to live on the return flow from past investment and therefore increased foreign investment is not only justifiable but most essential to the American balance of payments.[16] This seems to be a logical result of the American type of foreign direct investment and as such it defeats its own ends. The USA seeks trade liberalisation of foreign countries but she has to increase her own protection for traditional industries. Why does not the USA increase domestic, instead of foreign, investment in order to strengthen the competitiveness of some traditional industries and to create further new products which should be retained for export purposes? It is also a dilemma for the American economy that it welcomes foreign direct investment from Europe and Japan in order to increase employment. Japanese investment is only profitable in American in industries such as textiles which are heavily protected except in minor speciality industries. This further blocks the reorganisation of north-south trade.

VI A NEW FORM OF FOREIGN DIRECT INVESTMENT

How can foreign direct investment or the activities of multinationals be subordinated to international trade growth and what sort of contribution can it make? There are three aspects of foreign direct investment or the activities of multinational corporations to be evaluated: (1) the complementation of capital, technological and managerial knowledge which are in short supply in the recipient economy; (2) the monopolistic element; and (3) the internationalisation of production and marketing for utilising various kinds of economies of scale.

To complement capital, technological and managerial knowledge which are in short supply in the recipient economy is a genuine function of foreign direct investment and 'a potent agent of economic transformation and development, not only in the more laggard "developed" countries but also in the developing countries of the world'.[17] Direct foreign investment, particularly in the case of labour-intensive manufacturing with simple technology, should play the role of 'tutor', teaching technology, management and marketing to local people, and encouraging the growth of local skilled labourers and managers, making them do and/or establish business by themselves. When the foreign firm successfully completes its job as tutor, it would be better if it faded out. Then the direct foreign investment must shift to the production of more sophisticated intermediate goods. This is the logical conclusion in the case of Japanese-type investment.

However, American investment usually involves monopolistic elements since it is undertaken by big, monopolistic or oligopolistic multinational corporations.[18]

The monopolistic or oligopolistic nature of multinationals, internal as well as global, should be rectified, for it results in a wastage of world resources. Therefore, to promote the real role of foreign direct investment but to reduce and/or eliminate the monopolistic element should be a major objective of investment policy and this conforms to free trade policy. A new role for foreign direct investment in a new form should be encouraged[19] in order to maximise its benefits especially in respect of investment in developing countries.

(1) The most important policy question concerns the sort of industry that should be gradually transferred from advanced countries and transplanted in developing countries, appropriate to the stage of

the latter's economic development. Foreign companies invest according to private profitability without any consideration of the entire range of (potential) comparative costs, national economic development plans and priorities in the recipient country.

Hence, there are many accusations against anti-trade-oriented or American investment but few in principle against the trade-oriented or Japanese investment, although there are complaints about the performance and behaviour of Japanese firms abroad. Therefore, investors should ensure in consultation with the competent authorities that the investment fits satisfactorily into the economic and social development plans and priorities of the host country.[20] It is not necessary for the USA to control and reduce the direct investment outflow in general but to select appropriate industries in each recipient economy. Unless this is done by the USA, a selective control of direct investment inflow by the host country is inevitable and reasonable from the viewpoint of national economic development.

(2) Instead of a package of capital, technology and managerial skill, the transfer of only parts of the package may be considered, if the recipient country desires, through loan-*cum*-management contracts or by transfer of technology through licensing arrangements rather than direct investment. This may be desired because the package deal is the source of extra monopolistic profits, on the one hand, and, on the other, wider spillover effects for genuine national economic development are derived from an 'unpacked' transfer even though it takes a somewhat longer time and is less efficient than a package transfer.

Technological knowhow should be in the public interest for the host country provided that there is enough incentive for innovation;[21] it should not be the source of monopolistic or oligopolistic gains.

Agricultural technology is improved by public institutions and made available to farmers in a developing country free of charge or even with training aid. Why should not the same be done in the manufacturing industry? Some special consideration should be given to technology transfer to developing countries.

(3) By the same reasoning, joint ventures with local capital are preferable to wholly-owned subsidiaries. It may be most desirable to establish multinational joint ventures in which each advanced country provides either capital or technology and managerial knowledge, whichever might be appropriate.

(4) It is also better to transplant technology suited to local factor proportions (rather than sophisticated technology) through small- and medium-sized enterprises rather than massive 'enclaves' which usually

operate under more competitive systems. In this sense, the Japanese style of investment is more appropriate to developing countries.

(5) Priority should be given to investment in industries that have wide spillover effects in technology transfer, labour training, employment and external economies, and on industries that benefit mass consumption rather than consumption by a small and privileged elite.

(6) In the field of natural resource developments, developing countries have strong reservations about foreign extraction of resources and such enterprises are occasionally nationalised. Therefore, new forms and new codes of behaviour should be devised particularly for this type of foreign investment. Import linked investments and production sharing methods, as have been adopted by Japan, may be recommended.

(7) A progressive transfer of ownership may be necessary if the genuine objective of foreign direct investment is not a permanent source of monopolistic profit but the complementation of deficient factors in the recipient country as a tutor. Equity may be gradually transformed into loan capital. Precontracted nationalisation, phasing out, and other divestment methods should be seriously examined.[22]

(8) One aim of the above is to make foreign investment more suitable and less expensive for the national economic development of developing countries. The other aim should be to promote the reorganisation and growth of north-south trade. Here, all the policies of advanced countries for increasing the exports of manufactured goods from developing countries should be so accommodated as to promote structural change on both sides and the harmonious development of north-south trade. Thus, an integrated aid, investment-*cum*-preference, structural adjustment policy is required.[23]

Finally, how should the so-called internationalisation of production and marketing which consists of the fifth category of foreign direct investment[24] be evaluated? The global logistics of big multinationals are a rational means of maximising economies of scale in production, in the case of the vertical integration of the firm, and pecuniary economies in the case of horizontal integration or conglomerate. This is a technical rationality which should be encouraged as long as it does not accompany monopolistic behaviour, although 'the multinational corporation reveals the power of size and the danger of leaving it uncontrolled'.[25]

International trade theory has been mainly concerned with the division of labour between firms, coordinated by markets, whilst multinationals realise the division of labour within firms, coordinated by entrepreneurs.[26] The latter is particularly useful and efficient in promoting horizontal (or intra-industry) trade between parts and components each of which is produced in a different country with economies of scale greater than minimum optimum.[27] The trouble with this kind of horizontal trade is the difficulty of reaching agreement on specialisation between countries.[28] This difficulty is easily overcome in the multinational corporation since agreed specialisation is part of the centralised decision making process of the firm. However, a rational specialisation programme is made possible in a free trade area only where there are no trade barriers and no fear of increased barriers exists. Certainly, monopolistic behaviour should be strictly controlled and this may be feasible if the integrated market is so wide that many enterprises within each industry have to compete with each other.

Alternatively, as far as new manufactured goods are concerned, horizontal trade mainly among advanced countries should be promoted instead of direct investment.[29] Innovation of new goods is required for the reorganisation of and new dynamism in the international division of labour, while innovative human resources are relatively scarce in the world as a whole. It might be desirable for advanced countries to arrange an agreement to specialise in the line of innovation in which each country concentrates its effort. Assurance of specialisation and accompanying economies of scale will promote liberalisation of trade in these commodities. They might also be able to spare innovative human resources to create technology which is more suitable to developing countries.

If all advanced countries liberalise imports of new goods and exporting countries make serious efforts at exporting, mutual trade in these goods among advanced countries will certainly expand and there is no need to undertake foreign direct investment. If firms still dare to undertake direct investment, it is because monopolistic profits are anticipated. This sort of direct investment should be disçouraged.

Such agreed international specialisation in the innovative activities may be the only way of avoiding the vicious circle resulting from the American style of foreign direct investment.

In conclusion, it is worth stressing that foreign direct investment and the activities of multinationals should be trade-oriented and subordinated to free trade policy so as to contribute to the reorganisation of the international division of labour and the growth of trade between advanced and developing countries and among industrialised countries alike. A code of behaviour for international investments[30] should be thought out along these lines.

NOTES

1. The following remarks by Harry Johnson are suggestive: 'the essence of direct foreign investment is the transmission to the "host" country of a "package" of capital, managerial skill, and technical knowledge. The major issues posed for theory are the reasons why the transmission of such a "package" of capital and knowledge is more profitable than the alternative of transmitting either the capital or the knowledge or both separately, and what the welfare implications are for the "home" and the "host" countries respectively. Along with the first issue goes the important empirical question of which industries are likely to be characterized by direct foreign investment and which are not. Economic theory offers two approaches to these questions, that of the theory of industrial organization and that of traditional trade theory. These approaches must be used as complements, since the former is microeconomic in character whereas the latter stresses the requirements of general macroeconomic equilibrium.' Harry Johnson, 'Survey of the Issues', in Peter Drysdale, ed., *Direct Foreign Investment in Asia and the Pacific*, Australian National University Press, Canberra, 1972, p. 2.
2. For an excellent explanation of Japan's direct foreign investment see Koichi Hamada, 'Japanese Investment Abroad', in Peter Drysdale, ed., *Direct Foreign Investment in Asia and the Pacific*, Australian National University Bress, 1972. According to a MITI report, in an accumulated total foreign investment of $3,596 m. between 1951-70, mining accounts for 31.4 per cent, or $1,127 m.; manufacturing accounts for 26.99 per cent, or $963 m.; commerce accounts for 10.3 per cent, or $370 m.; and others (that is, agriculture and forestry, fisheries, construction, finance and insurance) accounts for 31.4 per cent, or $1,126 m.
3. According to the MITI report, in a total accumulated foreign investment in manufacturing industries of $963 m. between 1951 and 1970, pulp and wood (this belongs rather to natural resource oriented) accounts for 22.1 per cent; textiles 19.7 per cent; steel and metals 14.3 per cent; transport machinery 10.6 per cent; electric appliances 7.4 per cent; other machinery 7.0 per cent; foodstuffs 6.3 per cent; chemicals 6.2 per cent; and others 6.4 per cent.
4. According to the Second Questionnaire Survey undertaken by the Export-Import Bank of Japan, 90 per cent of manufacturing firms established abroad with Japanese direct investment use Japanese technology, 86 per cent of them import Japanese machinery and equipment and their imports of Japanese raw materials and intermediate goods account for 58 per cent.
5. As regards Japanese accumulated foreign direct investment by the end of 1969, the four largest investment projects were: Arabian oil in the neutral zone between Kuwait and Saudi Arabia; Minus steel in Brazil; pulp industry in Alaska; and oil extracting in North Sumatra. If these are taken separately, the average amount of investment per unit is $1.7-1.8 m. in mining, $0.5-0.6 m. in manufacturing, and $0.32 m. in commerce and others.
6. For example, Raymond Vernon, 'International Investment and International Trade in the Product Cycle', *Quarterly Journal of Economics*, May 1966; G. E. Hufbauer, *Synthetic Materials and the Theory of International Trade*, Duckworth, London, 1966.
7. Raymond Vernon, 'The Economic Consequence of US Foreign Direct Investment', *United States International Economic Policy in an Inter-*

dependent World, Papers 1, Washington, D.C., July 1971, pp. 930-7.
8. *Ibid.*, p. 930.
9. Stephen Hymer, 'United States Investment Abroad', Peter Drysdale, ed., *Direct Foreign Investment in Asia and the Pacific*, ANU, 1972, p. 41.
10. *Ibid.*, p. 29.
11. For example, see, Emergency Committee for American Trade, *The Role of the Multinational Corporation in the United States and World Economies*, February 1972.
12. An American labour union researcher states that: 'US-based multinational operations may adversely affect host countries as well as the US. The balanced economic and social development of developing economies, for example, is not necessarily promoted by the establishment of electronic subsidiary plants, with high productivity and low wages – with production for export from countries that urgently require basic educational, health and housing facilities, as well as balanced growth of domestic investment and consumer markets.' Nat Goldfinger, 'A Labor View of Foreign Investment and Trade Issues', *United States International Economic Policy in an Interdependent World, Papers 1*, Washington, D.C., July 1971, p. 927.
13. Stephen Hymer, 'United States Investment Abroad', pp. 30-1.
14. Stephen Hymer, 'The United States Multinational Corporations and Japanese Competition in the Pacific', a paper presented for Conferencia del Pacifica, Vina del Mar, Chile, 27 Sept.-3 Oct. 1970. Also see, Louis Turner, *Invisible Empire: Multinational Companies and the Modern World*, London, 1970.
15. Helen Hughes, 'Trade and Industrialization Policies: the Political Economy of the Second Best', Kiyoshi Kojima, ed., *Structural Adjustments in Asian-Pacific Trade*, Japan Economic Research Centre, July 1973, pp. 89-115.
16. See, for example, C. Fred Bergsten, 'Crisis in US Trade Economy and International Trade', *ibid.*, pp. 385-413.
17. Harry G. Johnson, 'The Multinational Corporation as a Development Agent', *Columbia Journal of World Business*, May-June 1970, p. 1.
18. 'The multinational producing enterprise has been acclaimed as an agent of development and has been condemned as a weapon of exploitation.

'Conflict between the multinational enterprise and the host government may derive from four sources: from the fact that is is *private* and hence may clash with the social and national goals; that it is *large* and oligopolistic and hence possesses market and bargaining power which may be used against the interest of the host country; that it is *foreign*, particularly if it is American, and hence may be serving the national interests of a foreign nation; and that it is "*western*" and hence may transfer inappropriate knowhow, technology or management practices, or products, designed with characteristics not needed in less-developed countries.' Paul Streeten, 'Costs and Benefits of Multinational Enterprises in Less-Developed Countries', John Dunning, ed., *The Multinational Enterprises*, George Allen and Unwin, 1971, pp. 240, 251.
19. This was discussed intensively at the Chile Conference. See, H. W. Arndt, 'Economic Cooperation in the Pacific: A Summing Up', a paper presented to Conferencia del Pacifica, Vina del Mar, Chile, 27 Sept.-3 Oct. 1970. Also, in Paul Streeten, *op. cit.*, pp. 251-4.
20. International Chamber of Commerce, *Guidelines for International Investments*, Nov. 1972.
21. Harry G. Johnson, 'The Efficiency and Welfare Implications of the International Corporation', Charles P. Kindleberger, ed., *International Corporation*, p. 36.

22. Albert O. Hirschman, *How to Divest in Latin America and Why?*, Essays in International Finance, No. 76, Nov. 1969, Princeton University.
23. See Chapter 7.
24. Even Vernon points out the need to build another model besides his product cycle sequence. Raymond Vernon, *Sovereignty at Bay, The Multinational Spread of US Enterprises*, Basic Books, Inc., 1971, pp. 107-12.
25. Stephen Hymer, 'The Efficiency (Contradictions) of Multinational Corporations', *American Economic Review*, May 1970, p. 448.
26. *Ibid.*, p. 41.
27. I have in mind the sort of logistical structure whereby 'Ford was making fender steel in Holland for car production in the rest of Europe and tractor components in Germany and motors for compact models in Britain to be used in US assembly plants'. Raymond Vernon, *op. cit.*, pp. 107-8. This kind of specialisation is applicable and beneficial to developing countries.
28. See Kiyoshi Kojima, 'Towards a Theory of Agreed Specialization: The Economics of Integration', in W. A. Eltis, M. F. G. Scott, and N. N. Wolfe, eds., *Essays in Honour of Sir Roy Harrod*, Oxford, 1970 (reprinted in *Japan and a Pacific Free Trade Area*, Macmillan, London, 1971, Chapter 2).
29. An excellent suggestion is given by Jagdish N. Bhagwati in his book review of Raymond Vernon, 'Sovereignty at Bay', *Journal of International Economics*, September 1972, pp. 455-9.
30. Cf. *The Pacific Basin Charter on International Investments*, PBEC, 19 May 1972, and *Guidelines for International Investment*, International Chamber of Commerce, 19 Nov. 1972. The Japan Chamber of Commerce has also issued independently a similar charter. See also, United Nations, *Multinational Corporations in World Development*, 1973, and *The Impact of Multinational Corporations on Development and on International Relations*, 1974.

5 A MACROECONOMIC THEORY OF FOREIGN DIRECT INVESTMENT

I INTRODUCTION

In the previous chapter, I identified the characteristics of two different methods or styles of foreign direct investment: the Japanese style compared with the American style, or trade-oriented versus anti-trade-oriented direct investment.[1] Since the difference has important implications for the role of foreign direct investment and its effects upon international trade expansion, it deserves theoretical elaboration through the construction of a model analysing the effects of each type of investment. This is the first task of the present chapter (Sections II to IV).

Secondly, whether foreign investment 'complements' or 'substitutes' for international trade is also an important subject which needs theoretical elaboration as some discussion has developed. This problem can be interpreted in terms of our distinction between trade-creating and trade-destroying direct foreign investment (Sections V and VI).

II A MODEL OF TRADE-ORIENTED DIRECT INVESTMENT

Comparative advantage between two countries or between one country *vis-à-vis* the rest of the world changes mainly due to differential rates of growth in factor endowments, as the Heckscher-Ohlin theorem and the Rybczynski theorem show. Direct foreign investment is trade-oriented, or more exactly trade-reorganisation-oriented, if it transfers a package of capital, technology and managerial skill from an industry which has a comparative disadvantage in the investing country to the recipient country, where it develops a comparative advantage and helps the reorganisation of the international division of labour and trade between them, upgrading the industrial structure of both countries. The point is that direct foreign investment must work in a complementary fashion to changes in the pattern of comparative advantage. On the other hand, if direct investment moves out from an industry in which there is a comparative advantage in the investing country, it prevents mutual upgrading of the industrial structure and blocks the reorganisation of international trade. This is direct foreign investment of 'anti-trade-reorganisation-oriented' type.

In order to make clear the difference between the two types of foreign investment, let us first construct a model of comparative investment profitabilities for trade-oriented foreign direct investment.

It should be noted that trade-oriented foreign direct investment works only in a competitive world in which standardised commodities are produced and traded and competitiveness is determined by traditional comparative advantage theory *à la* Ricardian theory or the Heckscher-Ohlin theory. In other words, it is not a problem of 'technological-gap trade' but of 'low-wage trade' in the product cycle.

To understand the determinants of direct investment, it may be useful to set out the following production function:

$$Q = f(L, K, T, M) \quad ,$$

where Q denotes the output produced, L and K labour and capital, T technology used and M managerial skills or organisational technique.[2] Foreign direct investments transfer the package of K, T and M, but it is assumed that endowment of K, besides L, is not affected, for international investment is *marginal* to total capital formation both in the investing and receiving countries. Technology and management used in country A (advanced industrialised country or Japan) are assumed to be superior to those in country B (developing country) before the direct foreign investment from country A to B takes place, but the direct foreign investment makes it possible for country B to use superior technology and management. This is possible because the technology and management are not specific but general factors which we assume are transferable as part of a package or separately between countries on a competitive basis.

Thus, the comparative advantage structure before the foreign direct investment takes place resembles that shown in Table 5.1 (a) in which the costs of the two countries are shown in a common monetary unit (say, the dollar) converted by the exchange rate. Country B produces more expensively than country A both X goods (traditional labour-intensive goods, e.g. textiles) and Y goods (new capital- and knowledge-intensive goods, e.g. computers) because of its inferiority or lack of technology and management as compared with country A. However, country A has a comparative advantage in Y industry whilst country B possesses a (potential) comparative advantage in X industry; or

$$\frac{P_{XA}/P_{YA}}{P_{XB}/P_{YB}} = \frac{100/100}{150/300} = 2 > 1 \quad ,$$

where P denotes production cost or price. This comparative advantage pattern results from the assumption that country A has a larger amount of K compared to country B (that is, $K_A/L_A > K_B/L_B$) while X goods are more labour-intensive than Y goods in both countries; that is

$$\frac{K_{XA}}{L_{XA}} < \frac{K_{YA}}{L_{YA}}$$

and

$$\frac{K_{XB}}{L_{XB}} < \frac{K_{YB}}{L_{YB}} \quad ;$$

according to the Heckscher-Ohlin theorem.

The situation may be illustrated well by Figure 5.1, where X and Y are the isoquants for the two sectors in country A and x and y those in country B, before foreign direct investment takes place. In country A,

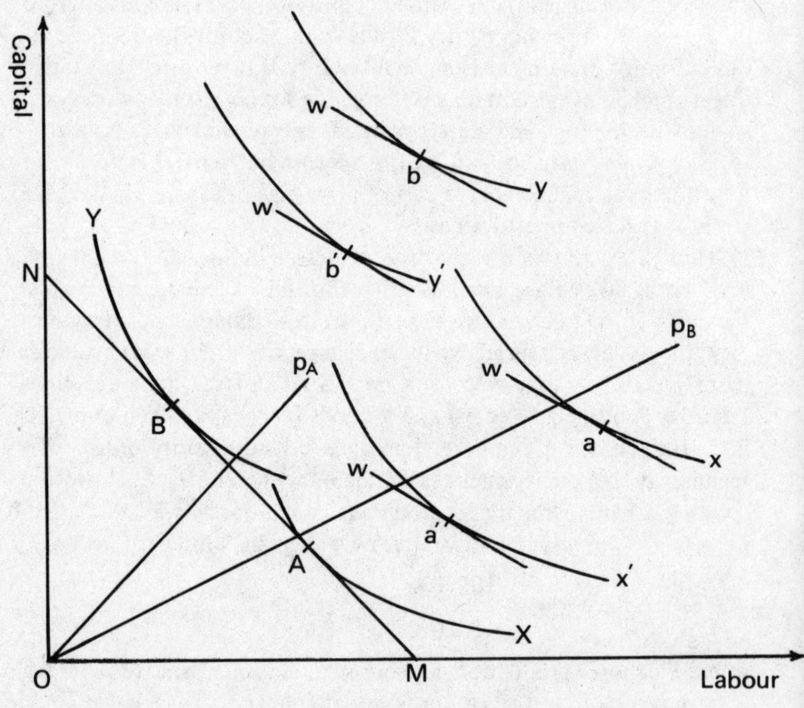

FIGURE 5.1

Table 5.1 A case of trade-oriented foreign direct investment

(a) Comparative costs before direct investment

	Country A	Country B
X goods	$ 100	$ 150
Y goods	$ 100	$ 300

(b) Comparative costs when direct investments are taking place in both industries

	Country A	Country B
X goods	$ 100	$ 75
Y goods	$ 100	$ 200

(c) Comparative profit rates for country A

	Domestic investment	Foreign direct investment
X industry	η_x 10 %	η_x' 12 %
Y industry	η_y 10 %	η_y' 5 %

(d) Comparative costs when direct investments have taken place only in X industry

	Country A	Country B
X goods	$ 100	$ 75
Y goods	$ 100	$ 300

the factor endowment ratio, K_A/L_A, is shown by ρ_A, the factor price ratio by MN, the equilibrium production points at A and B, and the costs of the two goods are 1:1. In country B, before the foreign direct investment, the factor endowment ratio, K_B/L_B, is shown by ρ_B, the factor price ratio by ω_s', the equilibrium production points at a and b, and the cost of X goods is lower than Y goods.

Now if direct investment takes place and T and M are transferred from country A to country B, the production function in country B is improved to the isoquants x′ and y′. It is assumed, as will be explained later in detail, that the degree of improvement in production function is greater in X industry than in Y industry because of the easier technology to be lèarned and a smaller requirement of skilled labour in the former industry. Now, given factor price ratio, w, in country B, the equilibrium production points would be at a′ and b′, leaving the product price ratio higher for Y goods. The new potential comparative costs when direct investment might take place in both industries may be shown as Table 5.1 (b) in which production costs of both goods in country B are reduced in different degree, strengthening the comparative advantage of X production. Thus, the cost of X goods in country B becomes competitive in an international market.

Now, what would be the expected profit rates for the investing country A? The profit rate from domestic involvement for X and Y industries, η_x and η_y respectively, is assumed to be the same, say 10 per cent, for in country A where free competition is assumed to prevail (see Table 5.1 (c)). The profit rate from direct investment to country B's x industry, η_x', would be higher than η_y', say, 12 per cent, for X industry in country B produces at lower cost than in the investing country and becomes competitive in an international market, thus retaining a greater profit margin. By contrast, Y industry in country B, even if foreign direct investment is taking place, remains at a comparative disadvantage and uncompetitive in the international market, and the foreign direct investment yields no or small profits compared with domestic investment, η_y, and foreign investment in X industry, η_x', under strong protection by the recipient country. In Table 5.1 (c), the profit rate from direct investment in country B's Y industry is thus assumed to be 5 per cent.

Obviously country A would be better off if it increased investment in Y industry at home and in X industry abroad. This can be seen by examining (a) the absolute profit rate differential between home and foreign investments for each industry or (b) comparative investment profitabilities, that is, [3]

$$\frac{\eta_x'/\eta_y'}{\eta_x/\eta_y} = \frac{12/5}{10/10} = 2.4 > 1 .$$

The core of our argument for trade-oriented foreign direct investment is that foreign direct investment should follow the direction indicated by comparative investment profitabilities which in turn are a reflection of comparative advantage under competitive conditions. Thus, foreign direct investment is not only complementary with trade but also an accelerator in reorganising trade patterns in the direction of potential and dynamic comparative advantage. This harmonious function of foreign direct investment is revealed in the fact that, because of comparative investment profitabilities, direct investment from country A actually takes place only in X industry in country B, and results in the new comparative cost pattern shown in Table 5.1 (d).

It reflects the fact that the comparative cost differential is widened due to foreign direct investment, as compared with Table 5.1 (a), transforming the X industry in country B from a potentially advantageous to a strongly competitive exportable industry. Due to such dynamic changes in the pattern of comparative advantage, country A is willing to promote structural adjustment to contract investment in and the production of X goods, which becomes an import industry, and to shift its resources towards foreign direct investment and domestic investment in the Y industry as well, the comparative advantage of which is strengthened as shown in Table 5.1 (d). Thus, this type of trade-oriented direct investment will bring about an upgrading of industrial structure both in recipient and investing countries alike.

III CORRESPONDENCE BETWEEN COMPARATIVE COSTS AND COMPARATIVE PROFIT RATES

Which line of production, either in X or Y goods, is more promising for a country is judged by the principle of comparative costs, which is however a theoretical criterion. Businessmen or firms determine cost by comparative investment profitability, which is a very useful criterion if it corresponds exactly to the comparative costs under a certain condition. The required condition is found as follows:

Let us assume that each firm behaves with a version of the 'full-cost' principle,[4] or, in other words, that it sells products at an average cost per unit of products *plus* a certain profit or 'mark-up'.

Let P stand for selling price, Q for the volume of sales (which is equal to the quantity produced), and PQ for total revenue which is denoted by T.

$$PQ = T \quad . \tag{1}$$

This consists of total cost, C, and total profit, R.

$$T = C + R \quad . \tag{2}$$

Using this, equation (1) is rewritten as follows:

$$P = \frac{T}{Q} = \frac{R/Q}{R/T} = \frac{\pi}{r} \;, \tag{3}$$

where $\pi \equiv R/Q \equiv P - C/Q$, which shows profit per unit of sales and $r \equiv R/T = R/PQ = (P - C/Q)/P$, which shows the profit rate of total sales.[5]

The relationship of equation (3) is established in the home country for each of the goods which are shown by the suffixes x and y:

$$\frac{P_x}{P_y} = \frac{\pi_x/r_x}{\pi_y/r_y} = \left(\frac{\pi_x/\pi_y}{r_x/r_y}\right). \tag{4}$$

This relationship is also applicable to the foreign country which is shown by the upper suffix:

$$\frac{P_x'}{P_y'} = \left(\frac{\pi_x'}{\pi_y'}\right)\left(\frac{r_y'}{r_x'}\right) . \tag{5}$$

Let us assume the home country has its comparative advantage in Y goods production:

$$\frac{P_x}{P_y} > \frac{P_x'}{P_y'} . \tag{6}$$

Under these comparative cost conditions, according to equations (4) and (5), the following relationship should necessarily exist:

$$\left(\frac{\pi_x}{\pi_y}\right)\left(\frac{r_y}{r_x}\right) > \left(\frac{\pi_x'}{\pi_y'}\right)\left(\frac{r_y'}{r_x'}\right) . \tag{7}$$

Let us add the assumption

$$\frac{\pi_x}{\pi_y} = \frac{\pi_x'}{\pi_y''} , \tag{8}$$

then, it follows that

$$\frac{r_x}{r_y} < \frac{r_x'}{r_y'}. \tag{9}$$

To sum up, as far as assumption (8) is satisfied, the comparative costs such as $P_x/P_y > P_x'/P_y'$ correspond to the comparative profit rates on total sales such as $r_x/r_y < r_x'/r_y'$. In other words, 'in the industry in which a country has comparative advantage, its profit rate on total sales is relatively higher'. This may be called the correspondence principle between comparative costs and comparative profit rates.[6] If the principle is well proved, firms are able to rely, as they usually do, upon the comparative profit rate judgements instead of the cumbersome theory of comparative advantage.

The crucial question is whether or not assumption (8) is plausible. The assumption requires that although the unit profit, π, may differ for each item, the ratio of unit profit for two items is the same in both countries. This is, however, a peculiar expression of free international competition in the case which uses 'comparative' comparisons as is usual in international economics. The cumbersome expression of the assumption comes from the fact that each item has its own unit and each country expresses prices in different currency units. If the unit of items is normalised and an equilibrium exchange rate is set, the assumption is expressed in an alternative way as $\pi_X = \pi_Y = \pi_X' = \pi_Y'$ or the profit per dollar's worth of total sales is the same in all commodities in both countries. This fully meets our condition and is quite compatible with free competition under the 'full-cost' principle.

Now, suppose that each country specialises in producing goods which are relatively cheap and thus more profitable, i.e. country A specialises in Y goods while country B specialises in X goods. As production of the items in which each country specialises expands, costs rise whereas costs of the relatively expensive items fall. Thus the cost plus unit profit which satisfies such a condition as $\pi_X/\pi_Y = \pi_X'/\pi_Y'$ for two items in both countries will converge through the competitive market mechanism to the international price ratio of the two items. To put it another way, according to the free trade condition, omitting transportation costs, the price ratio of the two items in both countries equalises with the international price ratio (i.e. $P_X/P_Y = P_X'/P_Y'$). Now, (a) $P_X/P_Y = P_X'/P_Y'$ subject to the free trade condition, and (b) $\pi_X/\pi_Y = \pi_X'/\pi_Y'$ according to our free competition assumption, it necessarily follows (c) $r_X/r_Y = r_X'/r_Y'$, or there is equalisation of profit rates of total sales in both countries. If we make an alternative assumption such as $\pi_X = \pi_Y = \pi_X' = \pi_Y'$ at the international equilibrium as mentioned above, it follows that $r_X = r_Y = r_X' = r_Y'$ which is a more explicit expression of the result of free international competition.

To sum up, in so far as free trade and free international competition prevail, comparative profit rates correspond to comparative advantages. Therefore, business decision-making in investment, both domestic and foreign, subject to the comparative profit rates will promote trade in the right direction along lines suggested by comparative costs. This is what trade-oriented foreign direct investment achieves. But what would happen if the comparative profit rates contradict comparative costs due to monopolistic elements in one of the industries? This is what the problem for American style or 'anti-trade-oriented' foreign direct investment is.

IV A MODEL OF ANTI-TRADE-ORIENTED DIRECT INVESTMENT

Let us turn to examine foreign direct investments of the American or anti-trade-oriented type. It is supposed that the pattern of comparative advantage between country P (say a pioneer country like the USA) and

Table 5.2 A case of anti-trade-oriented foreign direct investment

(a) Comparative costs before direct investments

	Country P	Country B
X goods	\$ 100	\$ 150
Y goods	\$ 100	\$ 300

(b) Comparative costs when direct investments are taking place in both industries

	Country P	Country B
X goods	\$ 100	\$ 75
Y goods	\$ 100	\$ 200

(c) Comparative profit rates for country P

	Domestic investment	Foreign direct investment
X industry	r_x 5 %	r_x' 12 %
Y industry	r_y 10 %	r_y' 50 %

(d) Comparative costs when direct investments are taking place only in the Y industry

	Country P	Country B
X goods	\$ 100	\$ 150
Y goods	\$ 100	\$ 200

country B is the same as in Table 5.1 (a) and (b). Even with such a pattern of comparative advantage, comparative profit rates for country P would be like Table 5.2 (c). The reason is, first, that due to the dualistic structure of the economy separating the new oligopolistic sector, Y, from the traditional competitive sector, X, the profit rate from domestic investment is not the same in the two sectors but low in the latter, say 5 per cent, and high in the former, say 10 per cent. Second, since X industry is assumed to operate under competitive conditions not only in the domestic market but throughout the world, its foreign direct investment, if it takes place, is able to obtain the same profit rate, η_x' being 12 per cent, as country A's foreign direct investment. Third, the profit rate from foreign direct investment in Y industry, that is, η_y', ought to be lower (or even less) than in domestic investment if the industry were under competitive conditions, but it is assumed to be 50 per cent, higher than in domestic investment and highest in the comparative profitabilities without any relationship to comparative advantages. This results from such entirely different causes as technological advantage, product differentiation, superior marketing, etc., any of which represents some monopolistic element as explained in the previous chapter.[7] In this case, the package of capital, technology and managerial skill brought in from country P to country B is not a general factor but a factor specific to that monopolistic firm.

More exactly, let us suppose that country B levies a protective tariff as high as 200 per cent on the import of Y goods, thus ensuring that the high cost ($ 300) domestic producer survives. For Y industry in country P, it becomes profitable, instead of trying hard to export, to get over the high tariff wall and to produce and sell by itself behind the wall. This foreign firm is able to produce Y goods at the cost of $ 200 and sell at $ 300, leaving a profit margin as high as 50 per cent.

Now in the anti-trade-oriented type, foreign direct investment takes place in Y industry, the new oligopolistic industry and top in the rank of comparative advantage in order to realise the higher profit rate, 50 per cent, than that in domestic investment, 10 per cent, for the sake of the company's profit maximisation ahead of its oligopolistic competitors. This has its rationale from a microeconomic point of view, but not from a macroeconomic point of view. The contradiction between the comparative costs shown in Table 5.2 (b) and the comparative profit rates shown in Table 5.2 (c) means that the market is not competitive but is disturbed by monopolistic or oligopolistic elements which bring about mal-utilisation of resources of each nation and for the world as a whole. A dualistic structure in country P between competitive and monopolistic sectors is exported to and spread throughout the world.

When the foreign direct investment takes place in Y industry, the new comparative costs would be as shown in Table 5.2 (d), so that the degree of comparative advantage of country P's Y industry is reduced when compared to the original situation shown in Table 5.2 (a). This makes the export of Y goods from country P less profitable and smaller in amount. Further, if foreign direct investment is successful from the point of view of the firm, production abroad becomes competitive and cheaper than in the investing country, resulting in *reverse* imports. This means that foreign direct investment of this type reverses the investing country's comparative advantage. Thus, it is obvious that this type of foreign direct investment destroys the export opportunity for the industry with a comparative advantage in the investing country.

Moreover, it is true that new products are successively created and new product cycles take place one after another in America. Multinational corporations grow larger and maintain monopolistic or oligopolistic gains. But, it is also true that the creation of new products does not keep pace with the spread of new technology, which is itself accelerated by foreign direct investment.[8] Thus, the American economy will lose its comparative advantage in new products (Y industry in our model) sooner or later and has already lost it in traditional manufacturing industry (X industry in our model) for a different reason. In the long run this creates export difficulties and adversely affects the US balance of payments. Where are labourers to be employed? They should be employed in the new industry sector. However in actuality the new industry sector does not offer many job opportunities, rather the reverse, because of foreign direct investment. Therefore, the labour force has to be absorbed in traditional, comparatively disadvantaged industries and by the service sector, requiring strong protection. This prevents needed structural adjustments to the economy.

What the American economy needs most is, first, to have its dualistic structure broken up into an entirely competitive system, to allow the traditional sector's resources to move freely into new growth sectors, to encourage the reorganisation of the industrial structure and the realisation of equal profitability between industries. From the point of view of world resource utilisation and welfare, foreign direct investment by monopolistic or oligopolistic multinational firms involves distortions and is therefore undesirable.

The situation would be improved if the USA were to invest abroad in traditional manufacturing industries (such as textiles, steel, shipbuilding, etc.) and in some agricultural concerns, for they represent her comparatively disadvantaged industries. It is puzzling that many economists have for so long assumed that such industries are not suitable for foreign direct investment[9] for the Japanese have made successfully foreign direct investments in such industries, as did UK companies a few decades ago.[10] Thus, although all foreign direct investment does not necessarily result in the 'export of jobs',[11] the anti-trade-oriented model usually does.

V INTERNATIONAL TRADE AND FOREIGN INVESTMENT: SUBSTITUTES OR COMPLEMENTS?

Recently, there has been some discussion about whether foreign investment 'substitutes' for or 'complements' international trade. First, Robert Mundell[12] showed that both are *complete* substitutes for each other under the assumption of identical production functions for two countries within the framework of the ordinary Heckscher-Ohlin-Samuelson theory of trade. Second, Andrew Schmitz and Peter Helmberger[13] and especially Douglas D. Purvis[14] demonstrated that foreign investment may work complementarily to international trade if production functions vary in the two countries. However, these writers do not seem to be able to show definite conditions for substitute or complementary cases.

Mundell and Purvis dealt with international movements of capital as one of the homogeneous factors of production, referring to it as a real, or physical capital.[15] I have called this 'money capital' for it is to be a general, homogeneous factor of production which is allocable and reallocable to any sector of the economy. It is money capital before it is allocated while it becomes real capital after allocation.[16] Schmitz and Helmberger had in mind foreign direct investment but dealt with it as if it were the same as money capital movement. But there is a critical difference, in the sense that foreign direct investment affects the activities of specific sectors of investing and host economies, whereas international money capital movement is absorbed by and results in the reallocation of factors of production (capital and labour) so as to attain a general equilibrium of both countries.

Keeping in mind this characteristic of foreign direct investment, we may be able to differentiate succinctly two cases in which foreign direct investment works as a complement to international trade (trade-creating) or as a substitute for it (trade-destroying). This is the main purpose of the remainder of this chapter.

Mundell's complete substitutes case

Mundell demonstrates that 'the substitution of commodity for factor movements will be complete' under rigorous Heckscher-Ohlin-Samuelson assumptions such as:

> (a) production functions are homogeneous of the first degree (i.e. if marginal productivities, relatively and absolutely, depend only on the proportions in which factors are combined) and are identical in both countries; (b) one commodity requires a greater proportion of one factor than the other commodity at any factor price at all points on any production function; and (c) factor endowments are

such as to exclude specialisation.

Practically, 'assume two countries, A and B, two commodities, cotton [textiles] and steel, and two factors, labour and capital'.[17] Country A is well endowed with capital but poorly endowed with labour relative to country B;[18] 'cotton is labour-intensive relative to steel. For expositional convenience we shall use community indifference curves.'[19] Therefore, country A has a comparative advantage in capital-intensive Y goods, or steel, whereas country B has a comparative advantage in labour-intensive X goods, or cotton.

In Figure 5.2,[20] T_aT_a and T_bT_b are initial (before capital movements) transformation functions (production possibility curves) for country A and country B respectively, production is at P and consumption is at C in each country. Country A is exporting P_aQ_a of steel and importing Q_aC_a of cotton, whereas correspondingly country B is importing C_bQ_b of steel and exporting Q_bP_b of cotton. In other words, since $C_aQ_aP_a$ and $P_bQ_bC_b$ are identical triangles, international trade between the two countries is in equilibrium.

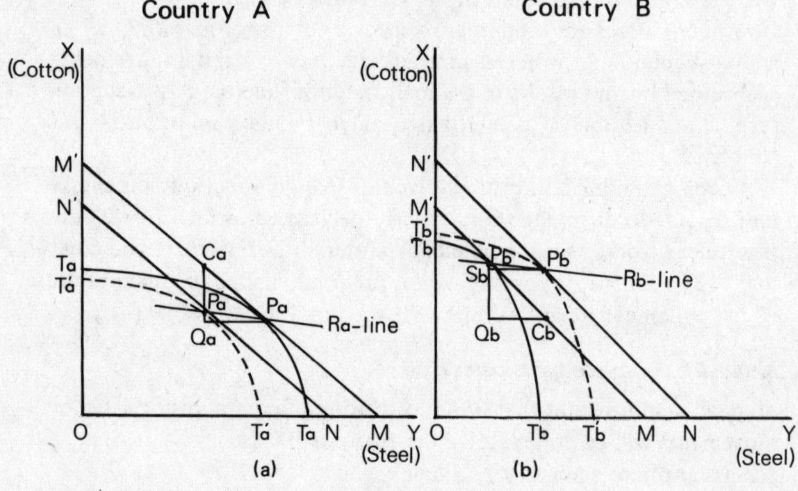

FIGURE 5.2

Suppose now, induced by the imposition of a tariff on steel by country B, capital as large as MN in terms of Y goods of M′N′ in terms of X goods moves from country A to country B. Country B becomes more capital-abundant and reallocates the increased capital and the original labour in general equilibrium fashion – this process is explained precisely by the aid of a box diagram, as in Mundell – reaching a new equilibrium production point at P_b' on a new expanded production possibility curve $T_b'T_b'$. Thus a Rybczynski line[21] for country B, i.e. R_b-line is drawn. Similarly, in country A which loses capital, a new equilibrium production point is achieved at P_a' and R_a-line is drawn. Both R_a- and R_b-lines are parallel to each other and result in identical triangles, $P_a'Q_aP_a$ and $P_bS_bP_b'$, i.e. an increased output of Y goods and a decreased output of X goods in country B and reverse changes of the same magnitude in country A. These results are due to the assumption of identical production functions between the two countries. If 'interest payments must be made to country A (instead of B in Mundell's original) equal in value to the marginal product of the capital inflow',[22] the value equivalent to M'N' in terms of X goods or MN in terms of Y goods is transferred as interest payments from country B to A, so income in both countries is unchanged, i.e. the situation remains as it was before the capital movements were undertaken. Thus, the capital movements are complete substitutes for commodity trade.

It should be noted here that in such a case as Mundell's, the capital abundant country A has a comparative advantage in capital-intensive Y goods while the capital moved from country A to country B will necessarily increase the production of capital-intensive Y goods, or, more generally, it will increase the production which uses the increased factor of production more intensively than the other goods. Thus, the potential for exporting capital-intensive goods from the capital abundant country and capital movements out of that country are substitutes for (and therefore competitive with) each other, the latter eliminating the former. Accordingly this case can be regarded as 'trade-destroying' or 'anti-trade-oriented'. And this will necessarily happen in the case of international movements of *money* capital which usually flow from a capital abundant country.

As far as Mundell's demonstration is concerned, there is no positive gain from capital movement for it is a complete substitution for commodity trade. Does this mean that there is no point in undertaking capital movement even if trade impediments exist?

In Mundell, it is not clear whether or not tariffs still remain with the new equilibrium situation in both countries after the capital movements, although he says that 'the tariff is now no longer necessary'.[23] If tariffs remain, capital movement must bring about some distortion and inefficiency in world production, especially in the host country. If this is true, free trade is preferable to capital movements with trade impediments.

Hamada demonstrates clearly that foreign investments induced by tariffs lead to falls in the host country's income at international prices for the tariffs give the advantage to foreign investors who can sell their products at a higher price than the international price within the tariff wall.[24]

Purvis' complements case

It might be advisable to make clear what the words 'complement' and 'substitute' mean in this context. Purvis defines complement as follows: 'A sufficient condition for complementarity is that the initial capital outflow generates an excess demand for imports and an excess supply of exportables at constant terms of trade.'[25] I agree with this definition. In other words, if foreign investment is complementary to product trade, it creates and/or expands the opportunity to import one product and to export another. Thus, this kind of foreign investment is 'trade-creating' or 'trade-oriented'.

Symmetrically, if the initial capital outflow decreases or eliminates the opportunity to import one product and to export another product,[26] this kind of foreign investment 'substitutes' for product trade and is thus 'trade-destroying' or 'anti-trade-oriented'. This is the case when foreign investment induces competitive production in the host country against the investing country's comparatively advantageous production (exportables).

We will not consider Schmitz-Helmberger's paper in detail for it deals with one product (particularly primary products and primary manufacturing) in a partial equilibrium model,[27] although it makes a significant contribution in pointing out the importance of different production functions between countries.

One of the focuses of Purvis' argument is to show the effect of different production functions between country A (capital abundant, investing country), and country B (labour abundant, host country), by varied Rybczynski lines.

Let us suppose that in Figure 5.2 (b), R_b, the Rybczynski line for country B is steeper than it is drawn and therefore steeper than R_a, the Rybczynski line for country A. This is possible if the expanded production frontier of country B, $T_b'T_b'$, is skewed towards Y goods much more than as it is drawn in Figure 5.2 (b). This, in turn, is possible if production functions in country B, which are supposed to be different from those in country A, are of *comparatively* higher productivity in Y goods than in X goods as compared with the same relationship in country A. How and why the production functions differ between two countries is a crucial element in the present arguments, but both Schmitz and Helmberger[28] and Purvis[29] do not give any rigorous specification.

It is still assumed here that the distance between the two parallel lines MM′ and NN′ is the same in both countries for it shows the value of the international movement of capital. In so far as the R_b-line is steeper than the R_a-line, the production of Y goods is increased in country B much more than that decreased in country A, resulting in a net increase in the output of Y goods for the two countries taken together. This may be counted as a gain from capital movement in a narrower sense.[30] But, in the production of X goods, the output decreased in country B more than output increased in country A, resulting in a net decrease. Therefore, whether or not capital movement brings about a net gain is still uncertain until we compare in value terms the net increase of Y goods and the net decrease of X goods.

Even if capital movement results in a net increase of Y goods, there remains another serious concern for both countries. Country A which, by assumption, is capital-abundant and has a comparative advantage in capital-intensive Y goods, now, after capital movement, shows a decreased excess demand for importables, X goods and an excess supply of exportables, Y goods. Country B now has a greater production and export capacity for Y goods which compete against country A's comparative production advantage. Again, capital movement may in this case decrease or eliminate product trade, as in the complete substitutes case. If the Rybczynski lines in both countries have the same direction, say, downwards to the right, even if they have different degrees of slope, capital movement will result in the destruction of product trade. This is true simply, as already mentioned, because money capital moves out of the capital abundant country which has its comparative advantage in capital-intensive goods and increases production of competitive goods in the host country.

In the above, it is suggested that two conditions must be satisfied for capital movements to be complementary to product trade: (1) capital movements must increase the total value of production of the two goods in the two countries taken together, for otherwise their welfare will not rise; (2) the capital must move internationally in such a way that it reduces the production of comparative disadvantage goods (instead of comparative advantage goods), in the investing country and increases those in the host country, or, in brief, the capital must move out from a *pro-comparative disadvantage line.*

Purvis himself realises the second condition when he says: 'In the present case, the capital abundant country A is initially exporting the labour intesnsive good X, so A must have a strong technological advantage in the production of X.'[31] But this is a rather unusual assumption in the context of the Heckscher-Ohlin-Samuelson model, and seems to me difficult to justify.[32] It has perhaps been used to evade the logic of a case in which capital moves from the capital abundant country and increases production capacity of capital-intensive goods in the host country whereas the capital abundant, investing country has a comparative advantage in capital-intensive production. This is a dilemma into which international movements of money capital necessarily fall, as we have already explained. This dilemma will be avoided in the case of foreign direct investment as will be explained in the next section.

As noted in an earlier footnote, Purvis assumes that the R_b-line is flatter than the R_a-line. This results in a net decrease in output of Y goods and a net increase in output of X goods for the two countries taken together. It is unclear whether or not this increases the total value of the two outputs and thus the welfare of the two countries. And it is rather peculiar that capital movement decreases the output of capital-intensive Y goods. Then, we have the question why and for what purpose capital was moved. Even if the Purvis' model can be used to bring about 'complements', its welfare effects may be neither definite nor dramatic.[33] This second difficulty will also be solved in the discussion of the role of foreign direct investment.

A distinctly 'complementary' case will be shown if the Rybczynski line of the host country moves upwards while that of the investing country shifts downwards to the right. This is expected from the effects of foreign direct investment.

VI ARGUMENTS FOR TRADE-ORIENTED DIRECT INVESTMENT

How is a foreign direct investment able to achieve the two conditions mentioned above and to 'complement' product trade? It comes from the two main characteristics, among others, of foreign direct investment which differ from international money capital movements.

First, 'the essence of direct foreign investment is the transmission to the "host" country of a "package" of capital, managerial skill, and technical knowledge.'[34] The international movement of money capital is not the main concern in direct investment: joint ventures are becoming popular; some part of the necessary money capital is procured in the host country; and a large part of capital contributed from the investor is transferred in the form of capital goods such as technical know-how, machines and equipment which embody technology. Thus, both decreased money capital in the investing country and increased money capital in the host country may be regarded as marginal in a theoretical model, as will be done here. The main role of foreign direct investment is to transplant superior production technology through training of labour, management and marketing, from the advanced industrial country to lesser developed countries. In brief, it is the transfer of superior production functions to replace inferior ones in the host country. The foreign direct investment acts as a starter and a tutor for industrialisation in less developed countries.

Second, the foreign direct investment is undertaken by a specific firm which belongs to a particular industry in the investing country, and undertakes that investment activity through a subsidiary or as a joint venture in the host country. A particular industry is affected in both the investing and the host countries. In this respect, direct investment differs from international money capital movement in which money capital as a general, homogeneous factor of production is reallocated in a general equilibrium fashion, instead of a specific way, according to its outflow from the investing country and its inflow into the host country. Thus it necessarily results in the competitive expansion of production that uses the increased general factor (capital) more intensively in the host country than the other production. However, the fact that a subsidiary or joint venture firm is established in the host country is not enough to analyse national (or macro) economic effects, although there is the so-called 'enclave' direct investment whose effects are limited. Foreign direct investment has a gradual effect spread over the specific industry in the host country through training of labourers, engineers and managers, making the establishment of competitive firms by local capital possible, and ultimately improving the overall production function of that specific industry. This is the role of foreign direct investment as a tutor. When the process is completed, it can be said that the new technology is properly transferred and established in the host country.[35]

There remains the problem of determining what type of industrial technology can be more easily transferred to the host country, and in what ways the production function there can be improved through foreign direct investment. There must be 'comparative advantages in improving productivity' of the host economy. Here it is assumed that the smaller the technological difference between the investing and host country industry is, the easier it is to transfer and improve the technology in the latter.[36] This means that low technology is easier to transfer and high technology often results in 'enclave' direct investment. Practically, the technology involved in labour-intensive and low technology industries such as textiles is more easily transferred to less developed countries than capital- and/or knowledge-intensive industries such as steel and large-scale computers.

Let us assume, as before, that country A is capital abundant and has a comparative advantage in capital-intensive Y industry while country B is labour abundant and has a comparative advantage in labour-intensive X industry. Both countries A and B are so small that international commodity prices are given exogeneously.

Also, the comparative advantages in improving productivity of the host country are assumed in such a way that the productivity of the host country is upgraded through greater direct investments in labour-intensive X industry than in capital-intensive Y industry, due to the smaller technological gap and the greater spread effects. More exactly, let us suppose that the production function of the host country becomes two times superior if direct investment flows into X industry, and 1.5 times superior if it flows into Y industry. Superiority of the production function means that the same amount of output is produced with proportionately smaller inputs of labour and capital resulting in effects similar to the neutral technological improvements *à la* Hicks.[37]

The initial (before direct investment) production possibility curve is TT for country A in Figure 5.3 (a) and tt for country B in Figure 5.3 (b), the latter being smaller than the former, because country B initially has inferior production functions in both industries, although there is no significant difference in the size of countries. The community indifference curve touches the production possibility curve at Q in country A and q in country B, and the commodity price ratio at an autarchy situation is shown by P- and p-lines respectively. This means that country A has a comparative advantage in capital-intensive Y goods, and country B in labour-intensive X goods, along the lines of the Heckscher-Ohlin theorem.

Let us suppose that the international commodity price ratio is given to be the slope of the P′-line in Figure 5.3 (a) to which both p- and p′-lines in Figure 5.3 (b) are parallel. Now, country A shifts the production point from Q to Q′ and the consumption point from Q to C, creating an

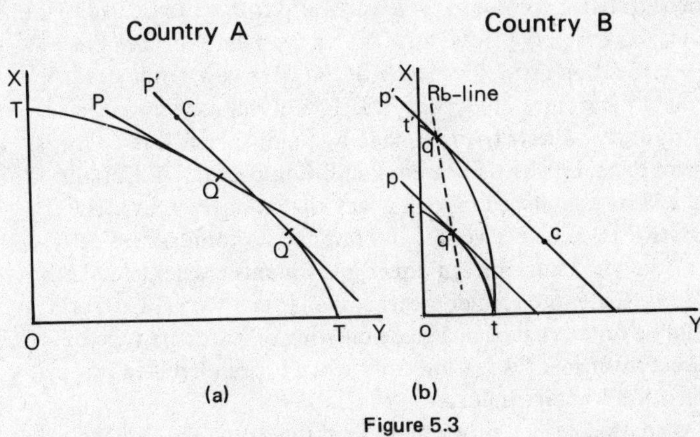

Figure 5.3

excess demand for X importables and an excess supply of Y exportables equivalent to the vertical and horizontal distance respectively between Q′ and C. However, international trade between country A and country B is not yet possible for the international commodity price ratio, shown by p-line, country B is an autarchy situation.

Let us now introduce foreign direct investments which are undertaken by a firm in X industry of country A so as to improve technology of the same X industry in country B. Such direct investment is stimulated by the fact that the production of X goods at Q under the international commodity price ratios, shown by the slope of P′-line, gives lower rewards both to labour and capital in that industry as compared with the other industry Y, and labour and capital must shift from the less profitable X industry to the more profitable Y industry[38] until Q′ point, where marginal productivity of labour and capital becomes equal in both industries. This is an internal structural adjustment. But there is another possibility, that is, for a firm in X industry to use its accumulated technology and managerial skills in foreign direct investment.

We assume that money capital movements are negligible[39] mainly in order to make our figures simple and also because the most important role of foreign direct investments is the improvement of productivity through the transfer and spread of superior technology into the host country. Then, since the technology and managerial skills do not decrease even when they are applied abroad and since labour and capital are assumed to remain unchanged in country A, the TT curve remains intact. In country B, it is assumed, the production possibility curve is expanded so that it is twice as large vertically from tt to tt′. Now, the international commodity prices ratio, shown by p′-line touches the expanded production possibility curve, tt′, at q′ (a new production point). Line qq′ becomes the Rybczynski line in this case, and directs definitely upwards. A new triangle made by points q′ and c in country B is identical to that made by points Q′ and C in country A. Harmonious trade will be established in such a way that country A exports its comparative advantage Y goods, and imports its comparative disadvantage X goods. Thus, foreign direct investments are complements to commodity trade, the former creating the latter.

It should be noted that such a trade-creating or pro-trade type of foreign direct investment is feasible only when it is undertaken in a pro-comparative disadvantage industry.

So far we have considered two manufacturing activities. But the logic is easily extended to foreign direct investment in the extractive industry,[40] which has a definite comparative disadvantage in production in the investing country.

Payments of profit returns to foreign direct investments must be taken into consideration and this complicates our analysis. However, it is certain that the returns are a part, perhaps smaller, of the distance between p- and p′-lines in Figure 5.3 (b) which is the direct and indirect contribution of foreign direct investments. This differs from the case of money capital movements. This may be true, first, to the extent that the rate of returns to foreign direct investments, i.e. royalties, knowhow fees, dividends and profits, etc., are determined on an internationally competitive basis, and, secondly, that gain comes not only from the direct contribution of the foreign subsidiary or joint venture but largely from the spillover effects of the foreign direct investments. In other words, foreign direct investment in our model has the same effect as technological progress. If foreign direct investment is undertaken in a pro-comparative disadvantage industry it creates harmonious commodity trade and, therefore, it is trade-oriented;[41] its direct and indirect contribution taken together brings about a net gain in the welfare of the two countries, similar to that of technological progress, not considering the distribution of the gain to each country.

In contrast to the pro-comparative disadvantage type of industry, what will happen if a foreign direct investment is undertaken by a firm of comparative advantage industry in country A? In Figure 5.4, it is assumed that country B's production possibility curve expands by 1.5 times horizontally from tt to tt″. Under the given international

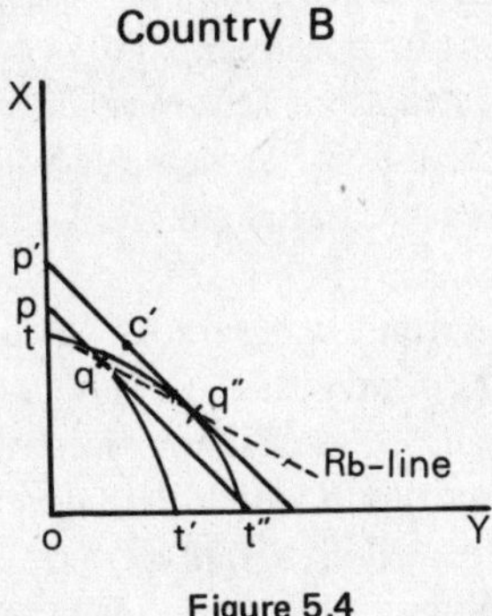

Figure 5.4

commodity price ratio, shown by p′-line, production point is at q″,[42] and consumption point at c′, creating an excess demand for X goods (importables) and an excess supply of Y goods (exportables) in country B. Country A's situation is the same as that shown in Figure 5.3 (a), and it has an excess demand for X goods (importables) and an excess supply of Y goods (exportables) equivalent to the horizontal and vertical distances, respectively, between Q′ and C points. The two countries are competing both in importing and exporting capacity. Foreign direct investment in this case will not open any commodity trade between the two countries, and may even destroy commodity trade which was opened by variation in the international commodity price ratios (for example, if P′- and p-lines are slightly less steep than shown in Figures 5.3 (a) and 5.4).[43] Thus, foreign direct investment of pro-comparative advantage industry is trade-destroying or anti-trade-oriented, similar to the money capital movements in the Mundell and Purvis cases.

Here, we have to remember that there is no proper motivation or incentive for a firm of Y industry in country A to undertake direct investment abroad. For the firm it is possible and profitable to expand production of Y goods from Q to Q′ in Figure 5.3 (a) and export them to country B[44] or even to third countries. Moreover, there is no sound reason under a free market mechanism to undertake foreign direct investment so as to create competitive production abroad against its exportables. If there is still some motivation, it must be of quite a different nature: for example the monopolistic or oligopolistic motivation of maintaining technological, marketing and other monopolistic superiority.[45]

Therefore, we have to pay attention to whether a foreign direct investment is undertaken in a pro-comparative disadvantage industry which is trade-creating, or in a pro-comparative advantage industry which results in trade destruction. This must be a primary criterion from the national economic point of view for both investing and host countries, although it is rather neglected from a firm's microeconomic point of view.[46]

We have a second criterion: 'comparative advantages in improving productivity' in the host country through foreign direct investment. It is usual, as we have assumed, that labour-intensive and low-technology industries such as textiles in which the investing country A has comparative overt or potential disadvantage have less difficulty in transferring their technology to less developed countries and improve productivity there far more than capital- and/or knowledge-intensive industries such as steel and large-scale computers. This may be true; the less developed country had a comparative disadvantage in capital-intensive goods because of its lower capital/labour endowments, the lack of capital, engineers, skilled labour (even neglecting the lack of demand), etc., needed for capital-intensive, high-technology industry. The same arguments apply in explaining the difficulty in transferring technology and in improving productivity. This case satisfies the two criteria: comparative advantages in trade and in improving productivity, and no conflict between the macroeconomic view of the international division of labour and the microeconomic interests of individual direct investors.

However, it is theoretically conceivable to have a case of conflict: while the investing country has a comparative advantage in Y industry, productivity in the host country increases in that industry through foreign direct investment much more than in the other industry, X. This type of investment should be restricted in the national economic interests of both investing and host countries since it destroys commodity trade, but it will be undertaken by individual firms seeking profits. It seems to me that no such conflicts will arise if comparative advantage in trade dominates the productivity improving criterion mentioned above, except where foreign direct investment is motivated by monopolistic or oligopolistic performance which usually results in 'enclave' activity in less developed countries.

Furthermore, it can be easily imagined theoretically that country A's firms undertake foreign direct investments in both X and Y industries, ignoring comparative advantages, so long as foreign investment provides higher profit than domestic investment for each industry. Then, country A incurs increased imports of X goods and decreased or even reversed exports of Y goods, resulting in a heavy trade deficit, and the export of jobs – which means erosion of the investing country's economy through excessive direct investments. This may be partly due to an excessively overvalued exchange rate of the country. If the exchange rate is devalued sufficiently, imports are cut; exports are increased; the annual flow of direct investments from both industries is decreased or one of them is eliminated; and it may be possible to regain the balance of trade or the balance of payments, including the return flow from past investments. If investment from comparative advantage Y industry is eliminated, the adjustment process is easier, but if not, it is difficult or impossible. Therefore, some direct and selective control of direct investment outflow is necessary especially in order to eliminate anti-trade investments. This applies also to the host country.

VII CONCLUSION

International money capital movements necessarily result in the destruction of commodity trade within the framework of the Heckscher-Ohlin-Samuelson theorem with either identical or different production functions between two countries. Even in the case of foreign direct investment, if it is undertaken from the investing country's comparative advantage industry, it results in the same trade-destroying pattern. Only foreign direct investment which is undertaken in the investing country's comparative disadvantage industry complements commodity trade and creates harmonious trade with the host country.

Thus, the most important criterion in undertaking foreign investment should be to take into consideration the present and potential pattern of comparative advantages between investing and host countries and to undertake foreign direct investment from the investing country's comparative disadvantage industry. This is trade-oriented investment and will bring about upgrading structural adjustment on both sides, resulting in trade reorganisation.[47]

Can the multinational firm ignore or oppose the pattern of comparative advantages in trade as is so often seen in American foreign direct investment? The trade-destroying effects of such investment should be carefully examined for the sake of better world trade conditions.

NOTES

1. I am grateful for valuable comments which I have received from: H. W. Arndt, 'Professor Kojima on the Macroeconomics of Foreign Direct Investment' and Kiyoshi Kojima, 'Reply', *Hitotsubashi Journal of Economics*, June 1974, pp. 26-35, pp. 36-8 respectively. G. C. Hufbauer. 'Multinational Corporations and the International Adjustment Process', *American Economic Review*, May 1974, p. 272. John Roemer, 'Features of Japanese Direct Investment; Some Comparisons with the American Pattern' (mimeograph). C. Fred Bergsten, ed., 'Introduction', *Toward A New World Trade Policy: The Maidenhead Papers*, Lexington Books, D.C. Heath & Co., 1975, pp. 6-7.
2. Cf. Bo Sodersten, *International Economics*, Macmillan, 1970, pp. 453-5, on the production function.
3. The *comparative* formula is useful in the same way as comparative advantage is, since the decision as to whether home or foreign investment should be undertaken takes place without considering such overall adjustments as changes in the exchange rate, inflation and deflation, etc. in both countries.

   If the investing country revalues its currency and the recipient country devalues its currency both in terms of a common unit, the dollar, both X and Y goods become dearer in country A and cheaper in country B than shown in Table 5.1 (b), making the profit rate from domestic investment in both industries proportionately smaller and that from foreign direct investment larger than shown in Table 5.1 (c); but this will not change at all the comparative investment profitabilities. The above illustrates the fact that an overvalued exchange rate stimulates foreign direct investment in general, whilst an undervalued exchange rate promotes domestic investment and exports.
4. See R. L. Hall and C. J. Hitch, 'Price Theory and Economic Behaviour', *Oxford Economic Papers*, 1939. R. F. Harrod, *Economic Essays*, London, 1952. Paolo Sylos-Labini, *Oligopoly and Technical Progress*, Harvard University Press, Cambridge, 1962.
5. The r is equivalent to the so-called 'mark-up ratio' which is usually shown as a percentage of total cost, whilst ours is shown as a percentage of total revenue. Therefore, $r/(1 - r)$ corresponds to the ordinary mark-up ratio.

   The r is not profit rate of capital invested but that of total sales. This may be a defect of our model, for the former is usually used as a theoretic concept of profit rate. However, it is not easy to determine how much capital is used in certain production and sales activities for a certain period, particularly in the case of foreign direct investment activity. The profit rate of total sales might be a more realistic concept in competitive market mechanism.
6. I am indebted to my colleague, Dr Makoto Ikema, for his help in proving the principle.
7. 'American direct investment cannot be explained simply in terms of better access to capital, better entrepreneurship, better technology or higher profits abroad . . . Analysis of oligopolistic bargaining strategy is however helpful; it is not unusual for leading oligopolists to establish inroads into their competitor's home territory to strengthen their position.' Hymer, 'United States Investment Abroad', Peter Drysdale, ed., *Direct Foreign Investment in Asia and the Pacific*, ANU, 1972, p. 41. Such global oligopolistic strategy is the main reason why US multinationals have a strong preference for the wholly-owned subsidiary. (See *ibid*., p. 44.)
8. 'Its (United States) great strength in innovation and organization cannot be denied. But a striking feature of the recent decade is the narrowing of lead-

times and the shortening of the product cycle. Direct foreign investment provides one way of meeting this challenge.' Hymer, *ibid.*, p. 44. Also see, Raymond Vernon, 'Future of the Multinational Enterprise', Charles P. Kindleberger, ed., *The International Corporation*, The MIT Press, 1970, pp. 386-7.

9. 'Their [multinational enterprises'] prominence will be more evident in the advanced technological sectors and in the industries that are reliant on raw materials that are subject to oligopoly control. Multinational enterprises will be less evident with respect to the more mature and standardized products. Indeed, mature industries that are now dominated by multinational enterprises, such as consumer electronics and cigarettes, could very well become more nationally oriented in their ownership and structure.' Vernon, *ibid.*, p. 389.

10. Dunning's studies, for example, show that foreign direct investment by the United Kingdom has long been the trade-oriented type. He makes an interesting comment on British investments: 'there is probably too much UK investment overseas in traditional-type industries and not enough investment at home in the newer technologically based industries.' John H. Dunning, *Studies in International Investment*, George Allen & Unwin, London, 1970, p. 91. Perhaps, a proportionate increase in investment of both types is desirable.

11. 'The decisions of executives of US-based multinationals to transfer American technology, for example, or to export American job opportunities may be rational and, perhaps wise, decisions, in terms of the firm. But the interests of the US, as a nation and of the American people are not identical with the interests of the multinational firm. The responsibility of the US government is to the American people – and not to US based multinational companies, without regard to the possibly adverse impacts of their decisions on American workers and communities.' Nat Goldfinger, 'A Labor View of Foreign Investment and Trade Issues', *United States International Economic Policy in an Interdependent World, Papers 1*, Washington, D.C., July 1971, p. 927.

12. R. A. Mundell, 'International Trade and Factor Mobility', *American Economic Review*, June 1957 (reprinted in his book, *International Economics*, Macmillan, 1968, Chap. 6.)

13. Andrew Schmitz and Peter Helmberger, 'Factor Mobility and International Trade: The Case of Complementality', *American Economic Review*, September 1970, pp. 761-7.

14. Douglas D. Purvis, 'Technology, Trade and Factor Mobility', *Economic Journal*, September 1972, pp. 991-9.

15. *Ibid.*, p. 992, n. 1.

16. In this sense, it might be better to refer to it as 'abstract' capital as Baldwin points out. R. E. Baldwin, 'Export Technology and Development from Subsistence Level', *Economic Journal*, March 1963, p. 841.

17. Robert A. Mundell, 'International Trade and Factor Mobility', *American Economic Review*, June 1957, pp. 321-2.

18. Here country A and B are reversed from Mundell's original usage in order to make the former an investing country.

19. Mundell, *op. cit.*, p. 322.

20. This is a combined figure of Mundell's figures 1 and 3 with only the reversal of country A and B.

21. Cf. T. M. Rybczynski, 'Factor Endowment and Relative Commodity Prices', *Economica*, November 1955, pp. 336-41.

22. Mundell, *op. cit.*, p. 324.

23. *Ibid.*, p. 325.
24. K. Hamada, 'An Economic Analysis of the Duty-Free Zone', *Journal of International Economics*, August 1974, pp. 231-5. Originally H. Uzawa proved the proposition geometrically, in his 'Shihon Jiyuka to Kokumin Keizai (Liberalisation of Foreign Investments and the National Economy)', *Ekonomisuto*, 23 December 1969, pp. 106-22 (in Japanese).
25. Purvis, *op. cit.*, p. 998.
26. Purvis mentions his second usage of the 'substitutes', i.e. 'impediments to trade will stimulate factor movements, and such relocation of factors of production will eliminate trade in goods'. (*Ibid.*, p. 991, n. 3.) My definition may be broader than this for it is not confined to refer to Mundell's result.
27. Schmitz and Helmberger, *op. cit.*, pp. 762-3.
28. *Ibid.*, p. 764, especially n. 12.
29. Purvis, *op. cit.*, p. 994, n. 1.
30. If R_b-line is flatter than R_a-line as Purvis shows in his Figure 3 (*ibid.*, p. 995), capital movements result in a net decrease of the production of Y goods. Practically this may be more plausible, for a capital abundant country usually has a comparatively superior production function in capital-intensive goods compared to a labour abundant country. If so, there must not be any incentive to invest abroad in this line.
31. *Ibid.*, p. 998.
32. In order to justify this, Purvis should show rigorously the specification of the technological differences between the two countries.
33. Purvis himself admits that 'it is essential to note that this complementarity is not a necessary result of differing technologies, only a possible one' (*ibid.*, p. 998).
34. Harry Johnson, 'Survey of Issues', Peter Drysdale, ed., *Direct Foreign Investment in Asia and the Pacific*, Australian National University Press, Canberra, 1972, p. 2.
35. The degree of ownership and managerial control is an important difference between direct and portfolio investments from the individual firm's microeconomic point of view. But this is not a great concern for macroeconomic analysis.
36. See, for example, Terumoto Ozawa, *Transfer of Technology from Japan to Developing Countries*, UNITAR, New York, 1971. Jan Kmenta, 'Economic Theory and Transfer of Technology', Daniel Spencer and Alexander Woroniak, eds., *The Transfer of Technology to Developing Countries*, Praeger, 1967.
37. J. R. Hicks, *The Theory of Wages*, Macmillan, London 1932, Chap. 6, Section 3.
38. Alternatively, we may assume that, under a given commodity price ratio, the labour-intensive X industry becomes less profitable than capital-intensive Y industry due to the rise in wage/rental ratio.
39. Even if we take into account the money capital movements, this will not change, but strengthen our results, for money capital accompanied in direct investments flows out from a specific industry in the investing country and is invested in the same specific industry in the host country.
40. This is what Schmitz and Helmberger had in mind as a 'complements' case and it is true that 'the larger the differences in production conditions among countries in primary products the greater will be the flow of international capital'. Schmitz and Helmberger, *op. cit.*, p. 763, n. 7.
41. It is an established theory that technological progress undertaken in an exportable industry is trade-oriented whereas in an importable industry it

is anti-trade-oriented. This is unambiguously true if the technological progress is neutral. Our dichotomy of foreign direct investment comes to the same conclusion. See Harry Johnson, *International Trade and Economic Growth*, George Allen and Unwin, London, 1958, Chap. 3.

42. A. Rybczynski line, R_b', is qq'' extended which directs downwards to the right, similar to the money capital movements.

43. This is applicable to the previous case and might have resulted in a better explanation but we refrained from doing so simply in order to avoid the complexity of figures.

44. Although our Figure 5.4 is not adequate to allow for country B to import Y goods, it is not unreasonable to modify the figure to allow it, as mentioned in the text, for country B has a comparative disadvantage in Y goods.

45. See Raymond Vernon, 'The Location of Economic Activity', John H. Dunning, ed., *Economic Analysis and Multinational Enterprise*, Allen and Unwin, London, 1974.

46. Almost all studies on multinational corporations including Raymond Vernon's product cycle theory ('International Investment and International Trade in the Product Cycle', *Quarterly Journal of Economics*, May 1966; *Sovereignty at Bay: The Multinational Spread of US Enterprises*, Basic Books, 1971) use a one commodity analysis and are based upon the location theory and the theory of oligopolistic firms, neglecting the theory of comparative advantage.

47. The theory of trade-oriented foreign direct investment presented in this paper may be an important fillip to guide trade expansion between advanced industrial and less developed countries with the help of foreign direct investment, although two way direct investment between advanced industrial countries may be explained by a different theory such as Bhagwati's theory of mutual interpenetration or my theory of agreed specialisation. See Joseph N. Bhagwati, 'Book Review of Raymond Vernon, *Sovereignty at Bay*', *Journal of International Economics*, September 1972, pp. 457-8. Kiyoshi Kojima, 'Towards a Theory of Agreed Specialization: the Economics of Integration', W. A. Eltis, M. F. G. Scott, and J. N. Wolfe, eds., *Induction, Growth and Trade, Essays in Honour of Sir Roy Harrod*, Clarendon Press, Oxford, 1970, pp. 305-24.

6 THE LONG-TERM PATH OF THE JAPANESE ECONOMY

I A RECONSIDERATION OF THE LONG-TERM VIEW

When the oil crisis struck, the Japanese economy was in its first period of export surplus and favourable balance of payments since the war. The balance moved towards surplus about 1965 and from 1968 to the outbreak of the oil crisis in October 1973 we earned huge export surpluses. Over that period trade restrictions were abolished over a wide range of goods and trade liberalisation was completed. At the same time liberalisation of capital movements both inwards and outwards was broadly achieved for the first time and we saw a rush to investment abroad (see Chapter 2). With the sudden increase in oil payments the current balance of payments again turned towards recovery. We had a switch in policy from the restriction of capital inflow and encouragement of outflow to the opposite. Is the trend of export surpluses and overseas investment expansion that continued from 1965 to October 1973 now to be reversed by the oil crisis? I believe that the trend has been only temporarily interrupted by the oil crisis and is likely to continue at least until around 1980.

Typical of thinking in the export surplus period before the oil crisis was the Industrial Structure Council's 'International Trade and Industry Policies for the 1970s' of May 1971. Is the 'Structural change towards knowledge-intensive industry' which it laid down as the long-term future path of the Japanese economy really in need of fundamental revision as a result of the oil crisis and the difficulty of obtaining raw materials and food from abroad? I believe that the oil crisis should inspire us not to fundamental revision, but to renewed determination to make that long-term future a reality and to bring it about with all speed and urgency. My own interpretation of the long-term future presented in 'Japan's Foreign Economic Policies in the 1970s'[1] is as follows.

Japan is a country which has carried through very rapid and large-scale adjustment of its industrial structure. By that I mean she has achieved a high rate of economic growth. The Japanese economy underwent its first structural transformation around 1900 centring on the textile industry and on that basis obtained export earnings which supported its development until the 1920s. Structural change in the direction of heavy and chemical industries started from the latter half of the 1930s but was interrupted by the war and it took until about 1965 to complete the second structural transformation consisting of large-scale development of the heavy and chemical industries. It was thanks to this that Japan enjoyed a basically favourable balance of trade from 1965 to October 1973. Even if we confine our attention to the postwar period, structural change from light industry centring on textiles to the heavy and chemical industries is most impressive. Despite this there is still an urgent need to revolutionise the structure of agriculture and traditional medium – and small – business. At the same time we are in a situation where, probably by about 1980, we shall be forced to carry through a third huge structural transformation from heavy and chemical industries to industries of the knowledge-intensive type. We may distinguish five internal and external factors that make this absolutely imperative.

i. There is an obvious shortage of coastal sites in Japan suitable for the location of new heavy and chemical industries.
ii. With the growing importance of the pollution problem there is concern at further expansion of the highly polluting heavy and chemical industries and in fact they are running into opposition from local residents.
iii. Supplies of raw materials and fuels necessary for heavy and chemical industries are getting beyond the level at which supply from overseas is economically manageable. For these reasons we are compelled to move in the direction of industries less dependent on raw materials and fuels and to transfer production of intermediate goods to sites overseas;
iv. Labour-intensive goods, represented by traditional light industries such as textiles, are losing their comparative advantage as labour becomes scarcer and wages rise. By 1980 a thirty-five hour five-day week is likely to come into operation. Under these kinds of pressures we shall be forced to move to new types of industry.
v. For similar reasons it has become imperative to revolutionise the structure of agriculture and medium- to small-scale business so as to concentrate production exclusively in efficient large-scale firms.

Thus, through the 1970s, the Japanese economy must carry through a structural transformation towards 'knowledge-intensive industries'. The kinds of knowledge-intensive industries whose growth should be promoted are:

i. R and D-intensive industries such as electronic computers, aircraft, electric cars, industrial robots, atomic power-related industries, integrated circuits, fine chemicals, new synthetics, new metals, special ceramics and the development of the oceans;
ii. sophisticated assembly industries such as communications equipment, business equipment, digital process control equipment, pollution control devices, large household coolers, teaching equipment, industrially produced housing, automated warehouses, large construction machinery and high grade plant;
iii. fashion industries such as high-quality clothing, high-quality furniture, household fittings, electric sound equipment and electronic musical instruments;
iv. knowledge industries such as information processing services, information provision, education-related video industries, software, systems engineering and consulting.

Of course, these new industries are not yet fully defined and many others will arise and develop in the future. Right from the beginning it has been argued that 'knowledge-intensive industries' is too vague a concept but I have summed them up as 'the more sophisticated products of heavy and chemical industry and software'.[2]

It was foreseen that a large-scale structural transformation towards these new industries would be progressively carried out by the early 1980s, using the favourable payments situation and the spare foreign currency holdings of that time to import knowhow and machine equipment and adding to it Japanese R and D. It was, in fact, the right time to carry through the third structural transformation. In the light of the heavy impact of the oil crisis a number of reconsiderations of the long-term future of the Japanese economy have been carried out. The following five are typical.

1. First, the Industrial Structure Council has issued a more detailed version of 'International Trade and Industry Policies for the 1970s' (May 1971) under the title 'The Course of Japan's Industrial Structure' in September 1974. This was published in November 1974 by the International Trade and Industry Research Association of MITI as 'A Long Term Vision for Industrial Structure' and is referred to below as the 'Industrial Structure Council's long-term vision'.

2. The Japan Economic Research Centre (JERC) under the direction of Mr Hisao Kanamori has produced a succession of excellent long-term forecasts comprising (a) 'The Japanese economy in 1975 – looking into the economy of the unknown' (December 1969); (b) 'The Japanese

Economy in 1985 – prospects for the trillion dollar economy' (April 1971); (c) 'Japan's economy in 1980 in the global context – the nation's role in a polycentric world' (March 1972); and (d) 'A three trillion dollar economic structure – Japan in 1985' (February 1974 – issued in English as 'A long-term outlook of welfare economy – The Japanese economy in 1985', April 1973). It has now issued a revised edition of (d) taking into account the oil impact under the title 'The future of world economy and Japan' (February 1975). This last will hereafter be cited as the 'JERC outlook'.

3. The Economic Council is preparing a follow-up and revision of its 'Basic economic and social plan – towards a vigorous welfare society' (approved in February 1973 to cover the period 1973-7) and has analysed the problems in the long-term outlook in its 'Follow-up of the basic economic and social plan: Annual Report for 1974' (December 1974). We shall call this the 'Economic Council outlook'.

4. Interestingly the business world has grave doubts about 'knowledge-intensive industrialisation' and as its comment on the Industrial Structure Council's long-term vision, the Industrial Policy Committee of *Keidanren* has put out 'The confused world economy and future industrial structure (an essay)' (February 1975). We shall cite this as the 'Keidanren essay'.

5. On the question of where Japanese agriculture should be heading opinions are divided. The Agricultural Policy Council's supply and demand section has published 'Outlook for the food problem and the direction of food policy' (January 1975) but this cannot be said to represent a well-articulated long-term forecast. It is referred to hereafter as the 'Agricultural Policy Council report'.

All these revisions have the following characteristics in common.

i. They take as their priority objective the satisfaction of popular aspirations for the construction of a welfare state.

ii. They are strongly aware of the restrictions on growth posed by oil and other raw materials, primary fuels and foodstuffs and stress the urgency of switching to energy-saving and resource-saving industrial structure and raising the rate of self-sufficiency in foodstuffs.

iii. They recognise the inevitability of a growth rate substantially lower than the high rate of growth (over 10 per cent a year) achieved in the past. The Industrial Structure Council's long-term vision foresees a 6.2 per cent rate over the period 1973 to 1985, the JERC outlook forecasts 7 per cent from 1975 to 1985, the

> Economic Council outlook makes alternative forecasts of 7 per cent and 5.5 per cent over a five-year period and the Keidanren essay also makes two assumptions of 5.7 per cent and 4 per cent up to 1985. This may be regarded as 'normalisation of growth' rather than as a 'switch to a low growth rate'.

Our problem is that we have no clear indication of the kinds of external economic relations that would be produced by the Japanese economy following a long-term development path with the characteristics outlined above. The Keidanren comment would seem to derive from this point. All three of the characteristics could be said to be inward looking policies. Is there not some way of clearly delineating our responsibility as an economic power to give a lead to the prosperity of the world economy?

Since the first three 'reconsiderations' listed are based on fundamentally the same way of thinking, in what follows I shall concentrate on the JERC outlook, as being the most comprehensive and refer to the other two as necessary where they differ from it. I shall follow this with some comments on the problems of agriculture and finally I should like to take up the comments advanced in the Keidanren essay to present my own views of the form which our international economic relations should take.

II THE JERC OUTLOOK

1. The future for the world economy

From 1960 to 1970 total world GDP grew at a nominal rate of 8.4 per cent. From 1975-85 it will grow by 12.0 per cent to reach $ 19,750 billion in 1985. World trade had a nominal growth rate of 9.6 per cent in the 1970s but between 1975 and 1985 this will rise to 12.7 per cent to reach $ 2,872 billion. In other words, they accept a relatively optimistic projection of the world economy and world trade.

> The shortage of oil supply may be eased thanks to increases in oil production in the areas other than OPEC countries and development of substitute fuels, and increases in oil prices are expected not to be equal to those of industrial manufactures in the future. As a result, the surpluses of current balance of oil exporting countries which are expected to reach $ 130 billion in 1980 and will be reduced to $ 110 billion in 1985. This is still large as an absolute figure, but is a meagre 0.5 per cent of world GDP and 4.0 per cent of world trade in 1985,

and not so large an amount as to be impossible to flow back through capital markets at large or through international agencies.[3]

2. *The scale of the Japanese economy*

The *growth rate* of Japan's GNP in the 1960s was 11.1 per cent in real terms and from 1975 to 1985 it is likely to grow at 7 per cent in real terms (somewhat above the total world rate of 5.3 per cent). Since prices will inevitably rise by 8 per cent per annum this represents a 15 per cent nominal growth rate and GDP will grow from $ 550 billion in 1975 to $ 2,200 billion in 1985 (expressed as a percentage of the world total, this represents a rise from 8.7 per cent in 1975 to 11.3 per cent in 1985). GDP per head at $ 18,000 will be higher than the United States figure of $ 15,000. How the rate of import dependence will move is difficult to forecast since it will depend on domestic industrial structure and on the difference between the rate of rise of domestic as against import prices; there are factors operating in both directions and it is not expected to change much from the current 10.7 per cent. Thus, in line with a nominal quadrupling of GNP over the 10 years, *imports* are expected to roughly quadruple (12.9 per cent per annum) and to grow from $ 70 billion in 1975 to $ 240 billion c.i.f. in 1985 (or $ 195 billion f.o.b.). Japan's share of world imports will rise somewhat from 8 per cent to 8.2 per cent. (The Industrial Structure Council's long-term vision forecasts the rate of growth of imports as 7.8 per cent in real terms, 18.7 per cent nominal, from 1970-80 and 7.2 per cent in real terms, 10.3 per cent nominal, from 1980-85. They anticipate that structural changes in the direction of energy- and natural-resource-saving industries will have substantial effects on imports.)

Meanwhile to achieve a balanced trade position *exports* will need to grow by 13.6 per cent or a little faster than imports, and expand from $ 66 billion in 1975 to $ 240 billion in 1985. Japan's share in world exports will rise slightly from 7.6 per cent in 1975 to 8.3 per cent in 1985. The difficulty of expanding exports in markets where Japan's share is already overlarge cannot be ignored. (The Industrial Structure Council's long-term vision expects that the rate of expansion of exports will be 8.6 per cent in real terms or 18.5 per cent nominal from 1970-80, and 7.1 per cent in real terms or 9.6 per cent nominal from 1980-5.)

Japan's *overseas direct investment* has increased rapidly in recent years and at the end of 1973 stood at $ 10.3 billion. By 1985 it should reach $ 100 billion. (The Industrial Structure Council's long-term vision has it reaching $ 45 billion in 1980 and $ 93.5 billion in 1985.) While direct investment by foreign countries in Japan was a mere $ 1.2 billion in 1973, from now on investment by the United States, Western Europe and the oil producers is expected to increase and to reach $ 25 billion in 1985.

Japan's total *foreign aid* reached $ 5.8 billion in 1973 representing 1.42 per cent of GNP and second only to the United States in scale. Despite increasing balance of payments restrictions, Japan must continue to provide aid at the level of at least 1 per cent of GNP and this will require $ 26 billion in foreign aid in 1985. Also official development assistance, which has been lagging up to now, must be drastically increased and brought up to some 0.6 per cent of GNP in 1985.

Since 1965 the structure of Japan's *international payments* has taken the form of an outflow of long-term capital covered by a surplus on current account. In 1973 and 1974 under the influence of the oil shock, the current account has gone into the deficit but the structure of payments should return to its previous form in the near future. In 1985 there will be a large favourable balance of trade amounting to $ 36.7 billion (exports $ 232.3 billion; imports $ 195.6 billion, both f.o.b.) and even after subtracting the deficit on service transactions, aid, etc., there will still be a $ 7.7 billion surplus on current account. This $ 7.7 billion current account surplus plus a long-term capital inflow of $ 24.2 billion will finance a net outflow of long-term capital of $ 31.9 billion.

3. *Industrial structure*

These are the macroeconomic dimensions which the Japanese economy should be able to reach in 1985. The problem, however, is its content, that is to say, the composition of industry and international trade. On these matters the Industrial Structure Council's long-term vision has come out with a clearer concept and I shall therefore deal with it first.

i. Responding to popular aspirations. The changeover in Japanese industry is brought about by changes in the structure of final demand in response to popular aspirations, namely 'realisation of a full and stable livelihood'. There are strong demands for qualitative improvement of food, clothing and housing, particularly for the provision of housing, maintenance of health (provision of medical treatment and social welfare facilities), fulfilment of intellectual aspirations (education), adequate leisure and adequate social capital (roads, sewerage, parks, elimination of pollution, etc.).

ii. Development of knowledge-intensive industries. 'International Trade and Industry Policies in the 1970s' (May 1971) indicates that with strong demands for resource and energy saving, preservation of the environment and transition to a high wage economy, gearing-up of the industrial structure will come through rapid growth of highly processed technology-intensive industries (the so-called knowledge-intensive industries). These trends show up in the detailed vision for the industrial structure in 1985. Looking at changes in the internal structure of manufacturing industry we find (a) a marked increase in the share of electrical machinery; (b) an increase in the share of 'miscellaneous industries' including furniture and consumption goods of all kinds; (c) a strong trend in the chemical industry and metal manufactures towards more sophisticated technology and more highly processed products with a progressive increase in their weight; (d) in processing industries such as textiles whose weight will decrease overall, a handing over of those sections with a low degree of processing and low value added to developing countries where wages are lower, and towards a higher degree of processing and improvement of product quality by raising the level of technology (see Table 6.1).

iii. Reduction in the weight of the intermediate goods (industrial materials) sector. Although Japan's industrial sector has achieved a high rate of transformation towards the heavy and chemical industries, nevertheless as compared to other advanced countries its internal structure contains a higher proportion of intermediate goods such as crude steel, non-ferrous metals, primary manufactures, pulp and basic chemical products. In the process of gearing up the industrial structure up to 1985 there will be a relative fall in the share of such industries as these in domestic production. This will occur because, as industrial sites become scarcer in Japan and restrictions on natural resources and energy bring to light barriers to increasing productivity, industries will move overseas to take advantage of new forms of international specialisation *vis-à-vis* the natural-resource-owning countries.

In summary, this view holds that the less sophisticated and low value added sectors such as the textile industry, as well as the intermediate goods (heavy and chemical industries) sector will be progressively transferred overseas and that much greater weight will be given to sophisticated technology-intensive industries (the machinery sector) which will become the main source of exports. The stages of development are traced from textiles to heavy and chemical industries and then to machinery. This will (a) raise value added, (b) contribute to

Table 6.1 Changes in production by industry (1970 prices, ¥ million)

	1970		1980		1985		1965-70	1970-80	1980-85	1970-85
	Production & proportion		Production & proportion		Production & proportion		Average annual growth rate	Average annual growth rate	Average annual growth rate	Average annual growth rate
Agriculture, forestries, fisheries	7,113	4.4	8,510	2.8	9,470	2.3	1.5	1.8	2.2	1.9
Mining	959	0.6	1,330	0.4	1,590	0.4	5.3	3.3	3.6	3.4
Food manufacturing	9,620	6.0	16,240	5.3	22,150	5.3	5.7	5.4	6.4	5.7
Textile manufacturing	5,349	3.3	7,240	2.4	8,310	2.0	5.7	3.1	2.8	3.0
Paper pulp	2,621	1.6	4,850	1.6	6,250	1.5	12.1	6.3	5.2	6.0
Chemical manufacturing	5,191	3.2	10,750	3.5	14,870	3.6	15.1	7.6	6.7	7.3
Oil and coal processing	3,019	1.9	5,820	1.9	7,720	1.9	17.1	6.8	5.8	6.5
Ceramics	2,670	1.7	5,150	1.7	7,190	1.7	12.0	6.8	6.9	6.8
Iron and steel	11,286	7.0	21,140	6.9	24,470	5.9	18.0	6.5	3.0	5.3
Non-ferrous metals	1,857	1.2	4,350	1.4	5,320	1.3	15.2	8.9	4.1	7.3
Metal products	3,777	2.3	8,870	2.9	12,480	3.0	19.1	8.9	7.1	8.3
General machinery	8,324	5.2	17,900	5.8	26,140	6.3	21.7	8.0	7.9	7.9
Electrical machinery	7,632	4.7	19,220	6.3	28,500	6.8	26.1	9.7	8.2	9.2
Transport machinery	7,624	4.7	14,090	4.6	17,920	4.3	27.4	6.3	4.9	5.9
Precision instruments	1,103	0.7	2,190	0.7	3,190	0.8	14.3	7.1	7.8	7.3
Other manufacturing	10,106	6.3	19,610	6.4	28,590	6.8	13.0	6.9	7.8	7.2
Building	16,259	10.1	31,120	10.2	45,380	10.9	13.6	6.7	7.6	7.1
Electricity, city gas	2,100	1.3	3,980	1.3	5,550	1.3	12.6	6.6	6.9	6.7
Transport and communication	7,444	4.6	14,510	4.7	20,060	4.8	13.4	6.9	6.7	6.8
Commerce	14,290	8.8	26,580	8.6	35,560	8.5	12.4	6.4	6.0	6.3
Finance and insurance	4,907	3.0	8,080	2.6	10,300	2.5	10.2	5.1	5.0	5.1
Service industry	28,267	17.5	56,140	18.3	77,290	18.5	8.8	7.1	6.6	6.9
TOTAL	161,518	100.0	307,670	100.0	418,300	100.0	12.8	6.7	6.4	6.6
Primary industry	7,117	4.4	8,510	2.8	9,470	2.3	1.5	1.8	2.2	1.9
Secondary industry*	93,397	60.3	189,870	61.7	260,070	62.1	14.8	6.9	6.5	6.8
(of which manufacturing)	80,179	49.6	157,420	51.2	213,100	50.9	15.1	7.0	6.3	6.7
Tertiary industry	57,009	35.3	109,290	35.3	148,760	35.6	11.0	6.7	6.4	6.6

* Secondary: mining, manufacturing, construction

Source: *Long Term Industrial Structure Vision*, p. 23.

eliminating pollution and preserving the environment, and (c) contribute to the conservation of natural resources and energy. If primary energy consumption in 1985 can be kept down to a total of 600 million kilolitres oil equivalent, oil imports might be expected to be 400-450 million kilolitres in 1980 and 500-600 million kilolitres in 1985 indicating an average rate of increase of 5 to 6 per cent.

On these points the JERC outlook comes up with a similar projection:

> Japan's industrial structure will change to that of an energy-economising type as a result of a decline of chemical and iron steel industries and rises of machinery and service industries in relative importance. The elasticity value of energy, or the quantity of energy necessary to increase the nation's real gross national product by one per cent, will fall from 1.15 in the past decade to 0.96. The dependence on oil will fall from 75 per cent of the total energy requirement in 1975 to 62 per cent in 1985 due to an increase in relative weight of nuclear power. As a consequence, the import requirement of oil will come to 500 million kilolitres in 1985 as compared with 320 million kilolitres in 1975. An oil import of this magnitude could be materialised to the full when the demand-supply balance of oil in the world is considered. The share of imported oil in the total energy supply will decline from 88 per cent in 1975 to 82 per cent in 1985. With respect to iron ore, coking coal, copper and other resources, their imports may need to be reduced by industrial restructuring and increased imports of semi-finished and manufactured goods.[4]

To effect this kind of transformation of the industrial structure will necessitate, (d) the opening up of overseas production of textiles, natural resources and intermediate goods by overseas investment amounting to a cumulative total of $ 100 billion by 1985 and at the same time (e) the promotion of creative technological development in all industries particularly in the sophisticated machinery sector.

4. *Composition of imports and exports*

In response to changes in the structure of industry, the *composition of imports* will change as follows (nominal terms). According to the Industrial Structure Council's long-term vision:

(a) Whereas in 1970 raw materials, mainly mineral fuels, formed the bulk of imports with a weight of 56.0 per cent, in future their weight will decline as basic industries like petroleum and iron and steel are developed abroad and in 1985 their share will be 51.2 per cent.

(b) As against this the share of manufactures will increase from 30.4 per cent in 1970 to 34.7 per cent in 1985. With the progress of industrialisation in the developing countries, it is expected that imports of textile products and miscellaneous manufactures, lower-grade machinery products and so on will steadily increase.

(c) Another feature will be an increase in imports of crude steel, basic petro-chemical products and other intermediate goods, as overseas investment increases.

Here too the JERC outlook is basically the same and may be summarised as follows. Comparing the commodity composition of imports in 1975 and 1985, foodstuffs will fall from 14 per cent to 10 per cent and raw materials from 22 per cent to 16 per cent. The proportion of mineral fuels will be much higher than the 20 per cent of the 1960s but, at 39 per cent, it represents a fall from the exceptional 1975 figure of 42 per cent. By contrast imports of manufactures will rise from 22 per cent to 35 per cent, with a continuing trend towards horizontal specialisation (see Table 6.2).

As regards the *composition of exports*, the Industrial Structure Council's long-term vision sees the following changes from the preponderance of heavy and chemical industry products in 1970, when metal products were 19.6 per cent, chemical products 6.3 per cent and machinery 46.2 per cent.

(a) From now on, as industrial sites become scarcer in Japan, there will be a fall in domestic supply capability for intermediate goods like iron and steel and petro-chemicals.

(b) In automobile exports, exports in knocked-down form will increase while the increase in exports of fully assembled vehicles will flatten out.

(c) The share of household electrical appliances and textile products in total exports will fall as rising wages lower their competitiveness and tariff barriers and import restrictions increase in various countries.

(d) In machinery exports, the share of high-quality, high-class products related to new technology, such as industrial machinery and the whole range of system commodities incorporating electronics, will increase.

(e) Exports of materials for plant construction will rise *pari passu*

Table 6.2 Japan's exports by commodity

	$ million						Annual rate of change (per cent)					
	1960	1965	1970	1975	1980	1985	1960-65	1965-70	1970-75	1975-80	1980-85	1975-85
Food	268	344	648	1171	1704	2485	5.1	13.5	12.6	7.8	7.8	7.8
	6.6	4.1	3.4	1.8	1.3	1.0						
Machinery	1024	2976	8941	34258	81814	160425	23.8	24.6	30.8	19.0	14.4	16.7
	25.3	35.2	46.3	61.2	67.7							
General machinery	222	624	2006	7162	23726	51720	23.0	26.3	29.0	27.1	16.9	21.9
	5.5	7.4	10.4	10.8	17.7	21.8						
Electrical	274	865	2865	3654	24614	50391	25.9	27.0	27.5	20.6	15.4	18.0
machinery	6.8	10.2	14.8	14.6	18.4	21.3						
Transport	433	1243	3443	15153	28392	48519	23.5	22.6	34.5	13.4	11.3	12.3
machinery	10.7	14.7	22.9	21.2	20.5							
Automobiles	107	237	1337	5985	14482	23154	17.2	41.3	34.9	19.3	9.8	14.5
	26	28	69	90	10.8	9.8						
Ships	288	748	1410	6661	9770	13782	21.0	13.5	36.4	8.0	7.1	7.5
	7.1	8.8	7.3	10.1	7.3	5.8						
Precision instruments	96	243	626	2289	5082	9795	20.4	20.8	29.6	17.3	14.0	15.7
	2.4	2.9	3.2	3.5	3.8	4.1						
Metal products	562	1718	3805	15087	19063	21988	25.1	17.2	31.7	4.8	2.9	3.8
	13.8	20.3	19.7	22.8	14.3	9.3						
Iron and steel	388	1290	2844	10855	13705	13518	27.2	17.1	30.8	4.7	0.3	2.2
	9.6	15.3	14.7	16.5	10.2	5.7						
Chemical products	169	547	1235	4992	11843	22410	26.4	17.7	32.2	18.9	13.6	16.2
	4.2	6.5	6.4	7.5	8.9	9.5						
Textile products	1223	1582	2408	4539	6709	7578	5.3	8.8	13.5	8.1	2.5	5.3
	30.2	18.7	12.5	6.9	5.0	3.2						
Non-metallic	145	265	372	1014	1652	2473	12.8	7.0	22.2	10.3	8.4	9.3
mineral products	3.6	3.1	1.9	1.5	1.2	1.0						
Other	664	1020	1909	5088	10975	19707	9.0	13.4	21.7	16.6	11.7	14.5
	16.3	12.1	9.8	7.7	8.2	8.3						
TOTAL	4055	8452	19318	66149	133760	237066	15.8	18.0	27.9	15.1	12.1	13.6
	100.0	100.0	100.0	100.0	100.9	100.0						

Source: Japan Economic Research Centre outlook, p. 12.

with the increase in overseas investment.

(f) In chemical products, exports of plastics and other petrochemical products, which currently form the bulk of exports will decrease while exports of new chemical products like fine chemicals, life science products and new compounds are expected to increase.

As a result of these factors the share of machinery products will increase from 46.2 per cent in 1970 to 64.6 per cent in 1985 and the share of chemical products from 6.3 per cent in 1970 to 15.2 per cent. Within the heavy and chemical industries the export share of intermediate goods products like iron and steel and petro-chemicals will fall, while in the fields of machinery industry and chemical industry the share of high value added, knowledge-intensive products will rise.

The JERC view is much the same.

(a) Iron and steel, until now Japan's top export, will suffer a fall in export capability. Shortage of sites within Japan and environmental problems indicate that it will become increasingly difficult to increase production of iron.

(b) While there is some room for expanding exports of textile products, exposure to competition from the developing countries will inevitably slow down export growth.

(c) Exports of automobiles, which have maintained an extremely high growth rate over the last ten years, will continue to grow strongly but in the later half of the 1980s the rate of growth will slacken as market saturation point is approached.

(d) Exports of shipping will also experience difficulties arising from stagnation of demand for tankers.

(e) Thus, the mainstay of exports will be general machinery and electrical machinery. This is because, in addition to a high rate of expansion of world demand for these products in general, the activities of Japanese firms overseas will bring an increase in export machinery for development of natural resources. They expect the share of machinery in the total value of exports to rise from 52 per cent in 1975 to 68 per cent in 1985 (see Table 6.3).

5. *Regional composition of trade*

The Industrial Structure Council's long-term vision does not go into this but the JERC outlook has something to say about the regional composition of trade and the balance of trade by region.

Table 6.3 Japan's imports by commodity

	$ million						Annual rate of change (per cent)					
	1960	1965	1970	1975	1980	1985	1960-65	1965-70	1970-75	1975-80	1980-85	1970-85
Food	547	1470	2574	9758	16017	23619	21.9	11.9	30.5	10.4	8.1	9.2
	12.1	18.0	13.6	14.0	12.3	10.0						
Raw materials	2207	3221	6677	15262	23436	37972	7.8	15.7	18.0	9.0	10.1	9.5
	49.1	39.4	35.4	21.9	27.9	16.1						
Textile raw	762	847	963	1970	2829	3264	2.1	2.6	15.4	7.5	2.9	5.2
materials	17.0	10.4	5.1	2.8	2.2	1.4						
Metal raw	673	1019	2696	6619	9380	17617	8.7	21.5	19.7	7.2	13.4	10.3
materials	15.0	12.5	14.3	9.5	7.2	7.5						
Other raw	772	1354	3018	6673	11227	17091	11.9	17.4	17.2	11.0	8.8	9.9
materials	17.2	16.6	16.0	9.6	8.6	7.3						
Mineral fuels	742	1626	3905	29224	55734	90971	17.0	19.2	49.6	13.8	10.3	12.0
	16.5	19.9	20.7	41.9	42.6	38.6						
Chemical products	265	408	1000	2672	6186	14450	9.0	19.6	21.7	18.3	18.5	18.4
	5.9	5.0	5.3	3.8	4.7	6.1						
Machinery	435	760	2298	5357	12451	26118	11.8	24.8	18.4	18.4	16.0	17.2
	9.7	9.3	12.2	7.7	9.5	11.1						
general	281	451	1262	2854	6424	12798	9.9	22.9	17.7	17.6	14.8	16.2
machinery	6.3	5.5	6.7	4.1	4.9	5.4						
electrical	34	111	478	1259	3325	7521	26.7	33.9	21.4	21.4	17.7	19.6
machinery	0.8	1.4	2.5	1.8	2.5	3.2						
tansport	87	154	406	730	1518	2951	12.1	21.4	12.4	15.8	14.2	15.0
machinery	1.9	1.9	2.2	1.0	1.2	1.3						
precision	32	44	151	514	1183	2847	6.6	28.0	27.8	18.1	19.2	18.7
	0.7	0.5	0.8	0.7	0.9	1.2						
Other manufactures	295	684	2426	7507	16885	42513	18.3	28.8	25.3	17.6	20.3	18.9
	6.6	8.4	12.8	10.8	12.9	18.0						
TOTAL	4491	8169	18881	69780	130709	235643	12.7	18.2	29.9	13.4	12.5	12.9
	100.0	100.0	100.0	100.0	100.0	100.0						

Note: The second rows of figures are percentages.

Source: Japan Economic Research Centre outlook, p. 8.

Table 6.4 Changes in Japan's trade by region (proportion of exports and imports, per cent)

	Export proportions						Import proportions					
	1960	1965	1970	1975	1980	1985	1960	1965	1970	1975	1980	1985
North America	30.1	31.9	33.7	27.8	27.9	28.9	39.1	33.3	34.4	23.9	25.0	25.9
USA	27.2	29.3	30.7	23.3	24.2	24.9	34.6	29.0	29.4	19.3	20.7	21.8
Europe	11.8	12.9	15.0	18.4	18.5	19.0	8.8	8.9	10.4	9.4	9.9	11.8
Oceania	4.1	4.4	3.6	4.5	4.5	4.2	8.4	7.5	8.8	8.1	8.6	8.4
South Africa	1.4	1.6	1.7	1.3	1.2	1.1	1.3	1.5	1.7	1.3	1.2	1.1
Southeast Asia	24.9	26.0	25.4	21.1	19.3	18.4	20.4	17.2	16.0	15.7	16.5	18.7
Middle & Near East	4.4	4.2	3.3	8.0	9.7	9.7	10.0	13.6	12.4	28.4	24.1	17.9
Africa	6.2	7.1	5.2	5.6	5.6	5.5	3.0	3.8	5.3	2.8	3.5	4.5
Central & South America	7.5	5.8	6.1	7.1	7.4	7.3	6.9	8.7	7.3	5.6	5.6	5.9
Communist Bloc	1.8	5.6	5.4	6.2	6.0	5.9	2.8	6.5	4.7	4.7	5.6	7.0
WORLD TOTAL	100.0	100.0	100.0	100.0	100.0	100.0	100.0	100.0	100.0	100.0	100.0	100.0

Source: Japan Economic Research Centre outlook, p. 10.

Table 6.5 Changes in Japan's trade by region (share in the partner region, trade balance)

	Export share to partner region						Trade balance (customs, clearance basis, $ million)					
	1960	1965	1970	1975	1980	1985	1960	1965	1970	1975	1980	1985
North America	6.0	9.4	12.6	12.9	14.1	15.1	53.8	30	14	1673	4696	7408
USA	7.4	11.9	15.2	15.1	16.8	18.0	657	113	380	2518	5317	7644
Europe	0.9	1.3	2.0	2.7	2.9	3.1	84	363	943	5623	11872	17213
Oceania	5.5	9.3	13.5	20.6	21.6	22.4	208	239	963	2694	5246	9989
South Africa	3.8	5.8	9.5	11.6	10.5	11.1	1	17	60	60	13	6
Southeast Asia	8.0	12.7	29.4	25.6	26.0	26.4	94	789	1889	3021	4158	2585
Near & Middle East	5.8	8.0	9.0	18.7	17.9	17.7	272	756	1703	14546	18582	19267
Africa	3.9	7.4	8.4	11.9	12.6	13.4	117	411	312	1711	2867	2501
South & Central America	3.8	5.2	6.4	8.7	9.6	9.5	7	219	186	810	2627	3625
Communist Bloc	0.5	2.3	10.7	11.0	11.1	11.1	52	49	158	828	671	2659
WORLD TOTAL	3.5	4.9	6.6	7.6	8.0	8.3	436	283	437	3631	3051	1423

Source: Japan Economic Research Centre outlook, p. 13.

(a) The fact that Japan's imports will be on such an extraordinarily large scale means that from the economic point of view apart from anything else, Japan must maintain friendly relations with all countries. It is unlikely that Japan could secure the raw materials she needs by building an economic bloc in Asia. Nor could she depend entirely upon the United States. If we look at the structure of Japan's import markets since the war we find that the US share fell from 30 per cent around 1970 to 24 per cent in 1973, and it will probably fall to some 22 per cent in 1985. As the Japanese economy gets larger, her export markets will spread out from the United States and Southeast Asia to the Middle East, Australia, Central and South America, the Soviet Union, China and so on.

(b) In some regions and in some markets the rate of penetration of Japanese exports is rather high. By 1985 it is expected that the rate of penetration of Japanese exports will be 20 per cent in Southeast Asia, 22 per cent in Oceania and 18 per cent in the United States. The share of Japanese export commodities in these regions is too high and there is danger of friction with the importing countries.

(c) Problems may arise in the balance of trade with particular countries. By the nature of her economy, Japan is bound to have a large import surplus in her trade with the Middle East and Australia. In 1985 we anticipate an import surplus of $ 20 billion with the Middle East and $ 10 billion with Oceania. Thus if Japan is to achieve an overall balance of trade she must have a large export surplus with other regions and this promises to be particularly large with Western Europe ($ 17 billion) and with the United States ($ 7.6 billion – both figures calculated on custom clearance basis). (See Tables 6.4 and 6.5.)

6. *The long-term vision for agriculture*

We do not really have a clear long-term vision of how Japan's food problem is to be solved or ameliorated. The following is taken from the Agricultural Policy Council Report.

Japan's overall rate of self-sufficiency in food fell from 82 per cent in 1963 to 73 per cent in 1972. The objective is to raise this to 75 per cent in 1985. If we take only cereals, the rate of self-sufficiency will fall from the already low level of 42 per cent in 1972 to an even lower 37 per cent in 1985. Poor harvests in the Soviet Union and Asia in 1972, the oil crisis, export restrictions by the United States (soybeans) and Thailand (rice) and the poor harvest in the United States in 1974 have combined to produce a sense of food crisis which, needless to say, has exerted strong pressure for redirecting Japanese agricultural policy towards raising the rate of self-sufficiency in food. Raising the overall rate of self-sufficiency from 73 per cent in 1972 to 75 per cent in 1985 may not seem much, but when one takes into account the growth of population (1.1 per cent per annum) and growth in consumption per head (expected to be 2,593 calories per head per day providing 83 grams of protein in 1985) we come up with a growth in demand of 1.6 per cent a year requiring substantial increase in food production. Hence, to achieve an increase in the rate of self-sufficiency from 73 per cent to 75 per cent will require agricultural production to expand somewhat faster than the 1.6 per cent rate of increase in demand – actually at slightly under 2 per cent. At the same time the area of agricultural land will expand from 5.6 million hectares in 1973 to 5.85 million hectares in 1985. Pasture land is put at some 250,000 hectares. Double cropping of paddy fields is to be actively expanded and raised from the current 240,000 hectares to 740,000 hectares in 1985. The rate of utilisation of arable land rises from 102.1 per cent in 1972 to 114.3 per cent.

The number of farm households will decrease at an annual average rate of about 1.3 per cent from 5.16 million households in 1972 to around 4.3 million households in 1985. Population engaged in agriculture will fall at an annual rate of 3.5 per cent to 3.0 per cent from 6.87 million persons in 1972 to 4.10-4.30 million persons in 1985 in full time equivalent. The proportion of agricultural workers to the total labour force will fall to some 7 per cent.

(a) Rice – total demand in 1985 will be 12.10 million tonnes with complete self-sufficiency.

(b) Wheat and barley – some 60 per cent of demand for wheat, for noodles and pearl barley and 50 per cent of beer barley will be domestically produced. Production of wheat will be raised from 2.84 million tonnes in 1972 to 5.53 million tonnes with a self-sufficiency ratio of 9 per cent.

(c) Soybeans – 60 per cent of human consumption demand will be met by domestic production and the overall self-sufficiency ratio will be raised from 4 per cent to 9 per cent.

(d) Meat – demand has already risen sharply and in 1972 annual consumption per head was 14.2 kilograms but it is not expected to go much beyond 19 kilograms in 1985 giving a total demand of 3.20 million tonnes. Of this over 80 per cent is to be domestically produced and for this purpose the number of beef cattle is to rise from 1,776 thousand head in 1972 to 3,305 thousand head and the number of pigs is to be increased from 7.168 million to 11.79 million.

(e) Marine products – demand will increase but because of resource limitations there will be difficulties in expanding the catch and 5 per cent of demand will be met from imports.

(f) Other foodstuffs – vegetables will be supplied entirely from domestic sources as will 94 per cent of milk and dairy products. For sugar the rate of self-sufficiency is to be raised from 20 per cent in 1972 to 28 per cent.

(g) Feed grains – there will be a steep rise in demand and there is a limit to the degree to which domestic production can be increased. Grain imports (mainly feed grains) will therefore increase from 20.81 million tonnes in 1972 to 27.89 million tonnes. It may, however, prove difficult to raise Japan's share in total world trade in feed grains much beyond the 21.9 per cent which it averaged in 1970-2. For this reason it is proposed to avoid raising that share by intensifying domestic production so far as possible (see Tables 6.6 and 6.7).

As we see from the above outline of the Agricultural Policy Council Report all these efforts to increase production will do no more than raise the overall rate of self-sufficiency by a mere 2 per cent from 73 per cent to 75 per cent. The rate of self-sufficiency in grains will fall from 42 per cent to 37 per cent and for both wheat and soybeans the rate of self-sufficiency will reach no more than a mere 9 per cent. We may well be faced with a choice of either increasing production of staple grains or concentrating on animal products.

On this point the JERC outlook makes the following comments. In food products the overall rate of self-sufficiency has fallen rapidly from 90 per cent in 1960 to 76 per cent in 1970 and 73 per cent in 1972. It would be undesirable for this rate of self-sufficiency to fall still further in the future. We need to increase stocks of rice in case of world harvest failure. On the other hand, raising the rate of self-sufficiency by means of strong agricultural protectionism would be economically expensive and would hinder the development of international specialisation and from these points of view it can hardly be called a wise policy.[5]

On the question of the rate of self-sufficiency, the JERC outlook's view is that there is no alternative to raising domestic agricultural productivity as far as practicable and relying on imports for the balance, and it rejects as unrealistic extreme arguments both of national security and of international specialisation. As an illustration, to produce domestically the amount of grain imported in 1973 would

Table 6.6 Forecast of food self-sufficiency ratios (per cent, 1972 real values)

	1972	1985
Overall self-sufficiency ratio for food-use agricultural products	73	75
Cereals self-sufficiency	42	37
Self-sufficiency in main food-use cereals	71	73
Self-sufficiency in important agricultural products		
rice	100	100
vegetables	99	100
fruit	81	84
eggs	98	100
meat (excluding fish)	81	86
milk and milk products	86	94
sugar	20	28
wheat	5	9
barley	18	36
soy beans for food-use	20	60
(including oil use)	4	9
feed	46	51

Source: Agricultural Policy Council Report, January 1975.

Table 6.7 Quantity of imports of cereals, etc. (Unit: '000 tons)

	1972	1985
Cereals	20811	27888
Cereals	17172	23072
Wheat, barley, oats, rye	6805	6958
Corn		
Kaoliang	10367	16114
Beans	3639	4816
(of which for oil)	2636	4000
Sugar	2542	2787

Source: Agricultural Policy Council Report, January 1975.

require a sown area of 9.15 million hectares (total arable area in 1974 was 5.62 million hectares), while on the other hand it has been computed that even if food imports were to stop entirely we would still be assured of the levels of nutrition of 1954.[6]

The JERC projection cannot be said to be either very clear or very sharp. As we have already indicated, we are faced with the choice of whether to put the emphasis on (a) completely self-sufficient production of rice, (b) increased production of other staple grains (wheat, barley and soybeans), or (c) encouraging animal husbandry. Here we should keep firmly in mind the future relative costs of production as between Japan and the rest of the world. It may be, for instance, that if we were to lower the rate of self-sufficiency in meat from over 80 per cent to around 50 per cent we could achieve a very substantial corresponding reduction in imports of feedstuffs and possibly raise the overall rate of self-sufficiency. The opinion is also put forward that increased production of pasture could replace imports of feedstuffs. By cutting down on animal husbandry, might it not be possible to put more effort into increasing production of wheat, barley, soybeans and other staple cereals? There is certainly concern about world shortages of staple cereals, but there might well be fewer worries about availability of meat imports.

III THE VIEW OF BUSINESS CIRCLES

The long-term projections of the Industrial Structure Council and JERC may be summarised as follows:

i. Location of labour-intensive goods production, such as textiles, in the developing countries and their import from those countries into Japan is accepted as virtually a *fait accompli*.

ii. To save natural resources and energy, to keep down pollution, and because of the shortage of appropriate sites in Japan a considerable part of the increase in productive capacity in intermediate goods (iron and steel and basic chemical products) should henceforth be transferred abroad.

iii. Hence, the mainstay of domestic industry and exports will in future be the knowledge-intensive and high value added machinery group (including high-grade chemical manufacture).

Interestingly enough, the Keidanren essay, reflecting the feelings of industry, has voiced the following grave concerns:

i. Transformation of the industrial structure should be through the operation of market forces and under the leadership of the private sector. This is in reply to the Industrial Structure Council's long-term vision of transformation of the industrial structure under the leadership of government implied in its idea of a 'planned market economy'. Basically, however, there does not seem to be any fundamental difference between the two positions.

ii. Conscious of Japan's role as a 'world industrial base' they believe that industry, of which heavy and chemical industry will remain the mainstay, should be located primarily within Japan. Heavy and chemical industries should not be lightly encouraged to relocate overseas.

Many countries that have close connections with Japan rely heavily on our comprehensive industrial capacity and technology and we should confirm the fact that we are performing the role of a 'world production base'. The developing countries of Southeast Asia in particular depend upon us for a large part of their basic materials, such as iron and steel, petro-chemical products and fertilisers, and there seems little hope that any alternative productive base will appear to take our place at least into the first half of the 1980s. Naturally, Japan will cooperate in making the developing countries more self-sufficient in industrial products, but we ourselves must continue to fulfil our responsibilities as suppliers of basic materials to the developing countries as we move towards becoming an industrial base for more highly processed goods. Thus it is important that we utilise what territory we have efficienctly and vigorously carry forward the development of anti-pollution technology so that we can push for the development of new large-scale industrial bases predicated on environmental conservation as a major national project.

Recent theories advocating the movement of Japanese equipment industries abroad and ideas of what would be a desirable industrial structure for our country look too much as though they are simply pushing out 'pollutant' industries and looking for ways of importing such products into Japan from plants located abroad. This seems to show a lack of a sense of cooperation in the economic development aspirations of the host countries, and it should be fully reconsidered.

The argument that intermediate goods industries should move abroad in the interest of saving raw materials and energy and solving the pollution problem neglects the fact that demands for a solution to the problems of natural resources, energy, and the environment are world-wide. The real problem is to continue to clean up industrial processes and to find increasingly efficient ways of utilising natural resources and energy. We need a full examination of resource- and energy-saving measures which would include a new look at the social system as a whole. In practice this would include a comprehensive check of the conditions under which resources and energy are being used in each industry followed by efforts to reduce the total amounts used, by raising output per unit of input consumed and by making use of recovery and recycling. On the product side we need to eliminate excess quality by setting standards and by standardising the life of parts and materials, by developing energy-saving products and avoiding excessive model changes. At the same time we should rationalise both commercial and physical distribution systems by abolishing excessive packaging, unnecessary cross hauling, etc.

iii. Knowledge intensification does not mean the building up of so-called knowledge-intensive industries such as space development, development of the oceans, or electronic equipment. Rather we should aim at knowledge intensification in all sections within existing heavy and chemical industry.

In recent years there have been strong demands for a switch towards knowledge-intensive type industrial structure. Knowledge intensification, however, does not only mean promoting the development of the so-called knowledge-intensive industries. Raising the degree of knowledge intensity means raising the degree of technological development of a resource-energy-environment and power-saving type, while at the same time working towards more highly processed products and higher value added.

Actually, the difference between the view of the Industrial Structure Council and Keidanren depends largely on the way they think about the content and specification of these two concepts, namely, on the one hand, intermediate goods identified with the materials producing industries and heavy and chemical industries and on the other hand knowledge-intensive industries identified with highly processed technology-intensive industries and the machinery industry. In effect their conclusions are not so very different. The main practical difference is that while the Industrial Structure Council is in favour of moving intermediate goods industries like iron and steel overseas,[7] Keidanren feels that since they are still the mainstay of domestic industries and exports they should not be lightly moved abroad.

To back up their argument the Industrial Structure Council stress the shortage of industrial sites, and the need to conserve resources and energy and avoid pollution. Keidanren, on the other hand, point out that the prevention of pollution is imperative whether at home or abroad, but claim that for some time to come it will still be more profitable to use the remaining sites within Japan, even after paying the costs of anti-pollution devices, than it would be to locate in the developing countries (the developing countries are not yet up to that stage). They consider that the way to save energy and resources is not by relocating intermediate goods industries overseas but by utilising resources and energy more efficiently and that promotion of research and development for that purpose is essential.

There is a further point. Whereas the Industrial Structure Council sees the Japanese economy being able to carry on the basis of a large-scale transformation towards the machinery industries, Keidanren is conscious of a lag in Japan's technological development and has grave fears as to whether the machinery industry could provide adequate employment, income and exports. In their view, apparently, we have not yet reached that stage, and the intermediate goods industries are still the backbone.

IV A NETWORK OF INTRA-INDUSTRY SPECIALISATION WITH NEIGHBOURING ECONOMIES

We can discern one basic difference between the two views. The Industrial Structure Council makes a distinction between (a) intermediate goods = materials industries = heavy and chemical industries on the one hand and (b) knowledge-intensive industries = highly processed technology-intensive industry = the machinery industry on the other (for convenience we shall refer to (a) as intermediate goods and to (b) as machinery). They advocate a shift in relative proportions from the former to the latter. By contrast Keidanren argues that writing off our current industrial structure completely will do nothing to solve the problem. Today's industrial structure supports today's livelihood and the kind of industrial structure that we would like to see tomorrow can hardly be wholly unconnected with the industrial structure of today. Thus, Keidanren favours raising the degree of technological intensity within each industry by promoting technological development of a resource-, energy-, environment- and power-saving type, while at the same time working towards more highly processed products and higher value added. In other words, they do not see intermediate goods and machinery as two distinct categories but claim that the two cannot be separated. They regard the intermediate goods or heavy and chemical industries as the matrix within which the machinery industry could be regarded as the more sophisticated, or technology- and knowledge-intensive section. On this point, Keidanren's view seems correct. I myself referred to the knowledge-intensive industries as 'more sophisticated heavy and chemical industry'.

The Industrial Structure Council's distinction between 'intermediate goods' and 'machinery' seems in need of some revision. In the first place, if you shift some intermediate goods industries (even iron and steel) overseas, one would expect those products which use these intermediate goods (machinery) to be produced on the spot and we can hardly think of the two as separate. To suggest, as the Industrial Structure Council does, that the intermediate goods should be shifted overseas while the machinery, etc., should be kept in Japan is simply not practicable. Faced with having to make a choice between sending either the intermediate goods/the materials sections of heavy and chemical industry overseas, or sending the machinery section which processes those intermediate goods it might very well turn out that from the point of view of comparative costs the intermediate goods, which require huge capital equipment and in which economies of scale are important, should be kept at home while the processing sectors which can take advantage of low-wage labour should be shifted to the developing countries – a conclusion which is just the opposite of that reached by the Industrial Structure Council. This was in fact the actual experience of standardised products like textiles, household electrical appliances and automobiles.

On the other hand, Keidanren's view that it would be premature to transfer the intermediate goods and materials-producing industries to the developing countries seems a little negative in the light of the remarkable industrialisation of the developing countries in recent years. The Keidanren essay itself states that we believe that location of our industries overseas will develop rapidly in the future but we must endeavour to establish a system of international specialisation by handing over to the developing countries those industries which should be handed over in the light of the aspirations of the host country as regards the upgrading of the degree of local processing and so on. Here they seem to have in mind labour-intensive goods like textiles and further processing of local natural resources.

What both the Industrial Structure Council and Keidanren have missed are the possibilities for detailed horizontal (i.e. intra-industry) specialisation based on a finer commodity classification.[8] In the case of labour-intensive goods like textiles, there is already wide acceptance that they should be located abroad and imported into Japan. This admits however of intra-industry specialisation under which some kinds of textiles would be imported and other higher quality textile products would be exported. Export of parts and imports of assembled products is another form of horizontal specialisation. We have reached the stage where we must increasingly consider the same kind of intra-industry specialisation in the heavy and chemical industries (including both intermediate goods and machinery).

It could, for instance, become necessary progressively to install integrated steel plants in neighbouring developing countries. Of necessity however these would remain small-scale. Nevertheless, iron and steel covers a great range of products and so by specialising in a particular product, each steel works could take advantage of the economies of scale and operate efficiently. In this way, it would not only supply local demand but also provide imports for Japan. Japan in turn could export other varieties of iron and steel. Through such regional dispersion of Japanese iron and steel firms, we could build up a system of intra-industry specialisation and a relationship of interdependence that would be mutually inseparable. In securing stable supplies of raw materials and oil, we would then need to consider not only Japan's requirements but those of neighbouring countries as well. The same kind of intra-industry specialisation might gradually be introduced in the petro-chemical industry or in iron and steel using and machine production.

This may be the only way in which we can raise the industries of neighbouring countries from the stage of light industry to the stage of heavy and chemical industry and finally raise their economies to the level and quality of Japan's. Until neighbouring countries reach an economic level equal to Japan's and we create interdependent relationships so close that they become mutually inseparable, Japan can never achieve international political and economic stability. The Industrial Structure Council's long-term vision seems implicitly to set up the composition of West Germany's industry and trade as a model for Japan. It must be remembered that the West German economy is based on the economic union of the European Community. We might well take as one of our objectives the building of the Western Pacific economic region into something resembling the European Community.[9]

V CONCLUSION

To recapitulate, the long-term projections for the Japanese economy that have come out since the oil crisis are vague in their vision of international economic aspects and their policy proposals are inward-looking and no more than passive reactions. These proposals seem to be as follows.

i. Japan must refrain from importing too much of the world's scarce natural resources and foods, and she should therefore transform her industrial structure along resource- and energy-saving lines and raise her rate of self-sufficiency in foodstuffs.
ii. The objective of structural transformation from heavy and chemical industries to knowledge-intensive industries is also something of an over-reaction to restrictions on the availability of natural resources, shortage of industrial sites in Japan and the prevention of pollution and does not provide any positive attractive objective for foreign economic policy.
iii. The switch from a high rate of growth with trade and private equipment investment as the leading sectors to a lower rate of growth oriented towards welfare will serve to reduce dependence on imports and restrain the rate of growth of exports from going too far above the rate of the growth of world trade.

These points are expressed as 'harmonisation and cooperation with the international economy' but they could be more accurately called an extremely negative and inward-looking reaction. Is this the way to fulfil our responsibilities as an economic power?

I believe that Japan should promote a network of intra-industry specialisation particularly with neighbouring countries of the Western Pacific region in all the sectors of natural resources, agriculture, light industry, intermediate products of the heavy and chemical industries and the machinery industries and should raise the level of their economies and build up relationships of interdependence that will be mutually inseparable. These are the kinds of attractive positive targets for international economic policy that should be forthcoming. We should re-examine in the light of this idea the relationships between Japan and Australia and New Zealand, between Japan and East Asia (North and South Korea, Taiwan, Hong Kong and China), between Japan and Southeast Asia, Japan and South Asia, the Middle East, and so on.

There is still a tendency to try to solve the problems of the world economy, such as inflation and the international trade and payment systems within the advanced countries alone, but such a solution will not be easy. This is an opportunity for the advanced countries to tackle in earnest the problems of the developing countries to which they have so far been paying only lip service. Here are possibilities for effectively using Arab oil money. Not only have the advanced countries run up against relative stagnation in technological progress but the technological innovation itself has taken some wrong turns, as in the production of luxuries and robot production. There is great scope for raising productivity by transferring existing technology and industries to the developing countries through effective direct investment. The scope for increasing purchasing power in those countries is practically unlimited. Only by doing their utmost to raise the economic level of the developing countries and reorganising north-south trade will the advanced countries find a way towards solving their problems of inflation and unemployment.

NOTES

1. Kiyoshi Kojima, 'Japan's Foreign Economic Policies in the 1970s and the Reorganisation of Western Pacific Trade', Kojima, ed., *Japanese-Australian Project,* Report No. 1, JERC, June 1975.
2. *Ibid.*
3. The Japan Economic Research Centre, *The Future of World Economy and Japan*, Tokyo, February 1975, p. 5.
4. *Ibid*., p. 10.
5. *Ibid*., p. 10.
6. *Ibid*., p. 91.
7. According to the Industrial Structure Council's long-term vision, domestic production in the iron and steel industry, for example, will grow from 103 million tons in 1972 to 162 million tons in 1980 (a rate of growth of 5.8 per cent from 1970 to 1980) and to 173-8 million tons in 1985 (a rate of growth from 1980-5 of 1.3-1.9 per cent). Exports are to increase from about 29 million tons in 1972 to about 46 million tons in 1980 but, as construction of steel works overseas proceeds, exports in 1985 will be only 21.1-26.2 million tons or about half the 1980 level. Cumulated overseas investment in the iron and steel industry will reach about $ 3 billion in 1980 and about $ 10 billion in 1985. Similar projections are given for the chemical industry, paper and pulp, aluminium and textile industry, miscellaneous industries, the machinery industry (general machinery, electrical machinery, transport machinery and precision machinery are shown separately), the forming industry (castings and forgings), the cement industry, the plate glass industry, non-ferrous materials and industrially produced housing.
8. An excellent study on this problem has been published: see Herbert G. Grubel and P. J. Lloyd, *Intraindustry Trade: The Theory and Measurement of International Trade in Differentiated Products*, Macmillan, 1975. Also, Kiyoshi Kojima, 'An Approach to Integration: The Gains from Agreed Specialisation', in his *Japan and a Pacific Free Trade Area*, Macmillan, 1971, Chap. 2.
9. See Chapter 8.

7 THE REORGANISATION OF NORTH-SOUTH TRADE

I A NEW STIMULUS FOR WORLD TRADE EXPANSION

The postwar economy has experienced setbacks to its rapid expansion around the end of each decade, but has resumed its expansionary course due to some new stimulus on each occasion. Following the problem of pound sterling convertibility in 1947 and devaluation in 1949, American aid to Europe and Japan, and the Korean War, both helped speedy recovery and a resurgence of world trade. The recession of 1957 was mitigated by the emergence and success of European integration, within the EEC and EFTA, which resulted in unprecedented growth in world trade throughout the 1960s. In 1967 the Kennedy Round was concluded in June and the SDR system agreed upon in September, both events preceding a series of monetary manoeuvres including devaluation of sterling in November, the gold rush, and revaluations in Europe, all of which ultimately resulted in the new United States economic policy of August 1971 and the international monetary realignments in December. Thus, talks on the reform of the international monetary system began and the Tokyo Round of GATT negotiations started, although the oil crisis disturbed this progress.

However, as a prerequisite for trade liberalisation and the smooth adjustment of balance of payments, structural adjustment is needed in every country's industries in response to change in comparative costs. Inefficient, old industries which have lost comparative advantage should be contracted and capital and employment transferred to other growing sectors through adjustment assistance policies. To do this development centres will have to be created.

The challenge is to create another major stimulus for trade expansion and the growth of economic interdependence. One such stimulus should come from the steady and dynamic economic development of the Third World. Another is likely to derive from the enlargement of the EEC. A third will come from functional economic integration in the Pacific region.

The creation of new products and technologies and the transformation of each country's industrial structure as part of an expansive and harmonious international division of labour should be complementary to these forces. Japan's aim throughout the coming decade will be to expand the new technology-based industries (the so-called knowledge-intensive industries) which consist of more sophisticated heavy and chemical industry products and software. Such expansion will open up wider opportunities for increased imports of processed raw materials and metals, both from advanced and developing countries, and of textiles and other labour-intensive manufactures, mainly from developing countries.

Japan should undertake positive, hopefully dramatic policy measures to promote the developing countries' economic progress. Japan has accumulated substantial foreign exchange reserves, trade with advanced countries cannot be expected to grow as smoothly as it has in the past, but assistance to the developing countries to ensure the expansion of mutually beneficial trade is promising. Trade between the Japanese and developing economies is already basically complementary. There is plenty of scope for Japan to adjust its industrial structure, thus increasing imports of developing countries' primary as well as manufactured imports. How to 'live on trade with developing countries' may be one of the main foci for Japanese economic policy in the coming decade.

The establishment of a new international division of labour between advanced (northern) and less developed (southern) countries is a task for Japan, the United States and other advanced countries.

However much involved they are in their own troubles, once they develop a common purpose, they can find new solutions to their mutual trade adjustment problems. Reorganisation of the north-south trade is a major target in the 1970s for Japan as well as other advanced countries; here Japan's role and responsibility is crucial. This will require cooperation in development assistance programme fostering their own structural adjustment in accordance with the developing countries' growing comparative advantages, and in expanding trade with developing countries. It may be that among advanced countries, those of the Pacific have the most incentive for such cooperation.

In the previous chapter, Japanese attitudes toward the changing international division of labour were examined from the viewpoint that structural adjustment in developed countries is essential to reorganisation of the trade between developed and developing countries. This chapter, first, in Section II examines the origins of Japan's successful industrialisation with the aim of drawing policy implications for developing countries. In Section III, Japan's aid and foreign investment policies are discussed and evaluated. Finally, in Section IV, Japan's trade policy towards developing countries is surveyed and experience with adjustment assistance policies reported. The conclusion stresses the need for an integrated aid, investment-*cum*-preference, structural adjustment policy.

II INDUSTRIALISATION AND TRADE GROWTH IN JAPAN

The success of Japan's knowledge-intensive industrialisation is not only important to her own economic development but also for the creation of a new division of international trade both with developing and developed countries. Although such industrialisation may not be an easy task, it can be undertaken determinedly and with the prospect of rapid progress, since the Japanese economy has had plenty of experience in fostering structural change successfully in the past.

In Japan, Dr Akamatsu, Professor Emeritus of Hitotsubashi University, propounded a 'catching-up product cycle' theory as early as the mid-1930s, predating Professor Vernon's 'product cycle' thesis.[1] He originally called it 'the wild geese-flying pattern' (*Ganko keitai*) of industrial development in developing countries since, as shown in Figure 7.2, the time-series curve for imports of a particular product is followed by that of domestic production and later by that of exports, suggesting, according to Professor Akamatsu, a pattern like 'wild geese flying in orderly ranks forming an inverse V, just as airplanes fly in formation'.[2]

The concern of Vernon and others[3] was to explain how a new product is invented and manufactured on a large scale in leading industrial countries (Figure 7.1). Exports of this product grew in so far as a 'technological gap' exists between the product developing country and foreign countries. Foreign producers imitate the new technology and follow suit. Then exports slow down and through direct investment an attempt is made to secure foreign markets. When the technology is standardised and widely disseminated and the limit of scale economies is reached, trade based on wage costs, or factor proportions, starts and the country turns to import this product from abroad.

In a developing, or catching-up, country, the product cycle starts from the importation of the new product with superior quality. 'Imports reconnoitre and map out the country's demand', and once increased demand approaches the domestic production threshold, domestic production can be economically started.[4] A learning process follows and is assisted by the importation of technological knowhow and/or foreign direct investment. The expansion of production then leads to the exploitation of economies of scale, increases in productivity,

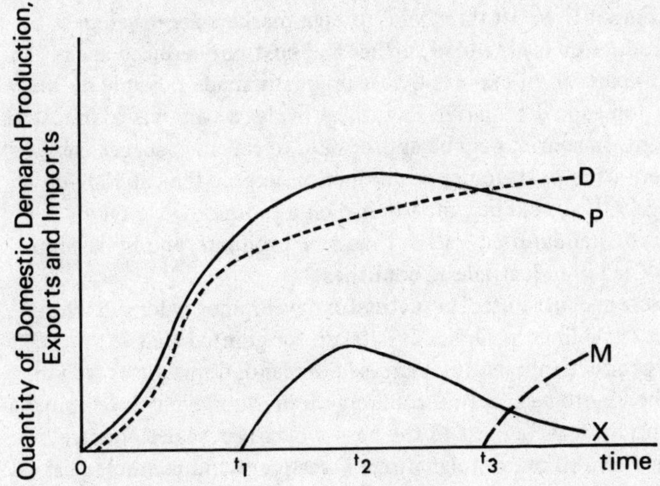

FIGURE 7.1 Vernon's genuine product cycle

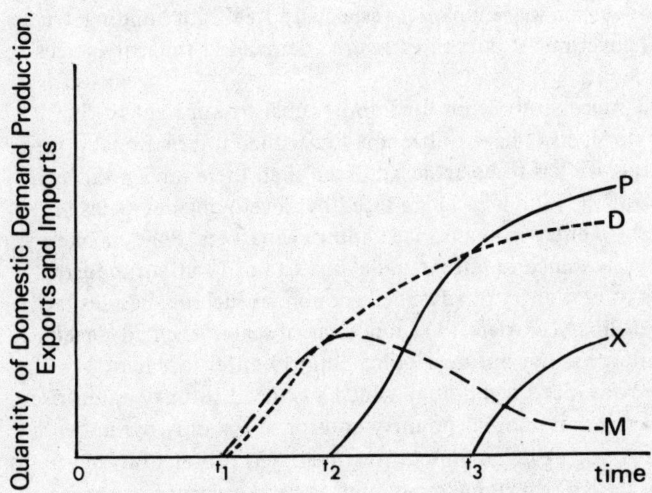

FIGURE 7.2 Akamatsu's catching-up product cycle

improvements in quality and reductions in costs. This involves an import-substitution process. But as domestic costs reach the international competitive cost threshold, foreign markets are developed, the scale of production is extended further and costs are reduced again. Thus, the expansion of exports that is originally made possible by the growth of domestic demand, in its turn, provides a stimulus to industrial development. In sum, it may be appropriate to call such successive development of import/domestic production/export the catching-up product cycle. It should be noted that such a product cycle takes place only for standardised, rather than new products, and in developing, rather than in industrialised countries.

What factors contributed to successful development along catching-up product cycle lines in Japan? It is taken for granted that each successive product enjoyed the increased demand, domestic as well as foreign. The key to a successful catching-up product cycle development was long-run decreasing costs of the nature clearly revealed for steel, automobiles, and so on. Foreign direct investment and technological knowhow were certainly important but the technological adaptability, active management and industrious skill of the Japanese were much more important. Foreign technology was often amended and assimilated in a way which made its application in Japan more efficient.

In the stage of import-substitution, various types of protection for infant industries were granted, including protective tariffs and subsidies.[5] For certain key industries (especially steel, shipbuilding, trucks and so on) government purchases assured demand in the early stages of development.

To grow successfully from the import-substitution stage to the exporting stage, costs have to become lower than international prices, and good quality has to be achieved. Even then there are a number of difficulties of the kind now being faced by developing countries in the barriers to new entry into advanced country markets. Policy makers may justify assistance to 'infant trade', instead of to infant industry.

Barriers to new entry in advanced economies include, besides tariffs and other ordinary barriers, (1) economies of scale which advanced country enterprise has but developing country enterprise has not realised; (2) advanced technology which advanced country enterprise monopolises and developing country enterprise can only use under royalty or through foreign direct investment; (3) product differentiation in brand or design which makes adaptation by developing countries difficult; and (4) other barriers such as marketing and information networks, vertical and horizontal integration in production and sales which are only possessed by large multinational corporations. Because of these barriers, developing countries may be wise to utilise the advantages of multinational enterprises through direct investment.

Japan's unique general trading firms[6] played an important role in the expansion of trade. Their hundreds of subsidiaries and branches throughout the world were able to identify where Japan's comparative advantage lay, and to participate substantially in Japan's direct investments abroad. Developing countries could establish similar organisations, use Japanese trading firms' facilities, or do both.

After World War II, the Japanese government established the Japan External Trade Organisation (JETRO) for trade promotion and information. The government also provided effective incentives for export promotion through tax reductions for export earnings and subsidised interest rates for export financing, long-term export credit on a deferred payment basis, and subsidies for export and export-oriented production which were designed to encourage exports by influencing the profitability of enterprises engaged in export activity. Export interest subsidisation worked particularly effectively. Incentive interest rates are accorded to foreign exchange bills which conform to the rule of standard settlement. Such trade bills become eligible to be discounted by, or qualified as collateral acceptable to, the Bank of Japan, and enjoy the benefit of discount or borrowing at interest rates lower than those prevalent in the country.

Marginal pricing practices in exports, particularly of mass production goods, is common in Japan and is even encouraged by the government, as can be seen from the *White Papers* of the Economic Planning Agency and the Ministry of Trade and Industry.

To diversify and upgrade the industrial sector of an economy is another difficult task which needs much broader macroeconomic consideration than the present paper can cover. I believe that the structure of comparative advantages is basically regulated and changed by factor proportions *à la* Heckscher-Ohlin theory.[7] Diversification and upgrading of the industrial structure usually implies progress toward more capital- and technology-intensive industry and production processes. To accumulate capital (inclusive of such human capital as scientists, engineers, managerial skill, skilled labour and so on) and to raise the capital/labour endowment ratio is the major force for economic development.

The Japanese economy accumulated capital by limiting the demonstration effect on consumption in the early period of industrialisation, and attaining a high rate of saving. A comparison of the capital/labour endowment ratio with those abroad should dictate the choice of industries with appropriate factor intensities. When the economy expands excessively through structural change, it must choose production processes with lower capital intensities in all industries, resulting in a setback in per capita income. But once the structural change is accomplished and capital accumulates further, then the economy can enjoy a steady growth. It is also usual for an economy to suffer from trade deficits in periods of structural change and enjoy trade surpluses in later periods.[8]

The Japanese economy has perhaps been fortunate because its industrial take-off was relatively early. The economy could find markets abroad for its industrial output, its domestic market rose with incomes, and it was large enough to enable large-scale intermediate capital goods industries to be established.

Compared with the Japanese experience, developing countries now confront two basic problems. First, many developing countries already have a clear comparative advantage in labour-intensive goods such as in textiles and clothing, and there is a considerable danger of oversupply of these goods and a consequent fall in the commodity terms of trade unless advanced countries foster accommodating structural change, thereby opening wider markets for developing country exports. This can be clearly understood when Figures 7.1 and 7.2 are compared.

Secondly, developing countries tend to be over-ambitious in wishing to establish intermediate capital goods industries. Some countries' economies have reached a stage where this is economic, but others must reconsider whether their factor endowments allow the establishment of such industries, or whether such investment is not over-ambitious. Many have to overcome the smallness of their domestic market either through economic integration among neighbouring countries, or through production integration with advanced countries.

The Japanese economy's move towards knowledge-intensive industrialisation implies a basic switch from the type of development characterised by the catching-up product cycle to the creation of its own product cycles. The Japanese economy should enter into innovative competition in new products on an equal footing with other advanced countries and promote horizontal trade with them in new products. The successful reorganisation in the international division of manufacturing production depends on such a trend. Although the patterns in Figure 7.1 and 7.2 look similar, the genuine product cycle is basically different from the catching-up product cycle. Imitation and learning are much easier than invention and innovation. The Japanese research and development investment in 1971 was 1.6 per cent of the gross national product which was far smaller than the 2.6 per cent of the United States, 2.3 per cent in the United Kingdom and 2.1 per cent in the Federal Republic of Germany. Making the coming structural changes effectively is therefore not easy for Japan. In addition, international specialisation and coordination in innovation of new products is needed among advanced countries for the benefit both of advanced and developing countries.

III JAPAN'S AID AND FOREIGN INVESTMENT POLICY

Another new task for the Japanese economy in the coming decade is how to increase its aid and direct investment to developing countries in such a way as to facilitate harmonious structural change both in Japan and developing countries, with the aim of successful reorganisation of the north-south trade. Current trends in aid flows make for a pessimistic outlook on the chances of fulfilling the Pearson Commission's recommendation that 'the one per cent target . . . be fully met by 1975, at the very latest', and that 'official development assistance should be raised to 0.70 per cent of donor gross national product by 1975, and in no case later than 1980'.[9] On the other hand, in Japan there is a growing realisation both at the public and government level, that the country must assume a greater responsibility in aid giving. A healthy balance of payments will render additional transfers relatively painless.

In 1974, Japan's total financial outflow to developing countries amounted to $ 2.96 billion, second only to the United States. This accounted for 0.65 per cent of GNP, although it reached to 1.14 per cent in 1973 due to a large increase in foreign direct investment and export credits. However, Japan's official development assistance is limited to $ 1.12 billion in 1974. It comprised only 0.25 per cent of GNP. Technical assistance was very limited. In addition, the terms of official direct loans were harder than the DAC average. Only a limited amount of Japan's official aid was in grant form, and future aid policy must be directed towards a significant softening of overall official development assistance terms.

Although the lag in the share of official development assistance is recognised, the rapid growth of total aid is very substantial. The total aid contribution in 1974, $ 2.96 billion, was ten times as large as that in 1962 ($ 290 million).

On the other hand, the largest financial flow from Japan to developing countries (62 per cent) consisted of export credits and private investment, both of which were provided from Japan's commercial interests in order to promote exports of capital goods and imports of raw materials, particularly mineral fuels and metals.

The political will is growing in Japan to mobilise larger resources for foreign aid. According to the Japan Economic Research Centre projection, Japan will be able to attain the 1 per cent target by 1985, with $ 26 billion worth of total aid, and Official Development Assistance must be brought up to some 0.6 per cent of GNP in 1985.[10]

Japan has already pledged herself to play a major role in postwar reconstruction in Vietnam. If the policies of postwar Vietnam allow such involvement, a large part of reconstruction in the Republic of Vietnam and nearby countries could be financed by Japan, as reparations payments cease elsewhere. This is an appropriate chance for Japan to offer a large scale 'Asian Reconstruction Programme' or 'Marshall plan for Asia'.

As in the case of direct investments, aid should also be provided in close conjunction with investments so as to facilitate the donor country's structural adjustment although major aid is directed towards in infrastructural investment. Untying aid is also an important objective.

Although there are commitments to a substantial increase in the 'official' component in Japan's total aid, foreign investments will play a more significant role in assisting LDC development. At the end of 1969, Japan's total foreign investments abroad (including advanced countries) amounted to $ 2,690 million. This has increased tremendously by $ 904 million in 1970, $ 858 million, $ 2,338 million and $ 3,500 million in 1971, 1972 and 1973 accumulating to $ 10,270 million at the end of March 1974.

Total investment will rise to $ 45,440 million by 1980 and $ 101,420 million by 1985.[11] By 1985, there will be an accumulated Japanese investment in Asia of around $ 24,000 million. These rapid increases in Japan's investments may well arouse Asian nationalist feeling against Japanese domination.

As pointed out in Chapters 4 and 5, Japanese foreign investment has to date been 'trade-oriented'. It was aimed at complementing Japan's comparative advantage position. The major part of investment was therefore directed toward natural resource development in which the Japanese economy is comparatively disadvantaged. Even investment in manufacturing has been confined either to such traditional industries as textiles, clothing and steel processing in which Japan has been losing its comparative advantage, or the assembly of motor

Table 7.1 Outstanding Japanese investments abroad by industry (authorisation basis) (million dollars, per cent)

					Actual projections							
	1960		1970		1973		1975		1980		1985	
		Share		Share		Share		Share		Share		Share
Resource-oriented industries	143	50.6	1428	40.4	3652	35.5	5881	35.7	16525	37.0	37888	37.4
Agriculture & forestry	3	1.0	56	1.6	152	1.5	240	1.5	639	1.4	1258	1.2
Fishing	4	1.4	26	0.7	77	0.7	114	0.7	304	0.7	683	0.7
Mining	86	30.5	1134	31.7	3061	29.8	4946	30.1	14253	31.4	32221	31.8
Lumber and pulp	50	17.7	212	5.9	362	3.5	581	3.5	1627	3.6	3726	3.7
Manufacturing	77	27.4	715	20.0	2898	28.2	5125	31.2	16525	36.4	39,600	39.0
Foodstuffs	2	0.7	51	1.4	167	1.6	261	1.6	561	1.0	931	0.9
Textiles	27	9.6	189	5.3	743	7.2	1171	7.1	2641	5.8	4516	4.5
Chemical	1	0.4	49	1.4	538	5.2	1077	6.5	4357	9.6	10462	10.3
Ferrous and non-ferrous	10	3.6	137	3.8	486	4.7	1034	6.3	4389	9.7	13339	13.2
Machinery	11	3.8	68	1.9	217	2.1	325	2.0	677	1.5	1167	1.2
Electrical machinery	1	0.5	73	2.0	328	3.2	572	3.5	1897	4.2	4524	4.5
Transport equipment	15	5.4	87	2.4	222	2.2	367	2.2	1033	2.3	2433	2.4
Others	9	3.3	61	1.7	197	1.9	318	1.9	970	2.1	2228	2.2
Services and others	62	22.0	1434	40.1	3720	36.2	5446	33.1	12094	26.5	23936	23.6
Construction	0	0	36	1.0	67	0.7	85	0.5	162	0.4	320	0.3
Commerce	40	14.0	412	11.5	1232	12.0	1912	11.6	4563	10.0	9178	9.0
Banking & insurance	11	3.7	318	8.9	917	8.9	1404	8.5	3239	7.1	6430	6.3
Others	12	4.3	669	18.7	1504	14.6	2045	12.4	4130	9.0	8008	7.9
TOTAL	283	100.0	3577	100.0	10270	100.0	16452	100.0	45442	100.0	101424	100.0

Source: Japan Export and Import Bank's and Finance Ministry's data for the actual figures. The Japan Economic Research Centre, *The Future of World Economy and Japan*, February 1975, pp. 108-9.

Table 7.2 Outstanding Japanese investments abroad by region (authorisation basis) (million dollars, per cent)

	Actual				Projections	
	1960	1970	1973	1975	1980	1985
Advanced countries	93	1833	5099	7960	20006	40694
	(32.8)*	(51.2)	(49.6)	(48.4)	(44.0)	(40.1)
North America	88	912	2462	3873	9181	18103
	(31.0)	(25.5)	(24.0)	(23.5)	(20.2)	(17.8)
Europe	3	639	1997	2830	6440	10923
	(1.2)	(17.9)	(19.4)	(17.2)	(14.2)	(10.8)
Oceania	2	281	640	1257	4385	11668
	(0.6)	(7.8)	(6.2)	(7.6)	(9.6)	(11.5)
Developing countries	190	1744	5172	8360	23982	57020
	(67.2)	(48.8)	(50.4)	(50.8)	(52.8)	(56.2)
Latin America	85	567	1811	2931	8261	18785
	(30.0)	(15.9)	(17.6)	(17.8)	(18.2)	(18.5)
Asia	49	751	2391	3839	10671	24014
	(17.1)	(21.0)	(23.3)	(23.3)	(23.4)	(23.6)
Middle & Near	56	334	716	1112	3072	6909
East	(19.8)	(9.3)	(7.0)	(6.8)	(6.8)	(6.8)
Africa	1	92	254	478	1978	7312
	(0.2)	(2.6)	(2.5)	(2.9)	(4.4)	(7.2)
Centrally Planned	0	0	0	132	1454	3710
Economies	(0)	(0)	(0)	(0.8)	(3.2)	(3.7)
TOTAL	283	3577	10270	16452	45442	101424
	(100.0)	(100.0)	(100.0)	(100.0)	(100.0)	(100.0)

* Figures in parentheses are percentages of total.

Sources: *Fiscal and Financial Statistics Monthly* and others, Ministry of Finance; JERC, *The Future of World Economy and Japan*, pp. 108-9.

vehicles, production of parts and components of radios and other electronic machines in which cheaper labour costs in Southeast Asian countries are achieved and the Japanese firms can increase exports, substituting for exports of final products, exports of machinery and equipment for the factory and technological knowhow.

Japanese foreign direct investment has thus been quite sensitive to change in its comparative advantage position. According to the progress of industrialisation in neighbouring Asian countries, Japanese foreign direct investment will step up to the second stage with the aim of establishing a network of intra-industry specialisation with those countries not only in consumer goods but also in intermediate goods production as well as machinery, as explained in Chapter 6.

Thus, both aid and direct investment are an important element in creating export capacity in developing countries and promoting the reorganisation of north-south trade.

IV JAPAN'S TRADE POLICY AND STRUCTURAL ADJUSTMENT

It becomes very clear that Japan and other advanced countries should develop an integrated aid, investment-*cum*-preference, structural adjustment policy in order to establish harmonious and expanding north-south trade relationships in the 1970s. Although the key factor is structural adjustment in advanced countries as has been stressed repeatedly, their trade policy, especially in relation to developing economies, is also important since the provision of wider market access in advanced countries to developing country manufactures is a crucial problem. Japan's trade policy was reviewed extensively in Chapters 1 and 2.

Currently, the north-south problem seems to be facing a turning point: there is a shift in emphasis from aid and trade expansion of a 'surplus disposal' type to that of a 'structural adjustment' type.

Structural adjustment in developed countries is an essential element if new development policies are to be successful. Multilateral and nondiscriminatory free trade is most important if world trade is to be increased. How to provide the basic conditions necessary to realise and maintain the free trade system is an important problem to be explored at present. The international monetary system must be revised so that balance of payments disequilibrium is quickly and frequently adjusted by *a more flexible adjustable peg system.* Then, many tariff and non-tariff barriers to trade which have been introduced, mainly for balance of payments reasons, can be eliminated. However, as a prerequisite for trade liberalisation and smooth adjustment of balance of payments, *structural adjustment* is needed in each country's industries in response to changes in comparative costs. Inefficient, old industries which have lost comparative advantage should be contracted and capital and employment must be transferred to other growing sectors through adjustment assistance policies. To do this development centres will have to be created. Overall unemployment is another difficult problem to be dealt with in structural adjustment.

Structural adjustment policy usually focuses its attention on contracting old, comparatively disadvantageous sectors of the economy; however, promoting the growth of new, comparatively advantageous sectors is equally important. Structural adjustment in declining, inefficient sectors is undertaken successfully only in a dynamic economy in which the growth sectors' expansion is rapid enough so that resources from contracting sectors may be absorbed smoothly.

Thus, there is a strong belief that upgrading the industrial structure in Japan (and other advanced countries) through knowledge-intensive industrialisation would also favour the industrialisation of developing countries and as such facilitate the reorganisation of north-south trade. But this solution crucially depends upon the prosperity of horizontal trade in knowledge-intensive products between advanced countries. The promotion of this trade also needs serious consideration. In this sense, the north-south trade problem cannot be separated from the problem of maintaining harmonious growth in trade among advanced countries.

While Japanese trade policy has been reluctantly changing in favour of manufactured exports from developing countries, our imports have increased rapidly in terms of their growth rate. For instance, imports of textile goods mainly from Asian countries increased from $ 43 million in 1965 to $ 383 million in 1971 and to $ 1,715 million in 1973. Recently, in 1975, Japan asked Korea, Taiwan, Hongkong and China to put voluntary export restraints on textiles in the same manner as a few years ago the United States was asking Japan to restrain textile exports. This resulted from the coincidence of serious slump in Japan due to the oil shock, but it also reveals at the same time that Japanese structural adjustment has been lagging and needs to be promoted more seriously.

Undertaking structural adjustments effectively therefore becomes a central issue for advanced countries if really wide markets for the manufactured goods of developing countries are to be created. Strong resistance, both economic and political, can be expected. Various steps will have to be taken to assist the adjustment, along the lines of those under the United States Trade Expansion Act of 1962 and the amended act of 1968.[12]

The Japanese economy has only limited experience of adjustment assistance policy. The first example is a recent policy of adjustment in rice cultivation, which should be examined since it is most important although it is not directly concerned with manufacturing. Heavy price supports have been provided for rice production, while imports of rice have been controlled by a state trading scheme. The implicit tariff rate on imports of rice is at least as high as 70 per cent and probably higher than 100 per cent, depending on the rice type and price quotations in Japan and abroad selected for comparison. Coupled with rapid productivity improvement, this has brought about overproduction of rice in Japan, resulting in difficulties for Asian rice exporting countries. A land-retirement scheme was introduced in 1970. The government provides compensation for those farmers who contract rice production acreage in the hope that they may switch to other occupations. This has not worked as expected. 'Rice is far more profitable than other farming enterprises, which prevents desirable shifts in the production pattern, and also more profitable than most nonfarm employment: this discourages farmers from making a complete shift to nonfarm work.'[13] The rice price was raised every year to take into account increases in nonfarm wages. Such price determination should be changed and the rice price should be lowered. Even if the rice price is lowered, the full-time farm unit can make enough profit if it attains a sufficient size. Agricultural pressure groups in Japan are still strong, but have declined substantially, and a more determined agricultural policy may be expected in the not too distant future.

How can job opportunities be created for those farmers who are discharged? Farms are diversifying their production from rice to dairy industries, cattle growing, poultry and fruit, which also necessitate protection. Many farmers already obtain income from outside farming. A Law for Promoting the Introduction of Industries into Rural Villages was introduced in 1971; retraining schemes for farmers and a farmer's pension scheme were also introduced. But structural reform has not yet been made effective. One hope is that natural contraction of the farm population will take place. Michael Tracy concludes, 'The age distribution of the farm population is heavily biased toward the upper age groups: in 1970, out of 4.0 million males engaged mainly in farming, 1.3 million were aged over 60 and 0.7 million were aged 50-59. It seems likely, therefore, that during the 1970s the control of nearly two-fifths of the farms in Japan will pass to the next generation.'[14] Agricultural reform in Japan is clearly a political and social problem rather than an economic problem.

In a second example[15] of Japanese experience with adjustment assistance policy, the Japanese coal industry has undergone dramatic structural adjustment since World War II. Immediately after the war, in December 1946, coal and steel industries were taken up as a priority industry for recovery. Governmental funds, steel and other inputs, including labour, food and clothing for labour were allocated with top priority to coal mining. The production of coal increased from a mere six million tons in 1945 to thirty million tons in 1947 and to fifty million tons in 1951.

The situation changed completely after the switch in policy toward the importation of oil in 1949. The change occurred because the price of coal was too high, and oil was more efficient in various uses. Perhaps also, the major international oil companies were interested in expanding markets in Japan. The coal industry changed to rationalisation and contraction under a law enacted in 1955, and amended in 1960. The law aimed at scrapping three million tons of old inefficient capacity and another twelve million tons later by using tariff revenue levied on imports of oil. The coal mining firms were confronted with strikes and other resistance from labourers who had to move to other jobs. The scrapping of old, inefficient mines was nevertheless rapidly accomplished during 1963 and 1964. The firms were keen to switch to other lines of activity because the superiority of oil to coal was obvious, and workers waited to find other jobs while the Japanese economy was growing dramatically.

A third example is the textile spinning industry. This industry was originally very capitalistic and depended little on government assistance before the war. It developed through the growth of small firms, their integration into big firms, the control of production through a cartel and the diversification of production from cotton to synthetic and chemical fibres. However, after the war, government intervention in spinning industries was introduced through the Textile Structural Adjustment Law of 1956, and the amended law of 1964 and 1967. Those laws aimed at scrapping old, inefficient spinning mills and building new, more efficient mills of optimum size. Governmental monies were provided as compensation for scrapping old spinning facilities. New spinning capacity was limited. But because of the superior efficiency of new capacity, the volume of production increased. In other words, the governmental assistance to the spinning industry contributed to increased production, to modernisation of the industry and to the strengthening of its international competitiveness, rather than to a reduction in production capacity and to the reallocation of resources to other industries. Since it consists of large firms, the spinning industry is more alert and adaptive to structural adjustment than smaller processing textile firms.

There is, as a fourth example, some experience in undertaking structural adjustment for small- and medium-sized firms, but this is a most difficult problem in Japan. Numerous adjustment assistance policies have been established. There are many laws, financial organisations, semi-governmental corporations and so on, specifically to assist the vast number of small- and medium-sized firms. They are perhaps too piecemeal, cumbersome and *ad hoc*, so that firms cannot make effective use of governmental assistance. They might well be better integrated into a single, comprehensive law and organisation. These policies intend to overcome the disadvantages or handicaps which, it is believed, small- and medium-sized firms have in comparison with large, modern firms. Their intention is to allow small- and medium-sized firms to survive, sometimes leading to their modernisation and rationalisation, but they are usually not assisted to move into growing industries. There is a tendency for new laws to be added to compensate unadaptable firms for whatever loss they suffer. For instance, the revaluation of the yen in December 1971 led to such legislation.

Other difficulties arise when a certain district is entirely specialised in producing specific export goods. For example, knives and forks are produced in the Tsubakuro area, and certain types of processed textiles in the Japan Sea districts. The problem is similar to that in agriculture. However there are good prospects for Japanese small- and medium-sized firms in establishing subsidiaries and joint ventures abroad, and moving to knowledge-intensive industries. The United States adjustment assistance policy is confined to curing unemployment caused by increases in imports, along the same lines as general unemployment insurance. Japan and other industrialised countries of Western Europe deal with the difficulties of business firms and works in a much broader and longer-term context. For them the adjustment problem is one of industrialisation and development. Such a broader but well-integrated policy is advisable since successful structural adjustment depends heavily upon the dynamic upgrading of the country's whole industrial structure.

Structural adjustment assistance policy for inefficient, declining industries should consist of two aspects.[16] The first is comprised of measures to promote the running down and transfer of inefficient industries to other sectors. For this purpose public infrastructural investment, low cost loans, investment grants and subsidies, tax benefits, technical assistance and training programmes, should be undertaken in a much more systematic way. Secondly, some safeguards for the gradual running down of inefficient protected industries are needed. But this safeguard should not be abused for protectionist purposes. It should assure the transfer out of inefficient industries. Therefore GATT Article XIX should include obligations to implement structural adjustment and to specify the duration within which the safeguard expires.[17]

There is one particular measure that would assist the adjustments desired. A fund for assisting structural adjustment should be established in every advanced country. This should become an international obligation similar to the one per cent of gross national product foreign aid target. A certain percentage (say, a half of one per cent) of gross national product could be collected through taxation for this purpose.[18] The fund should be used to eliminate uneconomic industries gradually and transfer factors of production to more productive activities where the advanced country enjoys a comparative advantage.

These funds would be more efficient than direct aid to developing countries, for they would serve to raise incomes and efficiency in developed countries as well as promoting industrialisation in the developing countries. From the point of view of advanced countries, there is a clear parallel between the reclamation of uneconomic industries suggested here and the urban renewal already widely undertaken by governments.

V AN INTEGRATED DEVELOPING COUNTRY POLICY

Trade preferences for developing countries are justifiable if divergence from the principle of non-discrimination within GATT is temporary, and if they foster liberalisation of world trade.[19] They are positively desirable if they encourage transformation in the international division of labour in such a way as to strengthen specialisation in the export of labour-intensive goods from developing countries. However, preferences alone may not bring about sufficient benefits. Aid and investment linked directly to preferential tariff and structural adjustment (an integrated aid, investment-*cum*-preference, structural adjustment policy) could offer more benefits to developing countries. First, directly productive aid and investment in the form of capital goods, advanced techniques of production, managerial knowhow and worker training should be provided to developing countries on an increasingly large scale if the efficiency of new export-oriented industries, primary as well as manufacturing, is to be improved to the point where they become increasingly competitive in world markets. Secondly, developed countries should provide preferential treatment to developing country export launched with the help of directly productive aid and investment, coupled with multinational firms' sales promotion. Preferences aimed at insuring wider markets would serve as a kind of aid and investment 'after-care', and might well be regarded as indispensable to realising the full benefits of aid and investment. It is important that the provision of preferences should be closely linked with the provision of aid and investment, since both are likely to be ineffective and wasteful of resources if applied independently. Thirdly, a receptive structural adjustment in advanced countries should be closely linked with the result of the aid and investment.

To conclude, structural adjustment to contract an inefficient sector, if it is done independently, is very difficult. It is most important for advanced countries to succeed in developing new growth sectors in which resources can be absorbed. In order to do this, specialisation and coordination in innovation in addition to prosperous horizontal trade in sophisticated new goods are most needed among advanced countries.

The policies of advanced countries for increasing exports of manufactured goods from developing countries should be such as to promote structural change on both sides, and the harmonious development of north-south trade. Thus, an integrated aid, investment-*cum*-preference, structural adjustment policy is required. Finally, it is clear that a large-scale aid, investment-*cum*-preference, structural adjustment scheme could be given more effect by a group of like-minded advanced countries. It is also desirable that aid giving and investment should be multinationalised, and freed as far as possible from bilateral tying. To realise these objectives, the possibilities for and advantages of closer cooperation among advanced countries in the Asian-Pacific region should be studied.

NOTES

1. Raymond Vernon, 'International Investment and International Trade in the Product Cycle', *Quarterly Journal of Economics*, LXXX, No. 2 (May 1966), pp. 190-207.
2. Kaname Akamatsu, 'A Historical Pattern of Economic Growth in Developing Countries', *The Developing Economies*, Tokyo, The Institute of Asian Economic Affairs, 1962, p. 11; *idem*, 'A Theory of Unbalanced Growth in the World Economy', *Weltwirtschaftliches Archiv*, 86, No. 2 (1961), pp. 205-8. This theory is widely recognised by now. For example, see Benjamin Higgins, *Economic Development: Problems, Principles and Policies*, rev. ed., New York, W. W. Norton, 1969, pp. 623-4; Miyohei

Shionohara, *Growth and Cycles in the Japanese Economic Development*, Tokyo, Kinokuniya Ltd., 1962, pp. 57-8; Christian Sautter, *Japan; Le Prix de la Puissance*, Editions du Seuil, Paris, 1973, pp. 233-51; William V. Rapp, 'A Theory of Changing Trade Patterns under Economic Growth: Tested for Japan', *Yale Economic Essays*, Fall 1967; *idem*, 'The Many Possible Extensions of Product Cycle Analysis', *Hitotsubashi Journal of Economics*, June 1975, pp. 22-9.

3. For example, Gary E. Hufbauer, *Synthetic Materials and the Theory of International Trade*, London, Gerald Duckworth and Co. Ltd., 1966.
4. Albert O. Hirschman, *The Strategy of Economic Development*, New Haven, Conn., Yale University Press, 1958, p. 121.
5. See Ippei Yamazawa, 'Industry Growth and Foreign Trade: A Study of Japan's Steel Industry', *Hitotsubashi Journal of Economics*, Feb. 1972; *idem*, 'Industrial Growth and Tariff Protection in Prewar Japan', (*Hitotsubashi Daigaku*) *Keizai Kenkyu*, 24, No. 1 (January 1973), pp. 23-34. indicates how such industries as computers, automobiles and steel in postwar Japan have developed in close cooperation between business and government.
6. The ten largest firms, in the 1970 fiscal year, handled $ 21.9 billion or 55.6 per cent of Japan's imports and exports.
7. Cf., Hal B. Lary, *Imports of Manufactures from Less Developed Countries*, New York, Columbia University Press, 1968.
8. Such a model is presented in Kiyoshi Kojima, 'Capital Accumulation and the Course of Industrialisation, with Special Reference to Japan', *Economic Journal*, LXX (December 1960), pp. 757-68.
9. Lester B. Pearson, *Partners in Development*, New York, Frederick A. Praeger, 1969, p. 18; the Tinbergen Report, Committee for Development Planning, *Preparation of Guidelines and Proposals for the Second United Nations Development Decade*, 1970, and UNCTAD III set even more ambitious targets.
10. The Japan Economic Research Centre, *The Future of World Economy and Japan*, February 1975, p. 13.
11. *Ibid*., p. 13.
12. US adjustment assistance policy is critically evaluated, and needed improvement is suggested by *US Foreign Economic Policy for the 1970s: A New Approach to New Realities*, National Planning Association, pamphlet no. 130, Washington, D.C., November 1971, pp. 194-211.
13. Michael Tracy, *Japanese Agriculture at the Crossroads*, London, Trade Policy Research Centre, 1972, p. 21.
14. *Ibid*., p. 25.
15. Cf. Nobuyoshi Namiki, 'The Japanese Economy – An Introduction to its Industrial Adjustment Problems', Kiyoshi Kojima, ed., *Structural Adjustments in Asian-Pacific Trade*, Japan Economic Research Centre, July 1973, pp. 241-81, reprinted in Hugh Corbet and Robert Jackson, eds., *In Search of a New-World Economic Order*, Croom Helm, London, 1974, pp. 70-106.
16. 'The optimum policy for bringing about the graceful retirement of uneconomic industries would be a "package" of subsidies to allow uncompetitive production to continue over the retirement period and of a cash grant to finance the closing down of productive capacity. Facilities should be provided, in addition, for the retraining and movement of redundant labour.' David Wall, *The Third World Challenge, Preference for Development*, London, The Atlantic Trade Policy, 1967, p. 51.
17. Gerald Curzon has proposed the adoption of an international adjustment assistance code. See Gerald Curzon and Victoria Curzon, *Global Assault*

on Nontariff Trade Barriers, Trade Policy Research Centre Thames Essays, No. 3, London, Ditchinling Press Ltd., 1972, p. 32.

18. See Kojima, *Japan and a Pacific Free Trade Area*, p. 125.

19. Where tariffs remain important, advanced countries ahould work towards the adoption of a system of value added tariffs on imports from less developed countries. Value added tariffs involve the levy of duties solely on that portion of the value of an imported commodity which is added to materials and components in the less developed country itself. This concession is important where manufacturing activity in less developed countries depends heavily on foreign capital equipment, and on parts and components imported from advanced countries. Value added tariffs would minimise the impact of tariff escalation in advanced countries, and encourage the migration of inefficient advanced country industrial capacity to efficient locations within less developed countries. United States Tariff Item 807 permits this kind of concession, although its terms are too restrictive. The Australian preference scheme for less developed countries can also be used to this effect. Japan has also recently extended value added tariff concessions to Korea on a limited number of items. Perhaps the most promising means of achieving generalisation of value added tariff systems is by negotiation among groups of interested countries. It is important to establish regional forums now through which these negotiations might take place.

(See, Kiyoshi Kojima, Saburo Okita and Peter Drysdale, 'Foreign Economic Relations', in *Southeast Asia's Economy in the 1970s*, London, Longman, 1971, pp. 297-9, and J. M. Finger, 'Tariff Provisions for Offshore Assembly and the Exports of Developing Countries', *Economic Journal*, June 1975, pp. 365-71.

8 ECONOMIC INTEGRATION IN THE ASIAN-PACIFIC REGION

I THE ORIGINAL PROPOSAL FOR A PACIFIC FREE TRADE AREA

The establishment of the European Economic Community was a major event of the 1960s. It has not only had a significant impact on international trade and investment but also wrought a profound change in world balance of economic power. The emergence of an enlarged European Community will have an even more profound influence in shaping the world of the 1970s. No country can ignore its existence and its policies.

Now, which free world countries are left outside the Eurobloc? They are mostly Pacific Basin countries: the United States, Canada, Japan, Australia, New Zealand and developing countries in Asia and Latin America. Is it not logical that these Pacific Basin countries should promote their economic integration, following the successful example of the European Community, in order to develop intensively this area of young and growing countries where there are plenty of resources and unlimited potentials as compared with an already well-developed Europe? Why should not the five Pacific advanced countries, the US, Canada, Japan, Australia and New Zealand, prepare for the formation of a Pacific Free Trade Area? Intensive economic development of a nation or a group of nations is a prerequisite to the growth and liberalisation of international trade. Could not the Eurobloc and a PAFTA be transformed into a world-wide Multilateral Free Trade Arrangement after a decade or so through measures similar to the dominant supplier authority in the US Trade Expansion Act of 1962? Thus both the Eurobloc and PAFTA could serve as useful routes toward global free trade.

It was this kind of double-faceted response to the emergence of the European Economic Community that led to the development of my original thoughts about Asian-Pacific economic integration and their presentation[1] at the International Conference on Measures for Trade Expansion of Developing Countries held on November 10-13 1965 in the Japan Economic Research Centre at Tokyo. My proposals set out two common aims for all the Pacific Basin countries.

Whether or not a Pacific Free Trade Area among the United States, Canada, Japan, Australia and New Zealand, is established, the transfer of markets in favour of Asian developing countries should be pursued since it could pose a quite promising improvement in the balance of trade and employment as well as national income of developing Asian countries. Moreover, it would be quite an economical and effective measure to support economic development of Asian countries and to promote trade between advanced Pacific countries and Asian developing countries.

Since structural adjustment and consolidated economic assistance are required for Pacific advanced countries, the establishment of a PAFTA is desired as a consolidated policy making body. Only with such an organisation can agreed measures be efficiently pursued and burdens shared. Moreover, due to the beneficial effects of tariff elimination and other indirect and dynamic effects, PAFTA countries would become more prosperous and expand their mutual trade in manufactured goods more rapidly. This would increase their trade with Asian developing countries and facilitate the structural adjustment required in relation to the latter.

It is hoped that the liberalisation of trade among advanced Pacific countries and, at the same time, the transfer of markets in favour of Asian developing countries will bring about a more optimal allocation of resources and a more prosperous trade in the Pacific and Asian region.[2]

I recall that the emphasis in my proposal at that time was upon the successful transformation and economic development of vast Asian developing countries. A slightly modified proposal with revised calculations of the effects of a Pacific Free Trade Area based on trade statistics in 1965 (instead of figures for 1963 used in the original proposal) was made in my book, *Japan and a Pacific Free Trade Area.*[3]

The Pacific ranks alongside Western Europe as one of the two major centres of world trade. Trade among the five advanced Pacific countries, the United States, Canada, Japan, Australia and New Zealand, increased by 96 per cent between 1958 and 1965, from $ US 9.16 billion to $ US 18.02 billion, and taken together their share in world trade rose from 7.99 per cent to 10.38 per cent. Trade within the EEC grew from $ US 6.86 billion to $ US 20.84 billion over the same period (see Tables 8.1-8.3).

Furthermore, mutual trade amongst advanced Pacific countries intensified over the years. Intra-area trade constituted 32.5 per cent of total Pacific country trade in 1958, but 37.3 per cent in 1965. In contrast, intra-area trade was 30.1 per cent of total EEC trade in 1958 and 43.5 per cent in 1965.

Table 8.1 Trade of PAFTA and EEC (in million dollars)

	Year	Intra-area exports	Total exports
PAFTA	1958	9161	28227
	1965	18022	48371
	1968	27959	64060
	1972	47615	105260
	1973	61935	144270
EEC	1958	6864	22776
	1965	20836	47916
	1968	28910	64200
	1972	61550	123580
	1973	83830	171560
World	1958		114704
	1965		173700
	1968		238680
	1972		408950
	1973		456880

Source: IMF, *Direction of Trade* and UN, *Monthly Bulletin of Statistics.*

Table 8.2 Extended Pacific trade and European trade (in million dollars)

	Year	Intra-area exports	Total exports
Extended Pacific trade	1958	23356	43138
	1965	37711	67150
	1968	60850	96150
	1972	90840	142120
	1973	129211	199540
European trade	1958	22228	41699
	1965	51158	79520
	1968	64710	101500
	1972	128180	187960
	1973	177160	257340

Source: IMF, *Direction of Trade* and UN, *Monthly Bulletin of Statistics.*

Table 8.3 Trade of Pacific Basin countries (in million dollars; figures in parentheses are ratios to total export)

	Year	PAFTA		Asia and Latin America		Total exports
US	1958	4504	(25.2)	5457	(30.5)	17904
	1965	8488	(31.0)	6440	(23.5)	27400
	1968	11860	(34.6)	9250	(27.0)	34230
	1972	17970	(36.7)	10970	(22.4)	48970
	1973	24670	(35.1)	16410	(23.4)	70220
Canada	1958	3200	(63.0)	329	(6.5)	5082
	1965	5132	(60.1)	392	(4.6)	8534
	1968	9295	(74.0)	644	(5.1)	12560
	1972	14885	(75.6)	1025	(5.2)	19700
	1973	19180	(76.1)	1300	(5.2)	25210
Japan	1958	839	(29.2)	1071	(37.2)	2877
	1965	3112	(36.8)	2592	(30.7)	8152
	1968	4960	(38.2)	4670	(36.0)	12970
	1972	11000	(38.4)	7090	(24.7)	28650
	1973	12020	(32.5)	11620	(31.4)	36970
Oceania (Australia & New Zealand)	1958	617	(26.1)	170	(7.2)	2364
	1965	1289	(32.3)	366	(9.2)	3985
	1968	1844	(42.9)	496	(11.5)	4300
	1972	3760	(47.4)	890	(11.2)	7940
	1973	6065	(51.1)	1375	(11.6)	11870
Asia*	1958	1869	(27.7)	2228	(33.0)	6756
	1965	2966	(34.5)	1431	(16.6)	8600
	1968	6927	(34.8)	4920	(21.6)	19900
	1972	7335	(44.7)	3385	(20.6)	16420
	1973	14740	(48.5)	6725	(22.1)	30390
Latin America	1958	3876	(47.5)	765	(9.4)	8155
	1965	4424	(42.5)	1075	(10.3)	10400
	1968	5072	(41.6)	1542	(12.6)	12190
	1972	8875	(43.4)	3655	(17.9)	20440
	1973	10336	(41.5)	4770	(19.2)	24880

* Asia includes countries in South and Southeast Asia, east of Pakistan and excludes China.

Source: IMF, *Direction of Trade* and UN, *Monthly Bulletin of Statistics.*

The formation of a Pacific Free Trade Area would, in fact, bring about a comprehensive trade liberalisation amongst participating countries, with the elimination of tariffs on a substantial proportion of their commodity trade. The impact effect of Pacific tariff elimination would be to increase trade by $ US 5,000 million. This represents an expansion of 28 per cent on intra-area trade, or 10.3 per cent on Pacific country exports to, and 11.9 per cent on imports from the whole world. In other words, there would be a significant trade expansion, a far greater trade expansion than can be expected under Kennedy Round tariff reductions, which will probably lead only to a 5.5 per cent increase in exports and a 7.7 per cent increase in imports.

Complete regional trade liberalisation would appear to have considerable advantages over partial trade liberalisation in world markets. This is especially true if, as is most probable, another major round of global tariff reductions is not feasible within the next ten or twenty years. In that event, the formation of PAFTA would seem an effective alternative for mutual trade expansion among the five advanced Pacific countries.[4,5]

Economic integration in the Pacific should take the form of a free trade area rather than a customs union or political union. A free trade area arrangement would have advantages over the alternatives from several points of view: it is consistent with the rules of the General Agreement on Tariffs and Trade; it preserves the autonomy of members with respect to their tariff policies *vis-à-vis* non-participants; and it is a purely commercial arrangement, carrying no obligation for eventual political federation of union.[6]

Concerning Asian developing countries, on the other hand, according to our estimates, imports from Asian developing countries would increase by $ US 425 million in the United States, $ US 27 million in Canada, $ US 50 million in Japan, $ US 58 million in Australia, $ US 11 million in New Zealand, and $ US 571 million in the five countries taken together, accounting for 16 per cent of their imports from Asian developing countries in 1965. This is not a large sum. For the five countries, the estimated increase in imports would be $ US 44 million on food, $ US 32 million in raw materials, $ US 371 million in light manufactures, and $ US 124 million in heavy manufactures.

These estimates suggest that the liberalisation of trade and free market access for Asian developing countries' products would not help much to foster their trade growth. Besides the liberalisation of trade, stronger measures for widening markets through structural adjustment in the advanced Pacific countries themselves and for assistance in increasing the export capacity of Asian developing countries would be necessary. These stronger measures could not be pursued unless consolidated action was made possible through the establishment of PAFTA.[7]

If the five Pacific countries were to establish PAFTA, they should welcome as associated members those developing countries in Asia and Latin America who wish to join. Or, they might provide PAFTA preferential tariffs in favour of the developing countries. Moreover, the five Pacific countries should provide more effective assistance on a larger scale to foster structural adjustment within their own economies in order to open wider markets for developing country exports.[8]

A more pragmatic step toward Pacific economic integration was suggested: before the establishment of PAFTA, several steps towards closer Pacific economic cooperation might be practicable immediately. Five main objectives suggest themselves:

1. To increase the flow of financial resources from the United States to other Pacific countries, as well as to Asian and Latin American developing countries.

2. To stimulate horizontal trade among the five advanced Pacific countries in heavy manufactures and chemicals and to expand production and trade of raw materials and intermediate goods more efficiently for the region as a whole.

3. To readjust production and trade in agricultural commodities among the five Pacific countries, taking into consideration their relationship with Asian and Latin American developing countries.

4. To readjust production and trade in light manufactures, which are labour-intensive, with the aim of providing greater access for Asian and Latin American countries in advanced country markets.

5. To coordinate the aid policy of the five advanced Pacific countries towards Asian and Latin American developing countries.

Practical steps towards closer Pacific economic cooperation can be taken by strengthening *functional*, rather than *institutional* integration, and thus attempting to attain the favourable benefits of a free trade area whilst avoiding the unfavourable impact effects. To realise these objectives, I suggest the initiation of three codes of international behaviour and the formation of two new regional institutions.

1. *A code of good conduct* in the field of trade policy should be promulgated under which countries would relinquish the right to raise tariffs or impose other forms of trade restriction, and would

gradually reduce those trade barriers particularly on the import of agricultural products and labour-intensive light manufactures.

2. *A code of overseas investment* to promote mutual investment among the five advanced Pacific countries, most effectively from the United States, and to foster the activity of joint ventures is much needed to promote trade expansion, especially horizontal trade expansion in heavy manufactures, and for the development of the vast mineral resources of the Pacific region. A code which minimises the fear of American capital domination and maximises protection for America's balance of payments would greatly facilitate overseas investment and the better allocation of regional resources.

3. *A code of aid and trade policies towards associated developing countries* is also required, so that Asian and Latin American countries might enjoy the benefits of larger markets for their agricultural products and light manufactures. The flow of developmental aid must be increased, appropriate aid projects selected, and domestic industrial structures adjusted to meet the legitimate trade needs of affiliated less developed countries.

An *Organisation for Pacific Trade and Development* (OPTAD) should be established in order to give effect to these codes of international behaviour. Its main features would be similar to those of the OECD, and it could be structured in the same way, with three committees on trade, investment and aid.

Further, a *Pacific Currency Area* and *Pacific Reserve and Development Bank* would be established with the aim of strengthening the international monetary system and facilitating economic development within the Pacific, Asian and Latin American regions.[9]

II RESPONSES TO THE PAFTA PROPOSAL

A decade has passed since I first proposed the idea of Pacific Free Trade Area. The response has been cautious in the sense that no concrete step towards institutional integration has been undertaken, but enormous attention has been paid to the proposal and functional integration has actually been intensified along the lines I suggested.

There are various reasons why the countries concerned in the Pacific Basin have been cool towards institutional regional integration. First, they tended to prefer a multilateral approach and negotiation through the GATT, IMF, UNCTAD, etc., and expected too much gain from such negotiations. Moreover the changes and chaos in the world economic order after the middle 1960s have been so rapid and serious that Pacific Basin countries have been preoccupied with accommodating to the changes, and have hesitated to take positive steps towards institutional integration.

Second, the estimate that the gains from tariff elimination would not be equally distributed among the five Pacific advanced countries involved, might have created antagonism rather than consensus towards the formation of PAFTA. It was estimated that Japan's exports would increase by $ US 1,740 million, or 56 per cent on her total exports to PAFTA countries, and her imports by $ US 430 million, or 14.7 per cent on her total imports from PAFTA countries.[10] Japan's trade balance with the Pacific, which was roughly in equilibrium in 1965, would have consequently improved by $ US 1,310 million. United States exports were estimated to increase by $ US 2,300 million, or 27.9 per cent, and imports by $ US 2,280 million, or 30.1 per cent, and the favourable balance in United States trade with the Pacific, of about $ US 850 million in 1965, would have been preserved. On the other hand, imports were estimated to rise more rapidly than exports for the remaining three countries. Canada's exports were estimated to increase by $ US 855 million but her imports would have risen by $ US 1,480 million; Australia's exports were estimated to increase by $ US 65 million, whereas her imports would have risen by $ US 650 million; and New Zealand's exports were estimated to grow by $ US 22 million, while her imports would have risen by $ US 140 million.[11] (See Table 8.4.)

The big gains for Japan from the establishment of PAFTA derive, firstly, from the fact that Japan's exports depend as much as 37 per cent upon the PAFTA markets. Compared with other PAFTA countries, European markets are not so important (13 per cent) for Japan.

Secondly, about 95 per cent of Japan's exports to other Pacific countries are manufactures which would have enjoyed a greater expansion from trade liberalisation, while about 71 per cent of Japan's imports are primary products, which would not have increased very much in consequence of tariff reductions.

If the time came for Japan to consider economic integration, a Pacific Free Trade Area would have certainly been her best choice. Japan is destined by geography to participate in political arrangements in the Pacific rather than in Europe. On the other hand, economic integration without the United States, which holds a 30 per cent share in Japan's trade, would have appeared a less attractive choice.

Thus, Japan would have benefited from the establishment of PAFTA, or from some other alternative, through the cheaper import of raw materials and other primary products, the expansion of her exports of

Table 8.4 Static effects of the formation of PAFTA

(a) Value of increase (million US dollars) (Base year = 1965)

		a USA	b Canada	c Japan	d Australia	e N. Z.	Pacific countries
a. United States	ΔX	–	1404.6	404.4	426.3	66.4	2301.7
	ΔM	–	791.5	1457.5	23.6	10.5	2283.2
	ΔX – ΔM	–	613.1	–1053.1	402.7	55.9	18.5
b. Canada	ΔX	791.5	–	17.2	39.5	7.2	855.4
	ΔM	1404.6	–	75.9	0.2	0.1	1480.8
	ΔX – ΔM	–613.1	–	– 58.7	39.3	7.1	–625.4
c. Japan	ΔX	1457.5	75.9	–	176.7	33.0	1743.1
	ΔM	404.4	17.2	–	7.6	3.5	430.7
	ΔX – ΔM	1033.1	58.7	–	169.1	29.5	1312.4
d. Australia	ΔX	23.6	0.2	7.6	–	33.2	64.5
	ΔM	426.3	39.5	216.2	–	8.1	650.6
	ΔX – ΔM	–402.7	–39.3	–208.6	–	25.1	–586.1
e. New Zealand	ΔX	10.5	0.1	3.4	8.1	–	22.1
	ΔM	66.4	7.2	33.0	33.2	–	139.7
	ΔX – ΔM	–55.9	–7.1	–29.6	–25.1	–	–117.6
Pacific countries	ΔX						4986.8
	X						18021.7

(b) Rate of increase (per cent) in trade due to the elimination of tariffs

		a USA	b Canada	c Japan	d Australia	e N. Z.	Pacific countries
a. United States	ΔX/X	–	26.06	19.85	61.48	53.13	27.92
	ΔM/M	–	17.03	58.59	7.24	8.56	30.10
b. Canada	ΔX/X	17.03	–	5.86	29.79	20.95	16.74
	ΔM/M	26.06	–	35.43	0.44	0.94	26.17
c. Japan	ΔX/X	58.59	35.43	–	50.25	54.17	55.97
	ΔM/M	19.83	5.86	–	1.37	7.02	14.69
d. Australia	ΔX/X	7.24	0.44	1.37	–	17.13	5.79
	ΔM/M	61.48	29.79	61.48	–	18.95	53.32
e. New Zealand	ΔX/X	8.56	0.94	6.85	18.95	–	9.76
	ΔM/M	53.14	20.95	54.17	17.13	–	33.77
Pacific countries	ΔX/X						27.67

Source: Kiyoshi Kojima, *Japan and a Pacific Free Trade Area*, p. 91.

light manufactures, and the promotion of horizontal trade in heavy manufactures and chemicals.

Thirdly, as already mentioned, the liberalisation of trade among the five advanced Pacific countries and free market access for Asian developing countries' products would not, as estimated, have helped much to foster their trade growth. They were inclined to feel that PAFTA would create another rich man's club and bring about little favourable effects to developing countries.

It is worth remembering that my estimate concerned only the static effect of tariff elimination among the five advanced Pacific countries. PAFTA's aim should be that of larger, broader and more dynamic trading. Tariff reductions would only be the beginning. Take, for instance, natural resources and markets in the vast Pacific area. Agriculture, extractive industries, processing industries and various manufacturing industries could be located in places best suited to the development and efficiency of the area as a whole. Development of each country in the area could be promoted greatly by the realisation of more optimal specialisation and scale. Transfer of capital, technology and management skill could be encouraged specially by more active direct investment, resulting in increases in regional productivity.

The divergence in benefits from the static effects of tariff elimination, and thus in reactions to the proposal, derives from the fact that the Pacific Basin, including Asian and Latin American developing countries, consists of many diverse economies. Political and cultural conditions differ: some countries are well endowed with natural resources; others are poor; still others are too small or too big, and there are large gaps in the level of industrialisation.

This makes the hasty establishment of institutional integration in the Pacific more difficult compared with the more or less homogeneous, highly industrialised economies in Western Europe.

The differential pattern of gains depends principally upon whether the country's exports are more or less heavily concentrated in manufactures, and suggests a need for fostering further industrialisation in Canada, Australia, New Zealand and developing countries especially. Indeed, the pursuit of this objective would be facilitated through the dynamic effects of establishing a larger and completely free regional market, and through the freer movement of capital, technical know-how and managerial skills among member countries. The most important fact to be noted, however, is that the expansion of intra-area trade would be larger if the five countries could effect tariff elimination.

At this stage, the PAFTA proposal still seems premature, unless there is some further unforeseen disturbance in the free world economy. It is as yet neither economically nor politically feasible. Firstly, American interests remain world-wide and the United States could not participate readily either in a Pacific or a European regional grouping. For the moment the United States appears committed to a global non-discriminatory approach to freer trade.[12]

Secondly, the five Pacific countries still lack the solidarity and degree of integration that would be necessary for dispensing with protective measures for the main sectors of their economies involved in regional trade – the labour-intensive industries in some countries, the agricultural and pastoral industries in other countries.[13]

Thirdly, the static gains from complete trade liberalisation would differ widely from one country to another because of the disparity in stages of industrialisation within the region.

These comments suggest, first, that any institutional integration in the vast Pacific region even of the simplest form is premature under the present circumstances, and only functional integration should be fostered as a prerequisite towards future institutional integration.

Under these circumstances, the suggestion that bilateral government-to-government consultations and negotiations should be developed within the framework of an Organisation for Pacific Trade, Aid and Development, would appear sound. OPTAD could be developed along similar lines to OECD, that is, not as a regulatory agency but as a place where government-to-government consultations could take place. Although this is already a function of OECD, Japan, Australia, the United States and Canada, are the four leading nations out of a total OECD membership of thirty-two and thus there would appear to be considerable advantages in having a smaller scale regional organisation to deal with problems of a more regional nature.[14] It is also desirable to establish a Pacific Policy Committee to study and promote practical means of achieving those objectives.[15]

Second, instead of the simultaneous institutional integration of all countries over a vast area, a limited number of countries comprising the more homogeneous economies should initiate and promote institutional integration. This is a realistic approach following the example of the establishment of BENELUX prior to the EEC.

The Canada-United States Automotive Agreement, which took effect from January 1965, should be given much attention as a pioneer project in selective industrial integration.[16] The Australia-New Zealand

Free Trade Agreement was initiated in January 1966,[17] and could be the foundation for Western Pacific economic integration in the future.

Besides the small Central American Economic Union, there is a large but loose Latin American Free Trade Area, and the more homogeneous and tightly-knit Andean Pact has emerged since 1969 alongside Mexico, Brazil and Argentine, the three giants in Latin America.

In Asia, ASEAN (the Association of Southeast Asian Nations) which consists of the Philippines, Indonesia, Singapore, Malaysia and Thailand, already has a long history (since 1961 if its predecessor is taken into consideration), but has remained a soft political and cultural forum. Recently because of the great changes in the Indochina situation, those countries may need to take a step forward towards stronger integration.

Similarly, there would be sufficient basis for the Northeast Asian countries (North and South Korea, Taiwan and Hong Kong), independently of mainland China, to act as a culturally and economically united group. The two groups have different racial and cultural backgrounds. In economic terms, the ASEAN group is better endowed with natural resources while the Northeast Asian Group has to rely overwhelmingly on the production and export of manufactures but actually has achieved a higher level of industrialisation. There are hopes for the harmonious development of vertical trade between the two groups.

With regard to the Big Three, the United States, Russia and China, the Northeast Asian countries of Japan, South Korea, North Korea, Taiwan and Hong Kong are all in the same boat and share the same fate. And including China, they are all of the same Mongolian race.[18] With these common features as a basis one may expect to see a Northeast Asian economic integration forged; indeed, this is the only path for the economic future of North and South Korea, Taiwan and Hong Kong.

Much attention to proposals for Pacific trade expansion has been paid by business and academic circles. The Pacific Basin Economic Cooperation Committee was established among business circles in the five Pacific countries in April 1967; and a number of bilateral cooperative activities have also been promoted within business circles. The committee has expanded since 1975 so as to include developing country members.

It is also worth noting that Mr Takeo Miki, Japan's former Foreign Minister and present Prime Minister, and Mr Kiichi Miyazawa, the present Foreign Minister are keenly interested in promoting economic cooperation in the Pacific and Asian region. Academic circles have also begun to probe hard the foundations for economic integration in this region.[19]

III PROSPECTS FOR PACIFIC ECONOMIC INTEGRATION

During the past ten years, since my first study on Pacific economic integration in 1966, many changes have occurred in the international, political and economic environment. Each time a shock was felt from outside the five Pacific countries, the necessity for closer Pacific integration was felt more seriously.

The first major event was the establishment of the European Economic Community in 1958, the completion of its internal tariff elimination in 1968, its enlargement to include the UK, Ireland and Denmark in 1973, and further extension enveloping the ACP (Africa, Caribbean and Pacific) nations through the Lomé Treaty of 1975. The successful economic growth of the EEC – which may not have been entirely a consequence of its institutional integration – holds lessons for other areas.

Second, the multilateral approach through the GATT and the IMF to the liberalisation and expansion of world trade and to the stabilisation of the international monetary system and inflation has been not only disappointing to those countries which preferred this approach, but has also brought in its train disorder and uncertainty, mainly due to the relative decline in the hegemony of the American economy in the world. In the post-Kennedy Round era much of the impetus to liberalise international trade further has been lost, although a new Tokyo round of multilateral trade negotiations in GATT was initiated by the Declaration of Ministers approved in Tokyo, September 1973. After a lengthy wait for authorisation of the US Trade Act of 1974, the negotiations resumed in early February 1975. Despite Nixon's New Economic Policy of August 1971, the international monetary and trade system remains confused and no sound new world economic order is anticipated to emerge in the future.

It should be noted that the growth of intra-area trade in the EEC exceeded that in the five Pacific advanced countries. Trade among the five advanced countries (the US, Canada, Japan, Australia and New Zealand), or PAFTA trade, in brief, increased by 97 per cent between 1958 and 1965 whereas the EEC trade tripled. Between 1965 and 1973, the former increased 3.4 times and the latter 4.0 times. The ratio of intra-area trade for PAFTA increased from 32.5 per cent in 1958 to 37.3 per cent in 1965 and to 42.9 per cent in 1973. In contrast, the similar ratios for the EEC were 30.1 per cent in 1958, 43.5

per cent in 1965, and 48.9 per cent in 1973.[20] (See Table 8.1.) The lag in Pacific trade growth must be of great concern in so far as it was brought about by the lack of institutional integration.

Third, the problems of the developing countries have become more serious. Although economic growth has been fairly rapid in their own terms, the gap between developing and advanced industrial countries widened. Most advanced countries have tended to neglect this difficult problem paying only lip service to development goals and trying to solve the problem of world economic order within advanced countries alone. Multilateral approaches through UNCTAD have been largely in vain. The oil crisis (the export cutbacks by OPEC countries in October 1973, a four-fold rise in price, and nationalisation of the major oil production facilities), is one example of rebellion by developing countries against the neglect of advanced capitalist countries. The oil crisis exacerbated, however, the difficulties of many other developing countries. Advanced countries too became seriously concerned about the security of national resource supplies.

Fourth, the emergence of China in the international economic society will have a profound impact.[21] A fact that also should not be ignored is that the USSR is greatly interested in Pacific economic integration in connection with the development of Siberia.[22] Latin American countries which were treated only briefly in my original paper have increased their interest in Pacific economic integration.[23]

Now, a new world economic order is being earnestly sought.[24] One of the most realistic plans is tripolar coordination, between North America, Western Europe and Japan, the three major powers in the Western capitalist world. The international monetary system could be stabilised and world trade further liberalised and expanded through closer and conscious cooperation of these three powers.[25] In so far as tripolar coordination is the key for a new world economic order, the Japanese economy must become more internationalised and create a strong basis of interdependence with neighbouring countries in the Western Pacific. Only then can she rank alongside North America and Western Europe as an equal partner.

The United States alone is a huge economy accounting for more than one third of the capitalist world's national income, and is integrated with the Canadian economy. The dollar is still the most important international currency and is widely circulated throughout the world. The original EEC or the enlarged EEC is also a huge economic unit and even the West German economy is strong and prosperous because it is not alone but integrated with the EEC. The EEC may establish common European currency by 1980, which would make a bipolar key currency system with the dollar more workable. Compared with these two blocs, the Japanese economy is aloof from neighbouring countries and the yen is not yet an international currency. International circulation of the yen is still limited. It is quite logical for Japan to recognise that economic integration in the Western Pacific region is valuable.

The original form of the proposal for Western Pacific economic integration between Japan, Australia and New Zealand (JANFTA) will now be examined.[26] In 1965 the total population of Japan, Australia and New Zealand was approximately 115 million, which is 35 million less than the population of the European Economic Community immediately prior to its formation. In 1965 Australia's Gross National Product was $ US 21,587 million, Japan's GNP $ US 84,324 million and New Zealand's GNP $ US 3,933 million giving a GNP for the entire area in 1965 of approximately $ US 110,000 million. On a per capita basis the relevant figures are Australia $ US 1,900, Japan $ US 861 and New Zealand $ US 1,490 which give an average per capita income for the area as a whole of $ US 981. In real terms this figure compared favourably with that of the EEC countries in 1965.[27]

Since the enforcement of the Australia-New Zealand Free Trade Agreement in January 1966, the two countries have endeavoured to promote economic integration but with some difficulty because the lack of fundamental complementarity and the small size of both economies prevents realisation of economies of scale. It is expected that closer union with a large complementary economy like Japan, would make Western Pacific integration more successful and fruitful. Thus, the gains from trade liberalisation among the three countries and the feasibility of sectoral integration in such key industries as motor vehicles, iron and steel, non-ferrous metals (especially aluminium), and meat and dairy products have been explored.[28]

The negotiability of a free trade area among these countries faces two main problems: firstly, the existing Japanese policies of agricultural protection, and secondly, Australian and New Zealand policies of protection for their manufacturing industries. Moreover, while JANFTA could be of considerable benefit to the Australian and New Zealand economies, the small increase in the size of Japan's market deriving from such a free trade union, diminishes the importance of the benefits.

The formation of a free trade area or the alternative of closer economic cooperation among Australia, New Zealand and Japan is important from two points of view. First, it would accelerate economic growth, based upon the highly complementary nature of the three economies, and it would strengthen their capacity to export to third countries outside the area, especially to North American and Western European markets. It would also be useful for the three countries to develop a negotiating bloc for obtaining concessions on a broader front, especially from the United States. A free trade area between these three countries is justifiable and necessary as a means of preparing a favourable position for their joining, or for their providing a jolt towards the formation of, a Pacific Free Trade Area or a wider free trade area among almost all industrial nations.

Secondly, closer cooperation between Australia, New Zealand and Japan is especially desirable in order to increase aid to and to facilitate trade growth with neighbouring Asian developing countries in which the three countries are greatly interested and commonly involved.

This proposal should be considered anew by taking into account changes in the international political and economic environment in the past ten years. Western Pacific economic integration need not in the first instance take the form of an institutional integration such as a Free Trade Area, but could be a built-in functional integration which would be the core of wider Pacific integration and leave room to develop interdependent relations with Southeast Asia, Northeast Asia, China and Russia, as well as the USA and Western Europe.

Japan, Australia (and New Zealand), three countries that have reached much the same high economic level (measured for example by national income per head) are situated at the northern and southern extremities of an area which includes the developing countries of Northeast and Southeast Asia. As the development of the European Community shows, no single country can have stable international relations and economic prosperity unless it is surrounded by countries of similar economic capacity with which it can develop horizontal (or intra-industry) specialisation in all fields of the economy and achieve a relationship of indissoluble interdependence. The same is true for Japan and Australia. Hence Japan and Australia should not only seek economic development by promoting their mutual interdependence but they should also cooperate closely in promoting the economic development and industrialisation of neighbouring developing countries through official aid, private investment, the transfer of technology and exchange of persons (one could ask how far the sphere of neighbouring countries should be extended, but I am thinking here mainly of Southeast Asia and Northeast Asia including China). The final objective should be to raise the incomes of these developing countries to Japanese and Australian levels.

We need to devise practical methods of Australian-Japanese economic cooperation to achieve this objective. A detailed plan must be the subject of future research.[29] Australia is naturally most concerned with its nearest neighbours such as Papua New Guinea, Indonesia, Singapore, Malaysia and Thailand. Administering development assistance in collaboration with Japan in this area would raise its efficiency. Japan on the other hand is interested in a wide area stretching from Northeast Asia (North and South Korea, Taiwan, Hong Kong and China) to the countries of Southeast Asia and here too it would be both politically and economically desirable to have Australian participation in her development aid.

The way to raise economic levels in these neighbouring developing countries is to transfer industry in stages, mainly through direct investment, beginning with labour-intensive industries such as textiles and moving on to some intermediate goods production, with Japan and Australia importing the products. This would present the neighbouring countries with opportunities for increasingly sophisticated industrial activity and expand their horizontal trade with Japan and Australia. This is based on the same principles as our advocacy of horizontal specialisation between Japan and Australia. It is necessary for Japan and Australia to spread the network of intra-industry specialisation over a wider area to include the developing countries of the region.

Japan and Australia now have the possibility of directly or indirectly applying oil money to long-term production-oriented investment in these developing countries. Following the oil crisis, the non-oil-producing developing countries are facing critical difficulties, and the provision of development aid through cooperation with Japan and Australia is a task of vital importance.

The key problem in fostering Western Pacific economic integration is how to harmonise interests between large and small economies. This is applicable even to a relationship between Japan and Australia and it is more serious in the relationship between Japan and other neighbouring countries. Therefore, the pursuit of subregional integration such as ASEAN or Northeast Asian group is to be welcomed. The principles for integration among economies which are unequal in size and stage of development may be different from those dealt with in the traditional theory of integration dealing with economies which are on a more or less equal footing. A new type of integration may be fostered through the establishment of horizontal (or intra-industry) specialisation. Foreign direct investment may have an important role to play in the development of horizontal specialisation.

NOTES

1. Kiyoshi Kojima and Hiroshi Kurimoto, 'A Pacific Economic Community and Asian Developing Countries', in *Measures for Trade Expansion of Developing Countries*, Japan Economic Research Centre, October 1966, pp. 93-134. Reprinted in *Hitotsubashi Journal of Economics*, June 1966, pp. 17-37.
2. *Ibid*., p. 33.
3. Kiyoshi Kojima, *Japan and a Pacific Free Trade Area*, Macmillan, London, 1971, Chaps. 3 and 7.
4. *Ibid*., pp. 165-6.
5. The effects of trade liberalisation in PAFTA was confirmed by Bruce W. Wilkinson, 'A Re-Estimation of the Effects of the Formation of a Pacific Area Free Trade Agreement', Kiyoshi Kojima, ed., *Pacific Trade and Development II*, Japan Economic Research Centre, April 1969, pp. 53-101.
6. *Japan and a Pacific Free Trade Area*, p. 167.
7. *Ibid*., p. 98.
8. *Ibid*., p. 171.
9. *Ibid*., pp. 168-9.
10. These gains would be far greater than in the case of global tariff reductions on the scale undertaken through the Kennedy Round, which are likely to increase Japan's exports by a mere 8.8 per cent.
11. *Ibid*., pp. 90-1.
12. See, for example, Sperry Lea, 'The Future Shape of US Trade Policy: Multilateral or Free Trade Approaches?', Kiyoshi Kojima, ed., *Paciifc Trade and Development, II*, The Japan Economic Research Centre, April 1969.
13. A comment opposing PAFTA is made by H. W. Arndt, 'PAFTA: An Australian Assessment', *Intereconomics*, Hamburg, October 1967 (reprinted in *A Small Rich Industrial Country, Studies in Australian Development, Aid and Trade*, Melbourne, 1968), to which there is a reply by Kiyoshi Kojima, 'A Pacific Free Trade Area: Reconsidered', *Intereconomics*, March 1968. There also exists a favourable Australian view of PAFTA, for example, Peter Drysdale, 'Pacific Economic Integration, An Australian View', Kiyoshi Kojima, ed., *Pacific Trade and Development*, The Japan Economic Research Centre, February 1968.
14. J. G. Crawford and G. H. Board, 'Japan's Trade Policy and Trade in Temperate Zone Agricultural Products', in H. E. English and Keith Hay, eds., *Obstacles to Trade in the Pacific Area*, Carleton University, Ottawa, 1972, pp. 39-40.
15. Communique of the Fourth Pacific Trade and Development Conference, Ottawa, 10 October 1971, in *Obstacles to Trade in the Pacific Area*, pp. iv-vi.
16. See Sperry Lea, 'Free Trade by Sector', NPA, *Looking Ahead*, September 1966.
17. F. W. Holmes, 'Australia and New Zealand in the World Economy', *The Economic Record*, March 1967.
18. There is an interesting observation by Edwin O. Reischauer, 'The Sinic

World in Perspective', a paper presented to the Williamsburg III Conference, Hakone, Japan, November 1973, that the Mongolian race may establish a cultural solidarity.

19. A series of six conferences on Pacific Trade and Development have been held: Kiyoshi Kojima, ed., *Pacific Trade and Development*, Japan Economic Research Centre, February 1968; Kiyoshi Kojima, ed., *Pacific Trade and Development, II*, Japan Economic Research Centre, April 1969; Peter Drysdale, ed., *Direct Foreign Investment in Asia and the Pacific*, Australian National University Press, Canberra, 1972; H. E. English and Keith Hay, ed., *Obstacles to Trade in the Pacific Area*, Carleton University, Ottawa, 1972; Kiyoshi Kojima, ed., *Structural Adjustments in the Asian-Pacific Trade*, Japan Economic Research Centre, August 1973; Kiyoshi Kojima and Miguel S. Wionczek, eds., *Technology Transfer in Pacific Economic Development*, Japan Economic Research Centre, January 1975.

The Japan Institute of International Affairs has continued the study headed by Saburo Okita and Kiyoshi Kojima, on the Asian Pacific Economic Region and published three volumes (in Japanese) in 1971, 1973 and 1975. Also the Institute of Developing Economies promoted a study which led to the publication of Seiya Yano, ed., *Studies on a Pacific Economic Region* (in Japanese), 1971.

The Japan Economic Research Centre undertook a Japanese-Australian Research Project in cooperation with a group working from the Australian National University, and has published three volumes (in both Japanese and English) of *Studies on Western Pacific Economic Region*, in 1973, 1974 and 1975. The Australian side has also published several papers.

Much interest has arisen in the USA including, among others, Harald B. Malmgren, *Pacific Basin Development: the American Interest*, published for the Overseas Development Council, Lexington Books, 1972; Jerome B. Cohen, *Pacific Partnership: United States-Japan Trade*, Japan Society, Inc., 1972; Richard Kosobud and Houton Stockes, 'Trade Peace in the Pacific Through a Free Trade Area?', *Journal of International Affairs*, Vol. 28, No. 1, 1974; William Diebold, Jr., *The United States and Industrial World: American Foreign Economic Policy in the 1970s*, published for the Council on Foreign Relations by Praeger, New York, 1972; Allen Taylor, ed., *Perspectives on US-Japan Economic Relations*, Ballinger Publishing Co., Cambridge, Mass., 1973; Keith A. Hay, *Japan: Challenge and Opportunity for Canadian Industry*, The Private Planning Association of Canada, 1971.

20. See, for example, Jean Royer, 'Greater European Economic Integration', Kiyoshi Kojima, ed., *Structural Adjustments in Asian-Pacific Trade*, Japan Economic Research Centre, July 1973.

21. See, for example, Shigeru Ishikawa, 'The Impact of the Emergence of China on Asian Pacific Trade', Kiyoshi Kojima, ed., *Structural Adjustments in Asian Pacific Trade*, Japan Economic Research Centre, July 1973.

22. See, for example, M. Maximova, *Economic Aspects of Capitalist Integration*, Progress Publishers, Moscow, 1973. V. Yakubovsky, 'Emergence of the Pacific Economic Complex and Some Aspects of the Economic Relations between the Societ Union and the Pacific Countries', and L. A. Lebedev, 'Integration Tendencies in Pacific Asia and External Economic Relations of the USSR', both in Kiyoshi Kojima and Miguel S. Wionczek, eds., *Technology Transfer in Pacific Economic Development*, Japan Economic Research Centre, January 1975.

23. For example, Chile held a big international conference on the Pacific at Vina del Mar from 27 September to 3 October 1970.

24. C. Fred Bergsten, *The Future of the International Economic Order: An Agenda for Research*, A Report to the Ford Foundation, Lexington Books, 1973; C. Fred Bergsten, ed., *Toward a New World Trade Policy: The Maidenhead Papers*, Lexington Books, 1975; Hugh Corbet and Robert Jackson, eds., *In Search of a New World Economic Order*, Croom Helm, London, 1974; Richard N. Cooper, ed., *A Reordered World: Emerging International Economic Problems*, A Potomac Associations Book, 1973; The Commission on International Trade and Investment Policy, *United States International Economic Policy in an Interdependent World*, Washington, D.C., July 1971; NPA Advisory Committee, *US Foreign Economic Policy for the 1970s: A New Approach to New Realities*, NPA, 1971; OECD, *Policy Perspective for International Trade and Economic Relations*, Paris, 1973.
25. See, Ernest H. Preeg, *Economic Blocs and US Foreign Policy*, National Planning Assicuation, 1974.

    There is also a series of tripartite reports published by the Brookings Institution. For example, *Reshaping the International Economic Order*, a tripartite report by twelve economists from North America, the European Community and Japan, the Brookings Institution, 1972.
26. Kiyoshi Kojima, *Japan and a Pacific Free Trade Area*, pp. 174-5. Harry Johnson pointed out that 'it would seem more realistic to concentrate attention on the probable benefits, drawbacks, and constitutional problems of a narrower Pacific free trade arrangement among Australia, New Zealand, and Japan . . . A free trade area among these three countries could in addition like EFTA in the European context serve as a possible model of free trade for the rest of the world, and possibly in the course of time be one of the building blocs out of which a worldwide system of free trade could be constructed.' Harry G. Johnson, 'A New World Trade Policy in the Post-Kennedy Round Era: A Survey of Alternatives, with special reference to the position of the Pacific and Asian regions', Kiyoshi Kojima, ed., *Pacific Trade and Development*, The Japan Economic Research Centre, February 1968, p. 250.
27. I. A. McDougall, 'Prospects of the Economic Integration of Japan, Australia and New Zealand', Kiyoshi Kojima, ed., *Pacific Trade and Development*, The Japan Economic Research Centre, February 1968, p. 115.
28. Peter D. Drysdale, 'Japan, Australia, New Zealand: The Prospect for Western Pacific Economic Integration', Kiyoshi Kojima, ed., *Pacific Trade and Development, II*, The Japan Economic Research Centre, April 1969; I. A. McDougall, 'JANFTA and Asian Developing Countries: Sectoral Analysis', *ibid.*; L. V. Castle, 'Alternative Policies in Trade Cooperation of the Advanced Pacific Countries in the Next Five Years', *ibid.*
29. See, *Australia, Japan, and Western Pacific Relations*: A Report to the Governments of Australia and Japan presented by Sir John Crawford and Dr Saburo Okita, Canberra and Tokyo, April 1976.

INDEX

adjustable peg exchange rate 66, 69, 157
administrative guidance 29, 35
Africa 21
Agricultural Policy Council 136-8
agricultural products 102, 121, 136-40, 159-60, 173;
  Japanese imports of 24, 25, 27-8;
  US exports of 61-2
agricultural technology 86
Akamatsu, K. 150-1
Asia 21-2; *see also specific countries*
Asian Pacific Region 168-87
Asian Trade Development Corporation 78
Association of Southeast Asian Nations 179
Australia 20, 136, 168, 182-4
Australia-New Zealand Free Trade Agreement 178-9
automobiles 130, 132

balance of payments 54;
  Japanese 10-11, 36-8, 120, 126;
  United States 10
barley 137
benign neglect policy 69
Bhagwati, J. N. 119n
bipolar key currency system 64-74
borrowing, overseas 39
Burma 22

Cambodia 22
Canada 20, 168, 172, 174-80
Canadian-United States Automotive Agreement 178
capital accumulation 163-4
capital flows, international 35-6, 85, 92, 103, 105, 107-9, 111, 115
chemical industry 173, 177
  Japanese 9, 14, 15, 18-19, 121, 127-8, 132, 140, 141, 142
China 179, 181
clothing industry 156
coal 160
comparative advantage 80, 84, 93, 101, 103-6, 110, 112-3, 153
complements 106-8
costs and profitability 97-9

dairy products 138
devaluation 71
developing countries 21-2, 58, 154, 158, 169, 173-4, 181, 183;
  and the oil crisis 42, 43, 61;
  exports 54, 56, 84, 163;
  integrated policy for 162-3;
  Japanese investment in 77-9;
  preference to 26, 162-3;
  type of industry transferred to 85-6; *see also specific countries*
development banks 42-3
dollars 65, 70, 181
dumping 31
Dunning, J. H. 117n

EEC 28, 51, 62, 72, 168, 170, 180, 181
EFTA 51
economic growth 12-14, 120, 123-6, 146
economic policy, Japanese 45n
economies of scale 54, 85, 152-3
electrical appliances 130
energy: saving 61, 129, 146;
  sources 40
Eurodollars 65, 68, 70
Europe: Japanese imports 10;
  trade with Japan 18-20, 32-3, 136
European Monetary Union 72, 181-2
exchange rates 23; floating 65, 66;
  Japanese 36-7; overvalued 115
Export-Import Bank 43
exports 51; discrimination against Japanese 31-5; embargoes 62;
  excessive competition 46n, 56;
  incentives 153; Japanese 9, 12-23, 125-6, 130-6, 174-80;
  of manufactured goods 15;
  promoting 30-1
extractive industry 112

factor endowments 92, 153
fair weather reduction rule 52
foreign aid 173; Japanese 126, 155-7
foreign direct investment 53, 58, 75-119; and international trade 102-8; anti-trade-oriented 99-102; by the United States 79-82, 86; code of behaviour for 88, 174; control of 115;
  in the United States 84;

foreign direct investment–*(cont.)*
Japanese 77-9, 86, 125-6, 155-7, 166-7; macroeconomic theory of 92-119; motivation for 76-7, 113-4; trade oriented 92-9, 108-15; transfer of ownership 87; versus free trade policy 82-5
foreign exchange reserves 10, 14, 149; Japanese 10, 14, 149
free trade policy 82-5; versus direct investment 82-5

GATT 31-3, 48-63 *passim*, 64, 180
government procurement 29
grains 138

Hamada, K. 106
heavy industry 173, 177; Japanese 9, 14, 15, 18-19, 121, 127-8, 132, 141, 142
Heckscher-Ohlin model 80, 83, 92, 103, 108, 110, 115
Helmberger, P. 103, 106-8
Hong Kong 22, 79, 158, 179
horizontal trade 19-20, 59, 88, 173, 177, 184, 185
Hymer, S. 80-81, 83

import substitution industry 77
imports 51; Japanese 9, 11, 12-23, 38, 56, 125, 129-30, 133-6, 138, 139, 158, 174-80
Indonesia 22, 179
industrial sites 130, 143
Industrial Structure Council 122, 140-5
innovation 88, 148-9, 150-1
intermediate goods industries 141-2, 143-5, 184
international liquidity 67-8, 69, 71
International Monetary Fund 9, 41, 180; oil facility idea 43
international monetary system 37, 48, 157, 181
international trade: and foreign direct investment 102-8; code of good conduct 173-4; Japanese 12-14; north-south 150-67
intra-industry specialisation 157, 183
investment: liberalisation of 35-8; research and development 154-5
invisible trade 13
iron and steel 132, 140, 145, 147n, 156

JANFTA 182-4
Japan Economic Research Centre (JERC) 122-40, 156
Japan External Trade Organisation (JETRO) 30, 153
Japanese economy 120-47; changes in production 128; industrial structure 126-9; intra-industry specialisation 143-5, 157; regional composition of trade 132-6; trade policy 157-62
Johnson, H. G. 89, 187n
joint ventures 43, 86, 109

Keidanren 123, 124, 140-5
Kennedy Round negotiations 24-5, 51
knowledge-intensive industries 15, 121-2, 127, 140, 142, 143-6, 149, 150-5, 158
Korea 22, 79, 158, 179

labour costs 121
labour-oriented investment 76
language barrier 30
Latin America 21
liberalisation of trade 23-35, 49, 84; regional 172
light industry 173, 177; Japanese 14
luxury goods 38

machinery industry 130, 132, 140, 143
Maidenhead Communiqué 55-6
Malaysia 22, 179
managerial knowledge 85, 92, 93, 108
manufactured goods 15, 16, 18-19, 102, 156; exported by developing countries 78; Japanese imports of 25, 27; tariffs on 49
marine products 138
market-oriented investment 76-7
marketing, internationalisation of 87-8
meat 137, 140
Middle East 20-1, 136
Mijazawa, Kiichi 179
Miki, Takeo 179
milk products 138
monopolies 58-9, 85, 102
multilateral trade negotiations 48-63
multinational companies 59, 75, 82-4, 90, 115; *see also* foreign direct investment
Mundell, R. 103-6

natural resource-oriented investment 76
New Zealand 20, 168, 172, 174-80,

New Zealand–*(cont.)*
182-4
non-tariff barriers 18, 20, 40n, 48-63, 64, 152-3; induced 28-30; liberalisation of 26-7; United States 48-9
north-south trade 148-67

OAPEC 60
OECD 35, 41
OPEC 61
oil: international commodity agreement on 61; Japanese imports of 129; revenues 184
oil crisis (1973) 9, 11, 38-44, 120, 124-5, 181; recycling funds 41-4
oligopolistic industry 81-2, 85, 101, 102
Organisation for Pacific Trade and Development (proposed) 174-80
Overseas Economic Cooperation Fund 43

Pacific basin countries 168-87; intra-area trade 180-1; prospects for economic integration 180-5; *see also* Asian Pacific region
Pacific Basin Economic Cooperation Committee 179
Pacific Currency Area (proposed) 174
Pacific Free Trade Area (proposed) 168-74; responses to 174-80
Pacific Reserve and Development Bank (proposed) 174
Philippines 22, 179
pollution 141
primary commodities *see* raw materials
product cycles 154
product differentiation 54, 152
production functions 106-8
production, internationalisation of 87-8
productivity 114
profitability (foreign investment) 75, 96; and costs 97-9; payment of profits 112
protection of infant industries 54, 55-6
Purvis, D. D. 103, 106-8

quota restrictions 24-6, 27-8, 46n

raw materials 9-10, 16, 149, 173; foreign investment in 87, 156; international commodity agreements 60-2;

raw materials–*(cont.)*
Japanese import of 15, 20-1, 24, 77-8, 121; supply access to 60-2
revaluation 71
rice 137, 140, 159
Russia 179, 181
Rybczynski line 105, 107

Schmitz, A. 103, 106-8
shipping 132
Singapore 22, 79, 179
socialist countries 21
soybeans 137, 140
Special Drawing Right 67-70, 71, 73
steel *see* iron and steel
structural change and adjustment 56-7, 97, 148, 154, 172-3; assisting 161-2; in Japan 14-15, 79, 120-2, 146, 157-62
subsidies 57, 153
substitutes 103-6, 152

Taiwan 22, 79, 158, 179
tariff barriers 18, 20, 46n, 48-63, 165n; Japanese 23-6; reduction of 48-63
technology 16, 54, 55, 143, 152; foreign 36, 80, 85, 86-7, 92, 93, 102, 108-15, 147
textile industry 127, 130, 132, 140, 156, 158, 160-1, 184
Thailand 22, 179
Tokyo Round negotiations 48-9, 180
Tracy, M. 159

UNCTAD 181
United Kingdom 28
United States 10, 28, 75, 168, 172, 174-80, 181; and exchange rates 68-70. 73; foreign direct investment by 79-82, 102, 116n, 117n; imports 48-9; trade with Japan 16-17, 34, 136, 168-87 *passim*

vegetables 138
Vernon, R. 80, 150-1
vertical trade 19-20, *see also* raw materials
Vietnam 22, 156
voluntary export restraints 33-4

wheat 137, 140
world trade 124-5; Japan's position in 10-23; *see also* international trade